SO-BRR-887

This book is an essential guide for managers and scholars seeking to understand how the national cultures of Latin America impact business. Elvira, Davila and their team of collaborators demonstrate the vital role HRM plays in translating the people-oriented cultures of Latin America into effective business organizations.

Denise M. Rousseau
H.J. Heinz II Professor of Organizational Behavior and Public Policy, Carnegie Mellon University and 2004–2005 President of the Academy of Management

Managing Human Resources in Latin America presents a fascinating study supported by research that helps one understand some of the complexities unique to Latin American culture. *Managing Human Resources in Latin America* is a must read for any manager who works in Latin America or employs people of Latin American origin.

Mike Yonker
Regional Vice President, Human Resources, Midwest & Canada Regions, Marriott International, Inc.

As more and more foreign firms establish themselves in Latin America, we need to better understand what human resource management practices are most effective in different cultural and institutional settings. This volume offers a state-of-the-art analysis and a set of specific recommendations. A must read for anyone interested in international human resource management.

Mauro F. Guillen
The Wharton School, University of Pennsylvania

Managing Human Resources in Latin America

Managing Human Resources in Latin America provides the reader with a thorough overview of the trends in HR strategies and practice as well as the challenges faced by HR executives in this region. Cultural issues critical to conducting business and understanding human resource management in Latin America underlie this exploration. Up-to-the-minute case studies from companies that conduct business in Latin America are used to illustrate the theory throughout the chapters.

The text moves from a general overview of the economic, managerial, and leadership styles found in Latin America to the current status, role, and strategic importance of the HR function in a variety of country-specific chapters. This text is invaluable reading for academics, students, and practitioners alike.

Marta M. Elvira is Academic Dean at Lexington College, Chicago.

Anabella Davila is a tenured Professor of Organization Theory at ITESM (Monterrey TEC), Mexico.

Routledge Global Human Resource Management Series

Edited by Randall S. Schuler, Susan E. Jackson, Paul Sparrow and Michael Poole

Routledge Global Human Resource Management is an important new series that examines human resources in its global context. The series is organized into three strands: Content and issues in global human resource management (HRM); Specific HR functions in a global context; and comparative HRM. Authored by some of the world's leading authorities on HRM, each book in the series aims to give readers comprehensive, in-depth and accessible texts that combine essential theory and best practice. Topics covered include cross-border alliances, global leadership, global legal systems, HRM in Asia, Africa and the Americas, industrial relations, and global staffing.

Managing Human Resources in Cross-Border Alliances
Randall S. Schuler, Susan E. Jackson and Yadong Luo

Managing Human Resources in Africa
Edited by Ken N. Kamoche, Yaw A. Debrah, Frank M. Horwitz and Gerry Nkombo Muuka

Globalizing Human Resource Management
Paul Sparrow, Chris Brewster and Hilary Harris

Managing Human Resources in Asia-Pacific
Edited by Pawan S. Budhwar

International Human Resource Management 2nd edition
Policies and Practices for the Global Enterprise
Dennis R. Briscoe and Randall S. Schuler

Managing Human Resources in Latin America
An Agenda for International Leaders
Edited by Marta M. Elvira and Anabella Davila

Managing Human Resources in Latin America

An Agenda for International Leaders

Edited by
Marta M. Elvira and Anabella Davila

To the students and scholars
at the University of St. Francis
who are devoted to an
enlightened new humanism
in service to the common
good,

Routledge
Taylor & Francis Group

LONDON AND NEW YORK

First published 2005
by Routledge
2 Park Square, Milton Park, Abingdon, Oxon, OX14 4RN

Simultaneously published in the USA and Canada
by Routledge
270 Madison Ave., New York, NY 10016

Routledge is an imprint of the Taylor & Francis Group

© 2005 Editorial matter and selection, Marta M. Elvira and Anabella Davila;
individual chapters, the contributors

Typeset in Times New Roman and Franklin Gothic by Taylor and Francis Books
Printed and bound in Great Britain by Antony Rowe Ltd, Chippenham, Wiltshire

British Library Cataloguing in Publication Data
A catalogue record for this book is available from the British Library

Library of Congress Cataloging in Publication Data
Managing human resources in Latin America : an agenda for international leaders /
[edited by] Marta M. Elvira and Anabella Davila.
    p. cm.
  Includes bibliographical references and index.
  1. Personnel management–Latin America. I. Elvira, Marta M., 1965-
II. Davila, Anabella.
  HF5549.2.L29M36 2005
  658.3'0098–dc22

                                                                      2004024600

ISBN 0–415–33917–0 (hbk)
ISBN 0–415–33918–9 (pbk)

To Eugenio y Fidela, my wise and loving parents.
Marta M. Elvira

To Raúl and María del Rosario, my loving and devoted parents.
Anabella Davila

Contents

Illustrations

Figures

Tables

Boxes

Contributors

Lydia A. Arbaiza is Lecturer/Professor of Management at Escuela de Administración de Negocios para Graduados (ESAN), Peru.

L. Fernando Arias-Galicia is Professor at División de Estudios de Posgrado y de Investigación, Facultad de Contaduría y Administración, Universidad Nacional Autonóma de México (UNAM).

Lourdes Casanova is Lecturer in the Asian Business and Comparative Management Department at INSEAD, France.

Anabella Davila is tenured Professor of Organization Theory and Business History at ITESM (Monterrey TEC), Mexico.

Marta M. Elvira is Academic Dean at Lexington College, Chicago, IL, USA.

Rubén A. Figueiredo is Associate Professor of Human Behavior at IAE, Universidad Austral, Buenos Aires, Argentina.

Carolina Gómez is Associate Professor of Management and International Business at the College of Business Administration, Florida International University, Miami, FL, USA.

Henry Gómez-Samper is Professor Emeritus at Instituto de Estudios Superiores de Administración (IESA), Caracas, Venezuela.

Gaston J. Labadie is Chaired Professor of Organizational Behaviour and Human Resources and Dean, at Facultad de Administración y Ciencias Sociales, Universidad ORT, Uruguay.

Ivan Martínez is Assistant Professor at Universidad Nacional de Colombia, Bogotá, Colombia.

Patricia G. Martínez is Assistant Professor of Management at the College of Business, University of Texas at San Antonio, USA.

Patricia Monteferrante is Professor at Instituto de Estudios Superiores de Administración (IESA), Caracas, Venezuela.

Enrique Ogliastri is Professor at INCAE, Costa Rica.

Asbjorn Osland is Associate Professor of Organization and Management at San Jose State University, USA.

Joyce S. Osland is Professor of Management at San Jose State University, USA.

Rene Ríos is Professor at Instituto de Sociología, Pontificia Universidad Catolica de Chile, Santiago, Chile.

Dario Rodríguez is Professor at Instituto de Sociología, Pontificia Universidad Católica de Chile, Santiago, Chile.

Francisca Rosene is Adjunct Professor at Escuela de Administración, Pontificia Universidad Católica de Chile, Santiago, Chile.

Jaime Ruiz is Associate Professor of Management and Organization at Universidad de los Andes, Bogotá, Colombia.

Juan I. Sanchez is Associate Professor of Management and International Business at Florida International University, Miami, FL, USA.

Eugenio de Solminihac is Consultant/Lecturer at Instituto de Sociología, Pontificia Universidad Católica de Chile, Santiago, Chile.

Mary F. Sully de Luque is Assistant Professor of Management at Thunderbird, The Garvin School of International Management, Glendale, AZ, USA.

Betania Tanure is Professor at Fundação Dom Cabral, Brazil.

Foreword

Routledge Global Human Resource Management is a series of books edited and authored by some of the best and most well-known researchers and teachers in the field of human resource management. This series is aimed at offering students and practitioners accessible, coordinated and comprehensive books in global HRM. To be used individually or together, these books cover the main bases of comparative and international HRM. Taking an expert look at an increasingly important and complex area of global business, this is a groundbreaking new series that answers a real need for serious textbooks on global HRM.

Several books in this series, **Routledge Global Human Resource Management**, are devoted to human resource management policies and practices in multinational enterprises. Some books focus on specific areas of global HRM policies and practices, such as global legal systems, global compensation, global staffing, and global labour relations. Other books address special topics that arise in multinational enterprises such as managing HR in cross-border alliances, developing strategies and structures, and globalizing the human resources function in multinational enterprises.

In addition to books on various HRM topics in multinational enterprises, several other books in the series adopt a comparative approach to understanding human resource management. These books on comparative human resource management describe the HRM policies and practices found at the local level in selected countries in several regions of the world. The comparative books utilize a common framework that makes it easier for the reader to systematically understand the rationale for the existence of various human resource management activities in different countries and easier to compare these activities across countries. This framework considers a range of national factors including culture, institutions, industrial sector, and dynamic changes in the environment. These books therefore help us to both understand the factors that still lead to unique HRM solutions in different countries around the world, the essential elements of localization, and also the opportunities to multinational enterprises for transfer of best practices. This book, *Managing Human Resources in Latin*

America: An Agenda for International Leaders, edited by Marta Elvira and Anabella Davila, is an excellent example of one of these books on comparative human resource management. In this book the reader will find detailed descriptions of human resource management activities in nine key countries in Latin America, including a broader coverage of human resource management activities and issues in Central America and Latin America. Before describing each of the nine countries, Marta Elvira and Anabella Davila provide an excellent overview of several key environmental conditions common to many countries in Central and South America. After the countries are described, they conclude with suggestions for research directions in Latin America.

In completing this fine book, the editors have brought together a series of prestigious authors of the various country chapters, who have been carefully selected for being experts in the subject area in their chosen countries. Each chapter is complete with useful and timely references that enable the reader to delve into each country in even more detail than provided in the chapter. Overall, Marta Elvira and Anabella Davila have given the reader a very valuable book that provides information on the human resource management activities and experiences in Latin America.

This Routledge series, **Routledge Global Human Resource Management**, is intended to serve the growing market of global scholars and professionals who are seeking a deeper and broader understanding of the role and importance of human resource management in companies as they operate throughout the world. With this in mind, all books in the series provide a thorough review of existing research and numerous examples of companies around the world. Mini company stories and examples are found throughout the chapters. In addition, many of the books in the series include at least one detailed case description that serves as a convenient practical illustration of topics discussed in the book.

Because a significant number of scholars and professionals throughout the world are involved in researching and practicing the topics examined in this series of books, the authorship of the books and the experiences of companies cited in the books reflect a vast global representation. The authors in the series bring with them exceptional knowledge of the human resource management topics they address, and in many cases the authors have been the pioneers for their topics. So we feel fortunate to have the involvement of such a distinguished group of academics in this series.

The publisher and editors have also played a major role in making this series possible. Routledge has provided its global production, marketing and reputation to make this series feasible and affordable to academics and practitioners throughout the world. In addition, Routledge has provided its own highly qualified professionals to make this series a reality. In particular we want to indicate our deep appreciation for the work of our series editor, Francesca

Heslop. She has been behind the series from the very beginning and has been invaluable in providing the needed support and encouragement to us and to the many authors in the series. She has, along with her staff, helped make the process of completing this series an enjoyable one. For everything they have done, we thank them all.

Randall S. Schuler
Rutgers University and GSBA Zurich

Paul Sparrow
Manchester University

Susan E. Jackson
Rutgers University and GSBA Zurich

Michael Poole
Cardiff University

Preface

Managing Human Resources in Latin America: An Agenda for International Leaders developed from the timely need to focus theoretical and empirical attention on understanding human resource management (HRM) in Latin America. Two main questions guide the book's contributions and frame its research. First of all, what are the cultural, economic and historical factors that affect management and leadership in local and multinational firms operating in Latin America? Second, what knowledge and country-specific considerations are required for HRM practices to fit various countries' idiosyncratic business environments? To date, little research exists to answer these questions and help build stronger HRM capabilities in the region. This book paves the way for an HRM research and practice agenda in Latin America.

Latin America (including Central and South America) is essentially different from its northern continental neighbors. In the popular business programs offered by many local universities, views of management largely follow North American models that are simply translated into Spanish or Portuguese languages but rarely adapted to the Latin American business and cultural context. Exploring management and specifically the management of human resources (HR) from a Latin American perspective has largely been ignored. Paradoxically, this is a region where *people*, social relationships, and by extension their management are paramount. Thus, this book aims to explain the cultural meaning that people give to their relationships at work in Latin America by analyzing human resource management (HRM) from an insider's perspective.

Due to the fundamental cultural values guiding life in Latin America, human resource management is really a critical competency for any firm seeking to conduct business successfully. This book highlights the growth and importance of HR strategies and practices in Latin America, the dominant HRM systems, along with the challenges faced by HR executives in these countries. Our research motivation was to understand how cultural and historical developments affect the business environment and organizational structures and how these in turn define what HRM means in the Latin American context. What we call a *humanistic* approach to culture and, generally, management informs the research presented here by managerial scholars and practitioners in Latin America. Thanks to the creativity in data gathering and reporting by chapter authors, new research is included in this volume that we hope will seed future work from a cultural and humanistic perspective in this emergent research area.

A brief background: trends in business and foreign direct investment in Latin America

The importance of Latin America's economy continues to grow among developing nations. Globalization and internationalization trends have opened opportunities for foreign investment from Europe, North America, and Asia, as evidenced by international trade agreements such as NAFTA, Trade Agreement European Union, and Mexico (TAEUPM).

Over the past two decades, Latin American countries have initiated a process of economic opening and a democratic transformation of their societies, attracting foreign direct investment (FDI) to the region. A critical factor in attracting FDI has been the privatization of Latin American industries of high value added, such as service industries, banking and telecommunications, but not manufacturing. Simultaneously, Latin American countries continue to experience cyclical economic crises. For example, recently Brazil, Argentina, and Venezuela suffered severe economic crises that halted FDI growth. However, multinational corporations (MNCs) operating in these countries rarely leave, for they have learned to overcome the volatility of this region's economies and exploit its potential contribution. Explaining this volatile environment and its relationship to HR practices is one of the goals of this book.

MNCs coexist in the economy with large family conglomerates, often MNCs themselves, as well as small entrepreneurial firms and a large informal sector. Obviously, the process of economic opening in the region has also influenced local corporations. Latin American researchers have documented the unusual concentration of wealth characteristic of this region resulting from diverse historical processes. This concentration of wealth accounts for the development of large Latin American-based global corporations that have developed world-class managerial practices in order to compete against foreign multinationals. The HRM practices of these firms and companies have contributed to their establishment as global competitors.

Latin American corporations have also capitalized on trade agreements and expanded their investments abroad. Consider Mexico, where several family-run businesses stand out. For example, Bimbo (bakery) has acquired Orowit in the United States, Ideal in Chile, and other operations in Central and South America. Cemex (cement) has acquisitions in Panama, Colombia, Venezuela, the United States, Europe, and Asia. IMSA (steel) has investments in Brazil and in Europe.

Overall, Latin American companies are playing an increasingly important role in the global arena. Among the list of Forbes 500 Top International Firms, 12 are from Brazil and Mexico. There are also 38 Latin American companies among the Forbes Top 2000 World Firms. This suggests that Latin American corporations have been able to use modern management practices in order to operate internationally and now they need to manage a diverse workforce. Therefore, local and foreign firms exist in a hybrid cultural environment where global and local management practices combine to different extents.

The development of human resource management has followed an idiosyncratic historical and institutional development in this region. Latin American countries have experienced specific political and social development processes which share elements of a common history, including the conquest by Spain and Portugal, which instilled a form of life and a religious faith. They also share the independence process at the same period of time by military leaders (at least in South America), the inheritance of ancestral traditions that are still practiced, and more recently, the immersion of the region in the global arena. In addition, organizations in Latin America face interventionist and authoritarian governments, widely involved in regulating the economy and organizational relationships. Finally, most Latin American organizations continue to be family-owned. While there are many differences among individual countries, we surmise that strong common values are shared by the countries in this subcontinent. This shared background distinguishes Latin America from other continents where language, history, spiritual traditions, and social structures are distinctly rooted in different countries.

As a professional discipline, HRM in Latin America is well institutionalized. Professional associations exist that promote the advance of the discipline, such as the Mexican Association of Human Resources Management. In addition, the discipline is developed academically. Major higher education institutions offer academic programs at the undergraduate and graduate level in HR. One also finds governmental agencies in each country overseeing and promoting adequate HRM practices. This historical development has naturally impacted work culture and HRM practices. Changes in the business environment indicate that leading HR in this region where social relationships are critical to success has become a critical issue for policy makers, managers, and academics.

Summary of book contributions

Managing Human Resources in Latin America is organized into two parts that parallel the two main questions stated at the beginning. With respect to culture, we take a regional approach to understand the shared values that are common to most Latin American countries. We then focus on each country in particular.

Part I: Understanding the Latin American cultural and economic context

Part I sets the stage for research from a cultural perspective and includes four chapters focused on regional characteristics that affect HRM. The four chapters describe a cultural framework to understand HRM, the macroeconomic business environment, social capital formation within MNCs in Latin America, and paternalism as a form of leadership.

In Chapter 1, Davila and Elvira provide a basic framework to explain HRM research and practice in Latin America. Building on cultural and managerial research, first we overview the cultural values underlying management, zeroing in on two central work values: social relationships and respect for authority. Then we explain how HRM practices, such as compensation, staffing, training, and labor relations, relate to those cultural values. This general framework guides the structure of later chapters focusing on country-specific HR management.

In Chapter 2, Casanova details the macroeconomic environment for business and workforce development in Latin America. She explains the key drivers for the deep economic reforms in the region during the1990s, focusing on the Washington Consensus and the increased political stability, privatization, foreign investment, and trade liberalization processes. An important shift took place as deregulation and privatization advanced: the role of state-owned companies diminished, leaving space for large private companies, especially MNCs seeking growth, efficiency, and resources. The chapter links these macroeconomic factors to structural changes in the labor market and explores the key economic, social, and geopolitical challenges facing Latin American economies in the years ahead. Casanova explains how, despite the short-term outlook, Latin America faces serious obstacles for high sustained growth.

In Chapter 3, Gomez and Sanchez explore how MNCs implement HRM in Latin America and examine the formation of social capital. They adopt a holistic perspective of both the global and local factors affecting strategy in MNCs. The authors discuss the role of HR as a function that helps companies implement their strategy while allowing them to be culturally acceptable. Finally, they propose a model for MNCs to build social capital through HR practices by taking into account Latin American culture. A helpful table concludes their chapter summarizing how the criteria of cultural understanding help explain a number of HR practices. By meeting these criteria, HR practices will be culturally congruent and more readily accepted by Latin American employees, resulting in a solid foundation of social capital.

In Chapter 4, Martinez reviews existing literature on paternalism and examines its role in understanding leadership and HRM practices within the Latin American context. Based on her interviews with Mexican leaders in US firms as well as across the Mexican border, she explains paternalism's benevolent aspects. From a social exchange theory viewpoint, paternalism reflects a positive employment relationship where leaders and subordinates calculate costs along with benefits and expect reciprocation. Her analyses suggest that paternalism may be positively related to employee job attitudes and performance in Latin America.

Part II: Human resource management in Latin American countries

The ten chapters included in Part II address the current status, development, and challenges ahead for HRM in selected countries (these are listed alphabetically). We were unable to obtain contributions from all Latin American countries, as was our desire, within the time required. Each chapter follows a relatively similar structure, initially providing a brief overview of the country's history and culture as they relate to business and management practices. Chapters then detail HRM strategies and practices, the institutions involved with HR, including professional associations and academic disciplines developed, as well as the legal environment and extent of governmental intervention. A review follows of some critical HR practices such as pay, staffing, unions, and training. Chapters dwell mostly on the current status of the HR field, examine changes taking place, present actual cases illustrating how companies conduct HRM in the various countries, and end noting future trends.

In Chapter 5, Figueiredo reviews the evolution of the human resources function in Argentinean companies from an international and domestic historical framework which combines social, political, and economic factors. He explains the tight relationship between Argentina's industrialization process and the development of HR competitive practices. Figueiredo analyzes key historical periods to understand the transition from "Personnel Administration" to a "Strategic HR" role in large MNCs as well as in Argentinean corporations. This transition was brought forth by local and professional HR associations and higher education institutions. The author suggests that the HR challenges in Argentina will lead research to seek a greater strategic contribution, turning change and cultural management into a business priority, and aligning HR practices to sustain organizational culture.

In Chapter 6, Tanure describes and analyzes the profound changes taking place in Brazilian HRM practices due to globalization. She also discusses how cultural characteristics like personalism, ambiguity, and flexibility impact HR management. Upon this foundation, Tanure elaborates on the critical issues for people management in Brazilian companies today, including the evolution of labor relations. She discusses widespread outsourcing, development, and retention of talent, as well as the challenge of balancing private and professional life. Her discussion ends with prescriptions for transforming HRM into a strategic partner within firms. She illustrates her points with the successful case of change at Xerox Brazil, where business objectives, processes, and people were integrated during the change process.

In Chapter 7, Osland and Osland explore HRM in Central America and Panama. Building on interviews with senior managers and HR scholars in several countries, these authors document the similarities and differences among the small countries in Central America and their influence on HRM practices. Labor conditions and labor relations developed with unique characteristics that require an understanding of the geopolitical composition of the countries. For example, *solidarismo* stands out as a unique way of organizing workers based on the premise that management and labor are interdependent and should share the common goal of helping the organization succeed. Strategic HR practices, on the other hand, have followed from the region's internationalization and the establishments of sophisticated and innovative practices by MNCs and large local firms. The authors also survey the status of women's labor and the importance of the public sector, ending with an explanation of the social construction of HRM structures in Central America and Panama.

In Chapter 8, Rodríguez, Rios, de Solminihac, and Rosene portray the detailed history of HR practices in Chile, the first Latin American country to adopt economic reforms. The development strategy established in the 1970s by the military regime and maintained during the *Concertación* governments was based in a free market economy, export driven, open to international trade, and investment. Despite this profound economic transformation, the deep cultural values underlying human relations in the workplace were not altered. HRM in Chile has experienced a gradual process of professionalization and incorporated modern management principles and techniques. In fact, modern Chilean firms exhibit similar HRM practices to those observed in developed countries. Trends include contractually based work relationships, individualized labor relations, compensation increasingly linked to productivity, and a dramatic change in the role of unions and organized labor. Social security has been transformed from a welfare type of labor taxation paid by the employer and distributed by the state to a system of individual capitalization of workers' savings administered by private funds. All these changes occur as labor laws increase the complexity of HR management. The challenges ahead include solving social welfare, economic competitiveness, and labor market issues in a modern Latin American economy.

In Chapter 9, Ogliastri, Ruiz, and Martinez present the evolution and development of Colombia's economy and society. They take a strategic HRM perspective to analyze staffing, compensation, training and development, negotiation, and labor relations. They also illustrate the influence of international theories and trends. The authors identify many differences in HRM practices between small or medium-sized firms and large companies such as multinationals and government agencies. They focus on common challenges for all firms, including outsourcing, employment flexibility, training and development, and new labor relationships. In this changed context, the role of HR managers continues to be one of administrative specialists rather than members of the strategic team. The authors conclude by pointing to the need for research on

HRM as a strategic variable for Colombian organizations, which are still anchored in combined paternalistic and bureaucratic practices.

In Chapter 10, Arias-Galicia takes a non-traditional approach to overview the status of HRM in Mexico based on his rich experience as an HR executive, consultant, and academic researcher. Arias-Galicia links HRM development with its historical language, legal, and economic roots. HR practices such as staffing, training, and pay systems are explained under the eye of the Mexican labor law. This cultural approach informs management style, motivation, and incentives in the Mexican workplace as well as the orientation toward quality of life. Arias-Galicia stresses that to bring HRM to strategic positions in Mexican companies, HR managers should develop relationships with finance departments and demonstrate how HR practices impact organizational performance.

In Chapter 11, Sully de Luque and Arbaiza provide an overview of HRM in Peru with a particular focus on labor markets, as well as selection, compensation, and retention. They explore in depth the role of the informal economy, a rarely studied yet important economic phenomenon. Their analysis reveals interesting research avenues for HR practices which are mainly based on implicit social contracts. The country's main HR issues concern succession management given the scarcity of talent, participation, and transparency in companies' privatization processes, and decentralization processes to assist in balancing Peru's dual economy.

In Chapter 12, Labadie reviews the status of HRM in Uruguay with a particular emphasis on labor relations. To understand the evolution in the role played by HR managers in private firms, he focuses on the changes that have taken place in the last twenty years in the Uruguayan labor market, institutions, and workforce. He stresses the changing role of unions which currently operate mostly at the firm and plant level, no longer at the industry level. Labadie identifies promising avenues for increasing HR's relevance. Young managers that are well-trained can introduce modern HR practices in Uruguayan firms. Additionally, an opportunity exists for institutional change to inject flexibility and innovation into labor relations.

In Chapter 13, Gomez-Samper and Monteferrante detail Venezuela's economic history and its impact on HRM practices. Employment conditions and labor relations are determined by tight labor laws. Furthermore, as is the case in many Latin American countries, Venezuela suffers from cyclical economic crises which limit a smooth implementation of HR policies. The chapter describes changes in HR practices since the mid-1990s until the present in light of such instability, ending on a provocative invitation for the development of HR research in Venezuela: HR specialists, academics, and consultants should have a unified agenda in order to broaden the country's limited HRM knowledge.

In Chapter 14, Elvira and Davila conclude by noting the consensus among chapter authors on important HRM challenges that will shape the direction of academic research in the future. The nature of challenges such as balancing global and local HRM approaches, focusing on people while aiming at performance, and, in general, managing in a hybrid cultural and economic system requires reframing strategic HR in terms of social contract theories. Such theories consider multiple stakeholders and focus research on the employment relationship as unit of analysis, as has been suggested by Kochan, which fit well the preeminence of person-centered management over merely profit-centered goals. This is a call for theoretically anchored research to guide HRM practice taking into account Latin America's culture-specific humanistic approach and its labor market institutions.

Besides laying out the agenda for HR research and practice, the book will be of interest to undergraduate and postgraduate HRM and International Management courses. Additionally, the book is a resource for cross-national HRM researchers and practitioners in Latin America, the United States, Canada, Asia, and Western Europe who wish to understand, contribute, and further develop this rich and promising region. We envision the network of researchers started with this book's contributors to be enlarged with other scholars equally committed to the research agenda.

Thanks is due to the many individuals and institutions who have helped to make this book a reality, beginning with the series editors for the opportunity to develop this book and following with the team of excellent contributors for their creativity in gathering original data and responsiveness to writing chapters within tight deadlines. Thanks also go to Lisa Cohen, Kathleen Jackson, and Amanda Murphy for their help editing the chapters, and importantly, Francesca Heslop for her assistance at various stages of this book's commission and production. Not least, the Monterrey TEC, the University of California, Irvine, Lexington College, and Shellbourne Conference Center provided the resources and place, respectively, to bring the book to completion. Sincere thanks to everyone.

Marta M. Elvira
Lexington College, Chicago, USA

Anabella Davila
Instituto Tecnológico y de Estudios
Superiores de Monterrey, México

Part I

Understanding the Latin American cultural and economic context

1 Culture and human resource management in Latin America

ANABELLA DAVILA AND MARTA M. ELVIRA

Defining the Latin American management model has been the aim of many studies. Most of these studies highlight two cultural emphases upon which the Latin American management model is based: social relationships and respect for authority (Davila, 2004; Diaz-Saenz et al., 2004). These characteristics themselves rest on work values that suggest an appropriate cultural frame for understanding how Latin American organizations manage human resources (HR). Understanding such values will help scholars explain HR practices and their influence upon organizational performance in Latin America.

In this chapter, we first review research on Latin American work values and then suggest a cultural framework to explain how such values influence human resource management (HRM) in the region. We conclude by suggesting cultural guidelines to improve such management.

Work values in Latin America

Several scholars and practitioners have described the Latin American management model as transitional or in the process of development (e.g., Abarca et al., 1998; Aguilar, 1993; De la Cerda and Núñez, 1993) because Latin American firms are trying out different theories, methods, and tools proposed by developed countries. This book is based on different assumptions. We assume that Latin America's work culture has developed through a unique historical process shaping its economic, political, and societal structure. We view Latin American organizations as embedded in their historical tradition even though globalization forces have deeply changed the region. These combined historical and global processes have determined unique characteristics for business management and created a *hybrid* management model. That is, we find that successful organizations in Latin America – international or local – use global as well as local management practices. Nevertheless, universally accepted practices are more effective to the extent that they respect and adapt to local idiosyncrasy. To contribute to the development of HRM in the region, we should therefore study the local culture in which these practices exist.

Geertz (1983) argued that local knowledge could only be acquired from the native's point of view. He used Kohut's method of distinguishing between local knowledge concepts of "experience-near" versus those of "experience-distant". Geertz explained these concepts as follows:

> An experience-near concept is, roughly, one that someone ... might himself naturally and effortlessly use to define what he or his fellows see, feel, think, imagine, and so on, and which he would readily understand when similarly applied by others. An experience-distant concept is one that specialists of one sort or another ... employ to forward their scientific, philosophical, or practical aims.
>
> (1983: 57)

Our aim in this section is to identify experience-near concepts of work that Latin Americans use naturally, and to relate these substantively to experience-distant concepts of HRM theory. Thus, we focus on Latin American work-related cultural values.

While work is intimately connected to organizations' technological context, work values derive from social, economic, and political environments and are thus rooted in history. Given this, the study of work values will require examining national culture as an institutional process (Guillen, 1994). Hofstede (1982: 21) defined culture as "a collective programming of the mind that distinguishes members of one group from another ... Culture, in this sense, includes the system of values; and values are part of the culture's infrastructure." Hofstede proposed the dimensions of power distance, individuality, masculinity, and uncertainty avoidance as critical to differentiate national cultures.[1] We use Hofstede's research as a point of departure because his work is widely recognized and used to study cultural differences. Then, we add a finer reading of work values in the region.[2]

The "power distance" dimension indicates the degree of inequality accepted as normal within a society. The power distance index (PDI) is measured such that the greater the level of equality in a society, the smaller the power distance, and the lower the equality the greater the power distance index. Based on this index, Latin American countries are characterized by a high power distance. PDI values for these countries are: Panama (95), Guatemala (95), Mexico (81), Venezuela (81), Ecuador (78), Brazil (69), Colombia (67), El Salvador (66), Peru (64), Chile (63), Uruguay (61), Argentina (49), and Costa Rica (35). Organizations in societies with high power distance tend to be centralized and pyramidal and have many supervisors, large wage differentials among occupations, a large percentage of unskilled workers, and a higher appreciation for clerical than for manufacturing jobs (Hofstede, 1982).

"Individualism" is the degree to which people of one country prefer acting individually rather than as member of a group. The dimension opposite to individualism is "collectivism". A collective culture is characterized by low individualism. Latin American countries rank high in collectivism and low in individualism according to the individualism index (IDV), as shown in the following measures: Argentina (46), Brazil (38), Uruguay (36), Mexico (30), Chile (23), El Salvador (19), Peru (16), Costa Rica (15), Colombia (13), Venezuela (12), Panama (11), Ecuador (8), and Guatemala (6). Organizations in collectivist societies are characterized by a concern for the individual and his/her family welfare, as well as reciprocity for loyalty and a sense of duty. This dimension includes collectivism at different levels: the primary group (in-group) or an entire community (out-group) (Hofstede, 1982).

According to Hofstede (1991) power distance and collectivism are positively correlated. That is, countries high on power distance tend to be more collectivistic: people who depend highly on primary groups also tend to rely on authority figures. Therefore, organizational management in a collectivist society is management of groups, not of individuals.

The "masculinity" dimension, whose opposite is "femininity," concerns the degree to which values for assertiveness, performance, success, or competition are manifested in society. In general, these values are associated with the social role of men and prevail over other values such as quality of life, personal and warm relations, service, concern for the weak, and solidarity, goals associated with women's roles in most societies. In this masculine dimension, Latin American countries projected a dispersed scale of highs and lows according to the masculinity index (MAS): Venezuela (73), Mexico (69), Colombia (64), Ecuador (63), Argentina (56), Brazil (49), Panama (44), Peru (42), El Salvador (40), Uruguay (38), Guatemala (37), Chile (28), and Costa Rica (21). Organizations in more masculine societies expect young men to advance in their careers, while few women occupy decision-making positions (even if women do work in low-skill jobs with low salaries) (Hofstede, 1982).

Finally, the "uncertainty avoidance" dimension concerns the degree to which people in any society prefer structured situations in which rules for appropriate behavior are clear. Here, Latin American countries scored high according to the uncertainty avoidance index (UAI): Guatemala (101), Uruguay (100), El Salvador (94), Peru (87), Argentina (86), Chile (86), Costa Rica (86), Panama (86), Mexico (82), Colombia (80), Brazil (76), Venezuela (76), and Ecuador (67). Organizations in societies high on uncertainty avoidance are bureaucratic, task-oriented, less willing to make individual or risky decisions, ritualized, and dependent on power to control uncertainty (Hofstede, 1982).

Montaño (2000) critically analyzed Hofstede's dimensions in the Latin American context. He stressed that high-power distance characterizes most Latin American countries, except for Argentina and Costa Rica.[3] Collectivism is also common in Latin America. However, the masculinity index shows greater dispersion and is only high for a few countries there. High uncertainty avoidance is not unique to Latin America as a developing region, since even established industrialized countries like Japan or France also exhibit this trait.

To understand the influence of national culture in the management and functioning of Latin American organizations, the dimensions of power distance and collectivism need to be explored more thoroughly. D'Iribarne (2001) further suggests the need for an anthropological perspective to highlight each culture's internal coherence. He argues that societies do not distinguish themselves through universal characteristics of action, but through the meaning they give to action.

Meaning is acquired locally and given to words that describe how common life is organized. It is easy to mistake words' local meanings because equivalent, similar-sounding words cross all cultures. Yet "the same word does not necessarily evoke in all of us the same reality"[4] (d'Iribarne, 2001: 8). It is the meaning of that word which makes us culturally different. Take for example a comparative study of automotive assembly plants in six countries – five European and one Latin American – by Wilkens and Pawlowsky (1997). They found no evidence of the concept "self-managed" work teams in France or Mexico, although managers in these plants described their plant operations as structured into self-managed work teams. Wilkens and Pawlowsky use a German definition of self-managed work teams requiring a high degree of self-organization. French and Mexican managers had their own separate definition: teams could be self-managed when workers had discretionary control in only selected parts of the production process.

This example of self-managed work teams illustrates how any concept can have a culturally determined meaning. For d'Iribarne (2001) concepts are legitimate to the extent they have a local meaning, for which the culture rejects other meanings of the word. For management models to be accepted in a given culture, they should be perceived as legitimate. Managerial models and concepts can sometimes face absence of meaning and rejection when words have different meanings in the society in which they are applied versus that in which they originated.

Given this background, we aim to understand the local meaning of power distance and collectivism in Latin American societies by first identifying within these two dimensions two value categories: respect for authority and social relationships. These categories reflect a hybrid cultural environment. We used Hofstede's definition of values: "a general tendency to prefer certain states of behaviors over others" (1982: 18). Next, we explain how these work values appear in organizational contexts and then interpret how HRM in Latin America reflects these values.

Respect for authority

Power distance is evident in different ways within Latin American organizations. Below, we review some empirical studies on power distance and interpret its manifestations with reference to HRM practices.

Benevolent paternalism

A Latin American supervisor has the personal obligation to protect his/her subordinates (Osland et al., 1999). In Mexico specifically, s/he is entrusted with safeguarding the personal needs of workers and their families (Greer and Stephens, 1996). Researchers describe this paternalism as the old *hacienda* (private, large land-field) leadership style now reproduced in current economic organizations (Diaz-Saenz and Witherspoon, 2000; Martinez, 2003). Characteristics of this leadership are those of a *patrón* (owner–boss) who, besides paying salaries, takes care of his/her workers by providing room and board for them and their families. Under this welfare system, the community living in a hacienda develops strong familial bonds. Upon this social structure paternalistic leadership is based: it evokes a "father" who cares for and nourishes his/her children benevolently. Such paternalism is permissive and provides moral support. The result might be that children tend to develop a dependency toward authority figures when they grow up and enter their work life.

We note that Page and Wiseman (1993) find this paternalistic style mainly at the top management level, not the immediate supervisor level. They found that Mexican workers felt free to skip their immediate supervisor and speak to the general manager about their problems – whether work or personal.

At the organizational level, we find that "family" is the metaphor used by management for leading Latin American firms. For example, d'Iribarne (2002) found a collectivistic mentality in a Mexican subsidiary of an international company: "we are like a family" his informants revealed. By this they meant a place to look for support and trust, a social unit based on strong solidarity and mutual understanding. The author found supervisors in roles as "brothers", not "authoritarian fathers" which everybody fears. This "family" metaphor fits well the Mexican mentality where individuals growing up are not fully independent and need the support of their community to reach maturity (Paz, 1950, cited in d'Iribarne, 2002). These findings suggest the existence of a paternalistic variant which d'Iribarne labeled *fraternalismo* (brotherhood). In *fraternalismo*, social relations are oriented to eliminate distances and create a community of support and respect.

Conflict and confrontation

Lenartowicz and Johnson (2002) found that Latin Americans prefer to depend on somebody else at work. They accept authority from and over other employees, if it is conferred on people in a systematized hierarchy. Accepting authority is demonstrated by behaviors that aim to avoid conflict and confrontation with superiors, such as developing friendly, buffering relationships with them. Confronting or entering into conflict with a superior in public could be considered offensive to the superior as well as to other colleagues (Osland *et al.*, 1999). Subordinates who exhibit these behaviors publicly in Mexico could be labeled as disobedient, and then transferred or punished (Page and Wiseman, 1993). The Latin American philosopher Zea (1992) stressed that Latin Americans avoid making and receiving public criticisms because they are considered denigration. Thus, to avoid conflict or confrontation in public, workers use jokes, gossip, or passive-aggressive behaviors (Osland *et al.*, 1999). Different subcultures exhibit different variations of this behavior. Abarca *et al.* (1998) found that Chilean executives with high levels of education consider themselves assertive and ready to face the consequences of their actions. This did not happen at lower organizational levels in Chile, where individuals depended on the experience of international experts to avoid risky decisions.

Social distance

Latin Americans value hierarchy because it defines status and social distance between superiors and subordinates. Hierarchy is thus used as a mechanism of social differentiation. For example, job titles are local symbols of power distance. As Flynn (1994) indicates, international recruiters agree that job titles in Mexico are inflated and do not necessarily reflect work abilities. Additionally, fringe benefits are more highly valued than wages by Mexican executives, because they symbolize social status. Abarca *et al.* (1998) also identified accepted social discrimination practices in Chilean companies, based on external status symbols such as appearance, age, and gender that are typically correlated with social status.

Egalitarian sense

Latin American societies and organizations have a positive perspective on paternalistic leadership and rarely consider individuals' autonomy. Latin American culture looks for a balance between "equals that do not cooperate" and "authority that intimidates" (d'Iribarne, 2001: 28).[5] The model that better adapts to this mental structure is a community which offers intense mutual support yet coexists with a managerial authority that gives orders, criticizes and controls. Thus, it appears contradictory for managers to approach lower-level employees and so reduce the power distance that both groups value. Davila and Garcia (2004) found that committees – cross-hierarchical and cross-functional – were legitimate managerial efforts to approach subordinates and recognize their problems. Subordinates interpreted these committees as organizational strategies that symbolized equality between managers and workers.

In a case study d'Iribarne (2002) described how a new and young management team introduced global high-performance job practices throughout a local Mexican plant. This hybrid practice allowed organizational members to differentiate between a hierarchy of strangers that used to govern them and a community of equals that emerged from the new team empowerment. The new management introduced methods showing concern for all workers, mutual support, and a genuine commitment to eliminate differences without detriment to managing the plant. D'Iribarne (2001: 28) argued that performing this supervisory role is difficult: the supervisor must "assume the role of the boss" without "behaving like a boss".[6]

Social relationships

Collectivism in Latin America has specific manifestations in the workplace, the meaning of which we discuss below.

Personal contact

Personal communication is extremely important in Latin America. This is deliberately promoted by demanding that interactions between organizational members be made in person. Latin Americans want their supervisors to interact with them face to face, because personal presence carries a strong meaning of power proximity. Personal interaction is also valued from the managerial perspective because it strengthens centralization. For example, Gilberto Perez, Cemex director for U.S. Operations, stated in an interview: "I spend a lot of time on those issues – from communication to having a physical presence in the plants to talking to our employees at all levels of the organization. That keeps me grounded, and allows me to know firsthand what's going on in every corner of the organization. That's extremely valuable for me" (*Cement Americas*, 2002: 6). Personal communication, then, reduces the reliance of supervisors on impersonal administrative systems, as well as middle management authority.

Moreover, personal relationships in the workplace carry high emotional content. Latin Americans expect and prefer cordial and affective interactions at work. Therefore, friendly relationships are promoted among organizational members. The manager of the company mentioned above in Davila and Garcia's (2004) case study recently confided to the researchers that he organized a fishing weekend for his management team because "we have to become friends". In this way "we can fight at work without getting angry".

In addition, personal relationships develop the structure whereupon organizations work. Loyalty, trust, organizational flexibility, and administrative efficiency grow from this type of relationship. It is common to find informal organizations based on and renewed by empathy among organizational members. People outside the circles of personal relationships are precisely those that tend to create conflicts and resist administrative innovations (Osland *et al.*, 1999).

Group loyalty

Lenartowicz and Johnson (2002) concluded that values related to integrity and civility are appreciated by Latin Americans and reflect the cultural importance of social relations. In a Globe project study, Ogliastri *et al.* (1999) found that for Latin Americans family, collectivism, and loyalty to the group ranked among the highest scores in the world. Their study also reviewed leadership among Latin American executives and identified a tendency to accept participatory styles such as work group orientation and group collaboration; although a single leadership profile was elusive. Davila and Garcia (2004) also describe the high sense of unity that characterizes organizational members. Specifically, they felt proud of organizational achievements because they knew that they were the main actors behind such success.

Loyalty to the in-group is very important for Mexican companies. Executives know that their organizations depend on social relationships and the family or governmental ties on which they are based much more than a supportive national financial system (Martinez and Dorfman, 1998).

Popular religiosity

Social relationships are also manifested in popular celebrations. These include religious traditions that play an important role in Latin American workplaces. Many of these traditions obey popular religion; some Latin Americans see their religion as a part of their identity yet separate from their everyday life (Davila, 1999).

Some tacit religious values related to all Latin Americans are dependency on God and devotion to Our Lady – Mary (Hall, 1987). For instance, the importance of the Virgin Mary to the Mexican culture surpasses the notion of religious devotion. She is Mother, Mediator, Defender, and Compassion (Levy and Szekely, 1983). This devotion is manifested in the workplace. For example, in Mexican manufacturing plants it is common to find images, sculptures, or even altars devoted to the Virgin of Guadalupe. The CEO of a large Mexican conglomerate declared in an interview: "our workers use the most advanced German machinery under the watchful eye of Our Lady of Guadalupe" (Nichols, 1993: 164), a wonderful instance of the hybrid management model.

Christmas parties and pilgrimages illustrate the importance and beauty of religious events. Latin Americans are taught to express their religious beliefs through behaviors and gestures. Special pilgrimages, processions, blessings, abstinence, candle lighting, holy water, promises to God, statues, icons, medals, rosary praying, funeral prayers and rituals are all popular and public expressions of their religious beliefs. Although Latin Americans are generally inconsistent in attending Mass, celebrations related to Christmas and the Passion of Christ exceed the notion of religious duty. Latin Americans prefer to attend such celebrations for their deep spiritual and cultural meaning (Levy and Szekely, 1983).

Latin American workers expect freedom to express their faith in public. Therefore, it might be important for organizations to factor in their employees' religion. Moreover, international executives that are not used to seeing religious practices in the workplace might be surprised by these traditions. These religious manifestations usually represent the prevalent Catholicism, but organizational members who practice different faiths exist, even though public demonstrations of other religions are not as explicit.

Human resource management in the Latin American context

Latin American HR practices developed with the region's industrialization. In some countries, this process began when foreign investment arrived; in other countries with the indigenous economic transition from agriculture to manufacturing. In both cases, HR practices have been widely influenced by dominant global theories or foreign multinationals' imported practices, illustrating a hybrid management system. Thus, not surprisingly, implementing such HR practices in their original design often failed. Montaño (1991) argued that the human relations theory developed in industrialized countries assumes a culturally mature worker who seeks individual achievement in the workplace. This description does not fit the average Latin American worker.

The Latin American economic context is characterized by a high concentration of wealth, monopolies and oligopolies, high governmental intervention in regulating the economy, high volatility, abrupt changes from closed to open economies, and large investments in industries of low value added. Some authors (Barba, 1991; Montaño, 1991) have traced the development of organizational structures to these contextual characteristics. On the one hand, we find big diversified bureaucracies, with rigid manufacturing processes and managerial control systems that stifle workers' development by reducing their decision-making autonomy. On the other hand, there is also room for informal structures which symbolically compensate for the impersonality of rigid bureaucracies. These informal structures allow social relationships to subsist in Latin American societies. According to Montaño, there is no need for complex theories to exert control over Latin American workers. As long as informal structures last, Latin American organizations will remain in the market.

Next, we review HR practices through the lens of Latin American work values.

Human resources practices

Most HR practices reviewed below date from two life cycles in Latin American organizations. Some practices developed during stable environmental times with a constant flow of foreign investment during the 1990s, while others are currently emerging to face today's volatile economic and international context. To understand this HRM development within the cultural framework outlined above, we focus on staffing and promotion, training and development, rewards and recognitions, work systems, communication, and labor relations (see Table 1.1).

Staffing and promotion systems

Staffing policies for personnel recruiting and selection in Latin America are heavily studied and, perhaps, the most culturally specific of HR practices. Staffing is generally based on personality traits and physical characteristics. De Forest (1994) found, for example, that Mexican manufacturing plants search for candidates willing to cooperate with authority. De Forest explained that this practice is based on companies' need for maintaining peaceful, stable labor climates. Another study by Abarca et al. (1998) highlighted the importance of physical characteristics such as appearance, age and gender for executive selection in Chilean companies. The same did not apply at the blue collar level. Specifically, in Chile it is important for executives to have personal connections with primary social groups for promotion and advancement. To be promoted in organizational hierarchies, relationship ties with wealthy families, university colleagues, country club members, or birthplace geographical bonds are more important than talent (Abarca et al., 1998). In fact, the main source for personnel recruitment in many Latin American companies is other employees (Flynn, 1994); personnel selection processes are often subordinated to social relationship ties.

Social relationships and personal appearance underlie the "glass ceiling" concept in Latin American companies: promotions and transfers are determined by these two characteristics. Whereas glass ceilings for women or minorities appear in developed countries due to gender or racial discrimination, in Latin America they relate to physical appearence and social contacts.

Additionally, family traditions in the workplace are so strong that many organizations retain a policy of hiring family members or close relatives. The assumption behind this policy is that trust, loyalty, and responsibility will be guaranteed by having family members at work. This assumption holds in Latin American countries that have small labor markets in which it is difficult to find jobs. However, the practice could also reproduce a pattern learned by subordinates from their executives' practices: many big and small companies have been family-run for several generations (Husted and Serrano, 2002).

Table 1.1 Human resources practices according to work values in Latin America

	Staffing and promotion	Training and development	Rewards and recognitions	Work systems	Communication	Labor relationships
Respect for authority						
Benevolent paternalism	Hiring a worker's family members or close friends		Family protection and welfare	Could be interpreted as exploitation systems for workers	Vertical and hierarchical communication	Immediate rejection of any kind of abuse
Conflict and confrontation	People that contribute to a good labor climate	Modern practices are rejected or modified	Rejection of performance appraisals	Shared responsibility with team members	Avoid confrontation of ideas and actions	Courtesy and political treatment
Social distance	Glass ceiling based on physical appearance and social contacts	Social mobility	Symbols of status for top executives	Difficulty in authority delegation	Centralization of information	
Egalitarian sense				Reduces power distance	Concern for employee's work and personal problems	
Social relationships						
Personal contact	Nuclear and primary groups (in-group)	Starting participation practices and responses in MNCs	Rejection of individual recognition	Face-to-face relationships	Emotional ties	Personal commitment and friendship
Group loyalty		Organizational commitment	Sense of community; group and seniority recognition	Managerial commitment Rejection of outsourcing		Concern for others
Popular religiosity					Public expression of religious faith	

In terms of promotion, family is again important in employment decisions, including placing the welfare of one's family over the employee's career advancement. Scarce empirical research on staffing and promotion practices for women in Latin America prevents us from thoroughly understanding women's advancement and participation in decision making. Women are always present in manufacturing operations yet absent from authority positions. This situation is due to women's delayed entrance into the labor market, their decision to take care of family, and/or organizations' negative attitude toward including women in authority roles.

Training and development

Training and development departments in Latin American companies often conflict. On the one hand, they see a need to train the workforce in modern management practices such as self-managed teams. On the other hand, these departments know that not all modern practices fit local idiosyncrasies and that some could be rejected by employees (Chantell et al., 1999) or modified according to the Latin American mindset and experience (Sargent and Matthews, 1998). For example, Peterson et al. (2003) found that Mexican employees of a US subsidiary learned to express their opinion at the workplace without fear of being sanctioned, as they would have been in a traditional Latin American company.

Moreover, training and development departments often search for strategies to broaden their reach. Besides developing employees' skills for specific work systems, these departments often offer basic formal education and technical training (De Forest, 1994). Chantell et al. (1999) and Lawrence and Lewis (1993) reported the lack of technical knowledge, formal education, and analytical and communication skills in Mexican workers as a serious obstacle. This deficiency impedes the functioning of management practices such as self-managed teams and "just-in-time" production systems.

Wilkens and Pawlowsky (1997) reported that 90 percent of the workers in an assembly plant in Mexico were unskilled or at most semi-technically skilled. The cause is mostly low budgets for firms' training programs in an overall context of a deficient educational system. Thus, training and development departments respond with internal training resources (De Forest, 1994), which might reproduce the status quo: accepting deficiencies rather than generating new knowledge.

Despite this scenario, we would like to mention some sincere efforts by big Latin American multinationals to train their employees in modern management and technical skills. For example, Cemex (Mexico) announced an investment of US$110 million for training and development in 2003 (Ortega, 2003). Such education in Latin American organizations has a powerful motivational appeal as a mechanism for social mobility.

Rewards and recognitions

To understand motivation schemes in Latin America, we must consider the meaning of work. Diaz-Saenz and Witherspoon (2000) discovered that Mexican employees base their work decisions and expectations on their family needs. Family is central in Latin American workers' lives. In general, work is seen as the means to a single and important aim: to provide a good quality of life for the employee's family.

Institutional support for this cultural feature comes from labor legislation. In Mexico, for example, labor laws were created to promote social welfare, especially in the face of recurrent economic crises (1976, 1982, 1986, and 1994). Underlying this legislation is the premise that economic crises impact workers' salaries but not their fringe benefits, which are tax free. This law's objective is oriented toward maintaining the workers' families.

Benefits in Latin American organizations include health care, food bonds, children's scholarships, discounts for school materials and clothes, and mortgage credit. Some companies offer memberships to recreational clubs for the employees and their families, promote cultural activities and sponsor museums (Nichols, 1993). In addition, big companies establish strategic alliances with public day-care centers to provide this service to their employees – i.e. Telmex and Monterrey TEC.[7] It is common for companies to have facilities such as recreational or country clubs for family gatherings. Offering these fringe benefits for workers' family welfare is seen as an additional cost besides wages, typically considered low-cost in countries such as Mexico (Flynn, 1994). These extra benefits are loaded with a strong cultural meaning: to help workers' purchasing power and benefit their families.

Organization–worker–family relationships also include activities that deliberately involve the employees' family. Many Latin American organizations hold yearly family-day visits to the workplace. Other organizations celebrate popular holidays such as Mother's Day or Children's Day, organize family picnics and family Christmas parties, or offer advanced training courses for workers' spouses. Most of the fringe benefits described here are found in major organizations. Small and medium-size companies offer the minimum required legal benefits (Carillo, cited in Cepeda, 2004).

From a different perspective, Pelled and Xin (1997) described work in Mexico as an unpleasant thing needed to enjoy more important things in life. In other words, if Mexicans had the option, they would not work. Yet they have to support their family, because family "is more important". The authors also found that workers are protected by a dismissal law and argued that Mexicans live with a national culture that does not glorify work. As a result, Mexican workers are not proactive in their work.

Pelled and Xin's (1997) conclusions should be interpreted with caution. Work culture tends to have different manifestations depending on factors such as hierarchical level, age, and educational level. These factors are not considered in their study. For example, Sargent and Matthews (1998) found that multinational manufacturing plants in northern Mexico considerably reduced the number of expatriates because young talent in the region was locally available. Multinationals found trained engineers with managerial capacity, university diplomas, and bilingual education. In this context, accepting modern management and production methods was significantly higher among the young managers than among the mature.

Work in Latin America also fulfills a worker's social needs. Social recognition becomes an important motivator to be cooperative and loyal, important traits in a collective society. Rewards and recognitions carry a different cultural meaning according to employees' organizational level. On the one hand, Diaz-Saenz and Witherspoon (2000) argue that financial compensation differentials potentially make a worker shine as "the favorite" and result in rejection by his/her group. Rejection is intolerable for a Latin American worker. On the other hand, fringe benefits (including specific car brands, children's tuition payment for private schools, or gym memberships) offer recognition for executives and symbolize social status, something highly valued.

Workers' loyalty is socially recognized through ceremonies rewarding seniority. Seniority is very important in Latin America and many job benefits depend on it. For example, legal protection in case of an unjustified dismissal, vacation days, and in some organizations, salary increases all depend on workers' seniority.

Reward systems could become contentious when based on performance appraisals. The impact of performance appraisals is tinted by a work culture that avoids conflicts between superior and subordinates (Osland et al., 1999). Therefore, performance appraisals are controversial by definition and their outcomes are rarely used.

Income remuneration generally comes in the form of fixed wages – except for sales personnel. This wage and salary system reflects individualistic and hierarchical organizations (Gomez Lopez-Egea, cited in Gomez, 1998). In other words, organizations with work cultures that value centralization are characterized by fixed wages and salaries. In contrast, variable pay promotes flexible organizations and teamwork. These two last factors are not compatible with the Latin American's cultural preference for centralization (Montaño, 1991). In fact, data point out that only big Latin American companies as well as multinationals reward top executives with variable compensation based on performance. Few organizations strive to link variable compensation to the value of the company; Cemex is one of those exceptions (Furlong, cited in Gomez, 1998).

Work systems

Collective Latin American culture tends to favor successful implementation of all work teams. That is, Latin Americans value social relationships manifested through personal communication and empathy among organizational members, both aspects being integral to work teams. Yet work teams, as globally understood, were not found in a Mexico assembly plant (Wilkens and Pawlowsky, 1997). A barrier to implementing work teams in the region is related to uneasiness over decentralization or sharing of authority.

Modern management systems rely on authority decentralization (Chantell *et al.*, 1999; Montaño, 1991), which clashes with the Latin American's preference for centralization and organizational hierarchy. Workers' decision-making scope within work teams is limited by partial integration of the control processes (Wilkens and Pawlowsky, 1997), training or job self-training, or task scheduling (Garza-Zambrano, cited in Castilleja, 1998). This explains why modern management systems enter and leave Mexican companies quickly (Montaño ,1991). Additionally, subordinates value depending on a superior for decision making; they avoid responsibility. Therefore, employees expect a directive leadership style and at the same time accept participating in modern management practices (Lawrence and Lewis, 1993; Page and Wiseman, 1993). Again their work systems exemplify the hybrid model.

Employees expect management to show a daily commitment to modern management practices. Lawrence and Lewis (1993) indicated two criteria that Latin American workers interpret as commitment to these practices: (a) a management that gives sufficient time to pursue modern initiatives; and (b) a management that learns Spanish. In other words, Latin Americans perceive that international executives accept international assignments for short periods of time which preclude any interest in learning the local culture. These two criteria reflect the cultural expectation that management should be concerned about employees.

An interesting variation of this condition was reported for Chilean companies: Abarca *et al.* (1998) found top executives with high levels of education ready to face the consequences of their actions. These attitudes were not found in lower levels of the organizations. Workers at the operational level of the companies expressed a need to depend on the experience of an expert superior so as to avoid taking risks in making decisions.

Participation in decision making with management is another manifestation of the hybrid model because Latin Americans want to avoid conflict and confrontation, not only with superiors but also with colleagues. Therefore, subordinates accept a directive leadership style that mediates among parties in conflict, a style that might occur in work team dynamics. This said, when a sense of community has developed, workers are willing to enter into conflict to defend their team (Davila and Garcia, 2004).

Finally, the use of work teams also facilitates the cooperation and commitment required in companies today. Workers are motivated by sharing teamwork responsibilities (Chantell *et al.*, 1999). This attitude can be interpreted as a way of reducing individual risk because decisions are shared with other organizational members.

Modern management systems might fail in Latin America because a historical rivalry between labor and management informed the industrialization process of the region. Businessmen and organized workers considered themselves opposites because of the perception that the first exploited the second. A critical vision of hacienda leadership reflects this feeling that an authoritarian *patrón* exploited workers and paid them miserable wages, a system derived from feudal systems inherited from the Spaniards (Novelo, 1991, cited in Diaz-Saenz and Witherspoon, 2000). Thus, diverse studies portray Mexican managers or workers as indifferent to the industrial development process or in opposition to it (De la Cerda and Núñez, 1993; Robles, 1998). Nevertheless, Diaz-Saenz and Witherspoon (2000) argued that this historical rivalry is transformed into a unifying feeling when Mexicans, for example, see their work in danger of disappearing after foreign investment. Latin American nationalism provokes in both management and workers a desire to produce better quality products and to use technology more efficiently, all of which makes top management learn to share information with employees (Davila and Garcia, 2004).

Outsourcing

A most recent HR practice is outsourcing. A common assumption is that economically unstable contexts in Latin America would benefit from reducing labor costs through more flexible labor arrangements. Yet employees there have difficulty accepting work on a contingent basis, and this cultural resistance might outweigh the purported economic benefits. In addition, labor markets in the region are small and could partially explain why work supply exceeds demand, thereby affecting employment.

Given this imbalance in labor markets, permanent jobs are of great value because they represent economic and tangible benefits. Developmental opportunities, fringe benefits, and seniority benefits provided by stable jobs cannot be obtained through an outsourcing company. Generally, such companies offer specialized personnel services at a low cost. Therefore, they limit all benefits and follow labor laws strictly. However, outsourcing firms remain because for many workers it is their only option in a recession.

Organizations in the information technology industry would best fit contingent work. But using this type of strategy is developing slowly in the region. Morales (2004) found that two Mexican companies dedicated to e-commerce still maintain full-time personnel, despite their greater flexibility in using temporary and outsourced workers.

Geographic mobility

Globalization, one of the forces that pressed Latin American companies toward internationalization, requires geographic mobility in executives and employees.

One already finds many Latin American executives in international operations, including the Mexican Jose Octavio Reyes, the President and Operations Chief Executive for Coca-Cola Latin America and Executive Vice-president for The Coca-Cola Company in Atlanta; Brazilian Carlos Ghosn, President and Executive Director of Motor Nissan Co.; and Mexican Eugene Minvielle-Lakes, who was appointed President of Nestlé France in July 2004. Nevertheless, a strong cultural value for closeness to the nuclear and extended family reduces executives' willingness to move in support of a firm's geographic expansion strategy. Reyes indicated in an interview: "by personality and culture, in general, Latin Americans do not have the flexibility that is needed. In the United States, families get together once a year, in Thanksgiving. In Mexico, as in Brazil, families meet every Sunday" (Puertas, 1996).

Organizational communication

In hierarchical and vertically structured Latin American organizations, information flows generally from top to bottom. Communication barriers for first-line managers result from centralization preferences favored by Latin American managers (Wilkens and Pawlowsky, 1997). In addition, emotional proximity prevents subordinates from confronting their superiors regarding their ideas or actions, and explains why hierarchical communication is perceived as deficient (Lindsley, 1999). This could also be the cause of reduced horizontal relationships, so important to modern management practices requiring empowerment.

Labor relations

Labor relations in Latin America derive from many historical processes. Unionism is a social and political phenomenon with extensive ramifications. Here we take a HRM perspective focusing on conflict resolution and negotiation styles.

Several values support negotiations and conflict management styles in the region. First, personal contact is very important, due to the harmony and good labor climate that companies seek. Social interaction and friendship are important conditions for good and stable labor relations here. Therefore, courtesy and diplomacy are highly valued in labor relations. Gabrielidis et al. (1997) found that Mexicans prefer styles of conflict management which incorporate concern for others. Latin Americans do enter into conflict, but they prefer a particular confrontation style. Argentineans, for example, favor a mediating style between parties in conflict. Dominicans, on the other hand, prefer a mediating or autocratic style (Cropanzano et al., 1999).

Moreover, conflict management style is perceived as a means to assert who is the better person among the parties (Condon, 1985, cited in Gabrielidis et al., 1997).

In these cases, Latin Americans tend to identify with their primary group (in-group) rather than with the organization as a whole. This happens because of the preference for social networks based on friendship.

A more recent union development evolves from globalization. Abuse and mistreatment of the workforce by some international managers is condemned immediately by Latin American workers. The first thing workers do under these conditions is to organize unions that directly confront the company, as was the case in assembly plants in Mexico (*El Universal*, 2003; *Reforma*, 2003) and in subsidiaries of multinationals (*Diario de Yucatán*, 2003).

Final considerations

This chapter has explained cultural values affecting work in Latin America as a means to understand HR practices in the region and help organizations with future decisions. We propose social, economic, and political options that could facilitate obtaining good results for Latin American companies. From a social perspective, modern HR systems would be more effective if they respected the collectivism, fairness, and internal supplements valued by Latin Americans. In other words, they should place the needs of workers and their families at the center of fringe benefits. From an economic perspective, HR systems should try to satisfy workers' basic needs so that improved performance follows. From a political perspective, HR systems would be more effective if they were related to job stability, good labor relationships, and sustainable development of the company. How to develop HRM strategically is as much a challenge for practitioners as it is for academics.

HR departments will not reach a strategic level in Latin American organizations until they directly contribute to performance (Diez *et al.*, 2003). And we believe that performance should be interpreted from a cultural perspective, including the importance of respect for authority (power distance) and social relationships (collectivism). The challenge is, therefore, how to capitalize on HR practices that are culturally determined and valued. The performance results of this qualitative approach to HR are difficult to predict because results depend on a strong social structure as well as an organization's financial situation.

International competition and recurrent economic crises undoubtedly strain HR practices in Latin America. But understanding the cultural foundation of this region will help us reevaluate its human resource management.

Notes

1. In 1993 Hofstede added another dimension important for Asian countries: long-term orientation. We do not consider it here because the study did not include Latin America.

2. Hofstede (1982) measured each dimension in 40 countries according to an index derived from average scores obtained in a survey.
3. These countries have a cultural proximity with Europe due to their current demographic composition.
4. Translated by the authors.
5. Translated by the authors.
6. Translated by the authors.
7. Telmex is a Mexican telephone company and it is the largest in Latin America. Monterrey TEC is the longest private university in Mexico.

References

Abarca, N., Majluf, N., and Rodriguez, D. (1998) "Identifying management in Chile: A behavioral approach," *International Studies of Management and Organizations* 28 (2): 18–37.

Aguilar, E.J. (1993) "Mexican corporate culture," *Business Mexico* 3 (8): 8–9, 38.

Barba, A. (1991) "Reflexiones sobre la administración desde el punto de vista del proceso laboral" [Management considerations from the labor process perspective], in E. Ibarra and L. Montaño (eds) *Ensayos Críticos para el Estudio de las Organizaciones en México* [Critical essays for studying organizations in Mexico], Mexico: UAM-I, Miguel Angel Porrua, pp. 199–224.

Castilleja, J. (1998) "Logran calidad con multihabilidades" [Quality through multiple skills], *El Norte, Seccion Negocios*, retrieved 1 July 2004 through Elnorte.com from: http://busquedas.gruporeforma.com/00006180

Cement Americas (2002) "A conversation with Cemex's President of U.S. operations Gilberto Perez" (July/August), retrieved 20 July 2004 from: http://cementamericas.com/mag/cement_conversation_cemexs_president/

Cepeda, F. (2004) "Aconsejan a Pymes ampliar prestaciones" [Small and medium size companies are advised to increment tangible benefits], *El Norte*, retrieved 4 August 2004 through Elnorte.com from: http://busquedas.gruporeforma.com/00373520

Chantell, E.N., Lane, H.W., and Brechu, M.B. (1999) "Taking self-managed teams to Mexico," *Academy of Management Executive* 13 (3): 15–25.

Cropanzano, R., Aguinis, H., Schminke, M., and Denham, D.L. (1999) "Disputant reactions to managerial conflict resolution tactics: A comparison among Argentina, the Dominican Republic, Mexico, and the United States," *Group and Organization Management* 24 (2): 124–154.

D'Iribarne, P. (2001) "Administración y culturas políticas" [Management and political cultures], *Gestión y Política Pública* [Management and Public Policy] 10 (1): 5–29.

—— (2002) "Motivating workers in emerging countries: Universal tools and local adaptations," *Journal of Organizational Behavior* 23: 1–14.

Davila, A. (1999) "Cultura organizacional en una escuela Católica mexicana: Un estudio de caso" [Organizational culture in a Catholic Mexican school: A case study], in A. Davila and N. H. Martinez (eds) *Cultura en organizaciones latinas: Elementos, injerencia, y evidencia en los procesos organizacionales* [Culture in Latin organizations: Elements, interference, and evidence in organizational processes], Mexico: Siglo XXI-ITESM, pp. 44–70.

—— (2004) "Culture and business practices in Latin America: Opportunities for research and challenges for management", pp. 559–79, in N. Schweickart and L. Kaufmann (eds) *Lateinamerika–management: Konzepte–Prozesse–Erfahrungen* [Management in Latin America: Concepts, processes, and experiences], Wiesbaden: Germany: Gabler.

Davila, A. and Garcia, E. (2004) "Cultural symbols as change agents: International joint ventures in the Mexican context," in V. Gupta (ed.) *Transformative organizations: A global perspective*, New Delhi/California: Sage, pp. 373–386.

De Forest, M.E. (1994) "Thinking of a plant in Mexico?" *Academy of Management Executive* 8 (1): 33–40.

De la Cerda, J. and Núñez, F. (1993) *La Administración en Desarrollo: Problemas y Avances de la Administración en México* [Developing management: Problems and advances in Mexico], 2nd edn, Mexico: Instituto Internacional de Capacitación y Estudios Empresariales.

Diario de Yucatán (2003) "El maltrato laboral de jefes extranjeros a los mexicanos es una realidad en Cancún" [Labor mistreat to Mexican workers by international executives is a reality in Cancun] (3 December), retrieved 16 December 2003 from: http://0-site.securities.com.millenium.itesm.mx/

Diaz-Saenz, H.R. and Witherspoon, P.D. (2000) "Psychological contracts in Mexico," in D.M. Rousseau and R. Schalk (eds) *Psychological contracts in employment: Cross-national perspectives*, Thousand Oaks, CA: Sage, pp. 158–175.

Diaz-Saenz, H.R., García, C., and Davila, A. (2004) *Interpretations of sense of community in Latin American organizations: A cultural approach*, 9th International Society for the Study of Work and Organizational Values, New Orleans, USA.

Diez, F., Heslop, B., and Ambrosio, L. (2003) "Cambio de papeles" [Role changes], *Harvard Business Review: América Latina* 81 (10): 26–28.

El Universal (2003) "Abusos contra empleados" [Abuses against employees], Seccion Financiero (15 September), retrieved 16 December 2003 from: http://0-site.securities.com.millenium.itesm.mx/

Flynn, G. (1994) "HR in Mexico: What you should know," *Personnel Journal* 73 (7): 34–42.

Gabrielidis, C., Stephan, W.G., Ybarra, O., Pearson, V.M.D.S., and Villarreal, L. (1997) "Preferred styles of conflict resolution," *Journal of Cross-Cultural Psychology* 28 (6): 661–677.

Geertz, C. (1983) *Local knowledge: Further essays in interpretive anthropology*, New York: Basic Books.

Gomez, R. (1998) "Dando nuevo valor al talento" [Giving new value to talent], *El Norte, Seccion Negocios*, 3 November, retrieved 1 July 2004 through Elnorte.com from: http://busquedas.gruporeforma.com/00073614

Greer, C.R. and Stephens, G.K. (1996) "Employee relations issues for US companies in Mexico," *California Management Review* 38 (3): 121–146.

Guillen, M. (1994). Models of manuscript: work, authority, and organization in comparitive perspective. Chicago: University of Chicago Press.

Hall, S. (1987) "Understanding the Hispanic presence," in C. Reck (ed.) *Integral education: A response to the Hispanic presence*, USA: National Catholic Educational Association, pp. 29–38.

Hofstede, G.H. (1982) *Culture's consequences: International differences in work-related values*, abridged edn, Newbury Park, CA: Sage.

—— (1991) *Cultures and organizations. Software of the mind*, London: McGraw-Hill.

—— (1993) "Cultural constraints in management theories," *Academy of Management Executive* 7 (1): 81–94.

Husted, B.W. and Serrano, C. (2002) "Corporate governance in Mexico," *Journal of Business Ethics* 37 (3): 337–348.

Lawrence, J.J. and Lewis, H.S. (1993) "JIT manufacturing in Mexico: Obstacles to implementation," *Production and Inventory Management Journal* 34 (3): 31–36.

Lenartowicz, T. and Johnson, J.P. (2002) "Comparing managerial values in twelve Latin American countries: An exploratory study," *Management International Review* 42 (3): 279–307.

Levy, D. and Szekely, G. (1983) *Mexico: Paradoxes of stability and change*, Boulder, CO: Westview.

Lindsley, S.L. (1999) "Communication and 'the Mexican way': Stability and trust as core symbols in maquiladoras," *Western Journal of Communication* 63 (1): 1–31.

Martinez, P.G. (2003) "Paternalism as a positive form of leader–subordinate exchange: Evidence from Mexico," *Management Research* 1: 227–242.

Martinez, S.M. and Dorfman, P.W. (1998) "The Mexican entrepreneur: An ethnographic study of the Mexican empresario," *International Studies of Management and Organization* 28 (2): 97–125.

Mills, A.J. and Hatfield, J. (1998) "From imperialism to globalization: Internationalization and the management text," in S.R. Clegg, E. Ibarra-Colado, and L.B. Rodriguez (eds) *Global management: Universal theories and local realities*, London: Sage, pp. 37–67.

Montaño, L. (1991) "Las nuevas relaciones-humanas: Un falso reto a la democracia" [New human relations: A false challenge to democracy], in E. Ibarra and L. Montaño (eds) *Ensayos Críticos para el Estudio de las Organizaciones en México* [Critical essays for the study of organizations in Mexico], Mexico: UAM-I, Miguel Angel Porrua, pp. 67–102.

—— (2000) "La dimensión cultural de la organización. Elementos para un debate en América Latina" [The cultural dimension of the organization. Elements for a debate in Latin America], in E. De la Garza (ed.) *Tratado Latinoamericano de Sociología del Trabajo* [Latin American sociology of work handbook], Mexico: COLMEX, FLACSO, UAM, FCE, pp. 285–311.

Morales, G. (2004) *Estructura Organizacional de los Negocios Electrónicos: Dos Estudios de Caso en México* [Organizational structure for electronic business: Two case studies in Mexico], Programa de Maestría en Administración de Tecnologías de Información, ITESM, Campus Monterrey.

Nichols, N.A. (1993) "From complacency to competitiveness: An interview with Vitro's Ernesto Martens," *Harvard Business Review* 71 (5): 162–171.

Ogliastri, E., McMillen, C., Altschul, C., Arias, M.E., Bustamante, C., Davila, C., Dorfman, P., Coletta, M.F., Fimmen, C., Ickis, J., and Martinez, S. (1999) "Cultura y liderazgo organizacional en 10 países de América Latina. El estudio Globe" [Culture and organizational leadership in 10 Latin American countries], *Academia, Revista Latinoamericana de Administración* 22: 29–57.

Ortega, M.D. (2003) "Recluta Cemex 'cerebritos'" [Cemex recruits 'brains'], *El Norte, Seccion Negocios*, retrieved 1 July 2004 through Elnorte.com from: http://busquedas.gruporeforma.com/00298536

Osland, J.S., De Franco, S., and Osland, A. (1999) "Organizational implications of Latin American culture: Lessons for the expatriate manager," *Journal of Management Inquiry* 8 (2): 219–234.

Page, N.R. and Wiseman, R.L. (1993) "Supervisory behavior and worker satisfaction in the United States, Mexico and Spain," *Journal of Business Communication* 30 (2): 161–181.

Pelled, L.H. and Xin, K.R. (1997) "Work values and their human resource management implications: A theoretical comparison of China, Mexico, and the United States," *Journal of Applied Management Studies* 6 (2): 185–198.

Peterson, D.K., Puia, G.M., and Suess, F.R. (2003) "'Yo tengo la camiseta (I have the shirt on)': An exploration of job satisfaction and commitment among workers in Mexico," *Journal of Leadership and Organizational Studies* 10 (2): 73–88.

Puertas, A. (1996) "El valor de una carrera internacional" [The value of an international career], *Expansión*, Seccion Especial, 692 (5 June), retrieved 24 August 2004 through Expansión.com from: http://www.expansion.com.mx/_asp/print.asp?cve=692_09

Reforma (2003) "Denuncian represión en fábrica coreana" [Report on repression in a Korean factory] (30 June), retrieved 16 December 2003 from: http://0-site.securities.com.millenium.itesm.mx/

Robles, L. (1998) "Estereotipos rotos. El debate sobre la cultura laboral mexicana" [Broken stereotypes. Debate over Mexican work culture], in R. Guadarrama (ed.) *Cultura y Trabajo en México. Estereotipos, Prácticas y Representaciones* [Culture and work in Mexico. Stereotypes, practices, and representations], Mexico: UAM, Juan Pablos Editor y Fundación Friedrich Ebert, pp. 125–156.

Sargent, J. and Matthews, L. (1998) "Expatriate reduction and Mariachi circle: Trends in MNC human resource practices in Mexico," *International Studies of Management and Organization* 28 (2): 74–96.

Wilkens, U. and Pawlowsky, P. (1997) "Human resource management or machines that change the world in the automotive industry?" *Management International Review* 37 (1): 105–126.

Zea, L. (1992 [1952]) "El sentido de responsabilidad en el mexicano" [The Mexican's sense of responsibility], in *Dos Ensayos sobre México y lo Mexicano* [Two Essays: Mexico and the Mexican], Mexico: Editorial Porrua, Coleccion "Sepan Cuantos ...," No. 269, pp. 105–114.

2 Latin America: economic and business context

LOURDES CASANOVA

The objective of this chapter is to outline the economic context in which Latin American companies have developed over the last ten years. This is intended to provide an insightful backdrop for executives of Latin American companies, and to aid them in formulating their human resource management (HRM) policies more effectively.

The chapter offers a view of key drivers for the wide-ranging economic reforms in the region during the 1990s, chiefly the "Washington Consensus" and the increased political stability. It highlights the key developments and results of the reforms in the areas of privatization (across industries), foreign investment, and trade liberalization. It further provides insight into how the opening up of the regional economies resulted in multinationals penetrating and thereafter increasing their ownership of business across sectors, and how as a result the public sector's share shrank during the period and local businesses adapted to this changed environment. The chapter also touches upon some key structural changes in the labor market as a result of the developments of the 1990s. This is followed by an exploration of some of the themes and challenges facing the regional economies in the years ahead – economic, social, and geopolitical.

Economic reforms in Latin American economies in the 1990s: the "Washington Consensus years"

In 1990, John Williamson, a US economist from the Institute for International Economics, coined the term "Washington Consensus" "to refer to the lowest common denominator of policy advice being addressed by the Washington-based institutions to Latin American countries as of 1989."[1] This reform agenda included: fiscal discipline; redirection of public expenditure toward fields that offered high economic returns and potential to improve income distribution; tax reform (to lower marginal rates and broaden the tax base); interest rate liberalization; competitive exchange rate; trade liberalization; liberalization of inflows of foreign direct investment; privatization of state enterprises (which accounted for 10 percent of Gross Domestic Product (GDP), on average, in Latin American countries in 1985); deregulation (to abolish barriers to entry and exit); and secure property rights.

Deregulation and privatization

Chile was the pioneer in opening up its economy and aggressively pursuing market-oriented reforms, starting in the late 1970s and further accelerating in the late 1980s and 1990s. Following Chile's example, and guided by the Washington Consensus, most of the regional economies' policies started liberalizing in the 1990s. A majority of governments in the region engaged in significant trade liberalization, far-reaching privatization programs, reduction in the role of government in the economy, and other, similar measures. Government finances were reformed through expenditure rationalization, privatizations and efforts to make tax collection more efficient (EIU Viewswire, 2003). These "structural reforms" were carried out in the hope of attaining renewed growth in the global economy, after the so-called "lost decade" – by the foreign debt crisis, hyperinflation and stagnation that the region experienced in the 1980s. By the end of the 1980s, structural adjustment had evolved into a long-term project of economic liberalization. In comparative terms, economic reform in Latin America has been both extensive and sustained.

With respect to trade liberalization, according to the Inter-American Development Bank, "Average tariffs fell from close to 50% in 1985 to around 10% in 1996, and maximum tariffs fell from an average of 84% to just 41%. By 1996, non-tariff barriers affected only 6% of imports, while in the pre-reform period they affected 38%." (Haque, 2000).

As a consequence of trade liberalization, privatization, market deregulation and fiscal reform in the 1990s, the region became much more attractive to multinational corporations (MNCs), and net foreign direct investment (FDI) inflows in Latin America grew from US$18 billion at the beginning of the 1990s to a peak of US$108 billion in 1999. The year 1999 was the first time that Latin America overtook Asia as the preferred destination of FDI since 1986. Since 1999, investment has receded by 40 percent to US$36.5 billion in 2003. Despite several challenges in the last few years, Latin America continues to be a region for active investments by MNCs.

Latin America has also been prominent among the developing regions in terms of the number and value of privatization transactions. In the 1990s, Latin America accounted for 55 percent of total privatization revenues in the developing world (Chong and Lopez, 2003).

Selling state-owned enterprises (SOEs) to private interests – individual and institutional, domestic and international – appealed to many leaders as an all-purpose option – a way to raise state revenues, help balance budgets, reduce government subsidies to failing public firms, improve the efficiency and quality of public services, and attract foreign investment (Smith, 2002). These sales were part of a broader restructuring of the public sector that included outright SOE liquidations, encouragement of competition in sectors previously reserved for the state, and shifting of public sector activities to private providers through concessions.

Dramatic differences in the extent of privatization were evident within the region. Countries with previously large SOE sectors, such as Ecuador, Nicaragua and Uruguay, barely privatized in the 1990s, while others such as Argentina, Bolivia, Guyana, Panama and Peru raised revenues from comprehensive privatization programs that amount to over 10 percent of GDP. The privatizations throughout Latin America and the Caribbean between 1990 and 1999 totaled over US$151 billion, with Brazil (US$72 billion), Mexico (US$25 billion), and Argentina (US$23 billion) leading the way (ECLAC, 2001).

Privatization in Latin America has been wide-ranging, encompassing key sectors such as telecommunications, mining, energy, petroleum, finance, airlines, transportation, and infrastructure industries. Most countries began cautiously by privatizing smaller enterprises in the services sector and progressively moving to larger enterprises in the industrial sector.

The mining industry

In the mining industry, the new conditions for mining investment aroused interest in increasing such activities in the region. As a result, exploration budgets in Latin America rose from less than US$200 million annually in 1990 to US$544 million in 1994, rapidly reaching US$1.17 billion in 1997, 29 percent of the world's total exploration budget in that year (Ocampo and Martin, 2003). Chile was the first country to attract the interest of MNCs after granting extensive guarantees and open access to mining resources. Subsequently, other countries such as Argentina, Bolivia and Peru adopted similar policies, attracting substantial new investments in mining activities.

The telecom industry

Privatizations in the telecommunications sector attracted perhaps the widest interest from foreign investors. Chile opted to carry out early deregulation and privatization, creating a competitive climate and attracting several international companies into the market. At the other end were Costa Rica and Uruguay, which maintained the state monopoly in basic telephony while gradually opening cellular telephony and value-added services to other players. Between the two extremes lay Argentina, Brazil, Mexico, Peru and Venezuela. By the end of the 1990s, the main state fixed-line incumbents in all these countries had been privatized, cellular telephony licenses had been auctioned off, and the deregulation of satellite and online services had been achieved to a large degree. The privatization of the Telebras system of Brazil in 1998 raised more than twice as much revenue from the sale than had been initially expected.

In recent years, the regional telecom industry has seen a consolidation trend, with the biggest players buying out minority stakes of relatively weaker players. The Mexican group Telmex became the biggest telecom player, by number of subscribers, in the region in 2003 with two key acquisitions by the subsidiary América Móvil: BCP (Brazil's no. 2 wireless operator) and BSE in Brazil from BellSouth, and El Salvador's CTE from France Telecom. It also took a 49 percent stake in Argentine operator CTI, and bought out minority shares in Ecuador's Conecel and Colombia's Comcel (BusinessNews Americas, 2003). In 2000, the Spanish telecom operator Telefónica, the second biggest player, acquired Motorola's five Mexican wireless networks for US$2.6 billion to add to its existing Latin American wireless and wire-line operations in Argentina, Brazil, Chile and Peru. It also made strategic purchases in Brazil – Brasilcel, the merger of its Brazilian operations with Telecom Portugal, acquired Brasilia-based mobile operator Tele Centro Oeste for almost US$1 billion in early 2003. AT&T sold its Latin American operations to Telmex, MCI intended to sell Embratel in Brazil (bought by Telmex in 2004), while Comcast was scouting around for acquisitions.

The banking industry

The banking sector in Latin America has been among the most aggressively privatized. Taking the top six countries in banking terms (Mexico, Brazil, Argentina, Venezuela, Chile, Colombia), there are 129 foreign-owned banks out of 293 banks, and they account for 45 percent of the collective bank assets in these countries.

The two biggest banks in Spain – Banco Bilbao Vizcaya Argentaria (BBVA) and Banco Santander Central Hispano (BSCH) – have led the "conquest" of Latin American banking, accounting for slightly more than half of all foreign banks assets (Barth et al., 2002). As of 2003, Latin America represented 38 percent of BBVA's operational profits. For the same time period, BSCH had 31 percent of its total assets in Latin America. Of its net profit, 67 percent is from its operations in Latin America. These two banks account for about one-fourth of the total banking assets in Latin America. Overall, Spanish-owned banks account for 19 percent of the collective bank assets of these top six countries, or 40 percent of the total for all foreign-owned banks in these same countries. The other big foreign banks are Citibank, HSBC (which acquired Mexico's Grupo Financiero Bital in 2002), and the Bank of Nova Scotia of Canada. Crédit Agricole of France and Intesa SpA of Italy quit the region in 2002 and 2003 respectively.

The energy industry

In the energy sector, the thrust of reforms in the 1990s was to accelerate the use of market forces, lower barriers to entry for private companies, and reduce the role of price controls and subsidies in the sector to counter inflationary pressures in the economy. This was done by introducing competition and regulatory mechanisms to usher in private investment or privatization as appropriate, price correction, restructuring and financial restructuring of SOEs. Privatization led to a number of foreign investors entering Latin America, the most prominent being Spanish firms (Endesa and Iberdrola) and a number of US firms (AES Corporation, Houston Industries Energy, Southern Electric, CEA, Dominium Energy and CMS Energy). Given the scale of the resources involved, consortia of foreign firms from different countries were created, and these acted in partnership with powerful local groups to take control of the privatized assets. Interests focused first on the privatizations in Argentina, and then on Brazil. Mexico, in a bid to encourage more private capital in the gas industry, introduced a new mechanism in 2003 called "multiple service contracts". The idea was to group into larger bid packages a number of smaller contracts that would otherwise have been offered individually. For instance, state oil company Pemex awarded bundled contracts for the Cuervito, Mision and Reynosa-Monterrey blocks in the Burgos basin. In Colombia, the government decided in 2003 to privatize natural gas transport company Ecogas, in a move to reduce transport rates.

The results of electricity privatization have been mixed, with some successes but overall a very patchy record of private investment, mostly the result of an uncertain regulatory environment and governments dithering on crucial and badly needed reforms. Successful privatizations include Duke Energy of USA purchasing Brazilian electric company Paranapanema for US$684 million in 1999, and Endesa of Spain's acquisition of two Chilean power companies, Enersis and Endesa, for US$4.8 billion between 1997 and 1999. In recent years, however, investors' confidence has been dented by regional governments in Brazil appearing to change the rules of the game and renege on contracts. Goias and Parana states both had disputes in 2003 with Spain's Endesa, and in the case of Parana the argument involved US power company El Paso and Brazilian energy giant Petrobras, too. In Mexico, power sector reform had long been a politically sensitive topic and had dragged on for years. Nevertheless, several projects awarded to private companies had been commissioned there successfully: Transalta's *Chihuahua III* and *Campeche*, Sempra's *Termoelectrica de Mexicali*, Unión Fenosa's *Naco Nogales* and *Tuxpan III* and *IV*, and a 245MW cogeneration plant in Monterrey from Belgium's Tractebel. Despite the reform limbo, some success in private participation was achieved in 2003: the *Altamira V* thermoelectric project (to Spain's Iberdrola), the 508MW *Valladolid IIII* (to Japan's Mitsui). In Peru, the sale of state generators Egasa and Egesur to Tractabel fell through in 2003, and bidding for the *Yuncan* hydro project and a decision on the *Olmos* hydro and irrigation project were delayed until 2004. In Ecuador, the government postponed until 2004 the deadline to receive bids for a three-year contract to manage 13 of the country's state-owned distributors. In the Dominican Republic, Spain's Unión Fenosa sold its distribution stakes back to the government in 2003, as the country's poorly privatized power sector lurched into further trouble on the weaker local currency and the spike in oil prices, which resulted in distributors being unable to pay generators who were, in turn, unable to buy fuel. In 2003, consumers had suffered tremendously due to frequent and widespread blackouts. In Argentina, the financial crisis led to a tariff freeze, freezing of debt repayments to foreign creditors, and the so-called *pesofication*. Because of this uncertain environment, private investments continue to be largely withheld. Chile finally sent long-awaited legislation to Congress in 2003, but a final vote has not been held (BusinessNews Americas, 2003).

The infrastructure sector

In the infrastructure sector, many countries privatized their state airlines in the 1990s, which were poorly managed. Government-owned carriers like Aerolíneas Argentinas, Viasa (Venezuela) and Air Panama were privatized or went out of business. In addition, a wave of consolidation reduced the number of carriers, including Grupo Cintra (Mexico), TACA (Central America), LanChile, Varig (Brazil) and Copa Airlines (Panama). However, aviation experts opine that in some countries the result was the substitution of protected and subsidized state monopolies with protected and subsidized private monopolies. Moreover, the privatizations typically did not address the problem of overly rigid labor regulations and discriminatory taxes that hurt the airlines. Recent years have seen increasing private participation in the management of regional airports. The Cerealsur Consortium took over operation of the Uruguayan capital Montevideo's Carrasco international airport in November 2003. Colombia's government had drawn up a plan for a concession to upgrade Bogota's El Dorado international airport by the end of 2003. Seaports have also seen similar movement in recent years. Puerto Rico's Las Americas will select an operator for a design–build–operate–transfer concession by May 2004 (BusinessNews Americas, 2003). The urban water and sewerage sector has also seen substantial private investment from the late 1990s onwards.

In the face of substantial private sector participation, some countries have put the brakes on any plans to privatize state water utilities. In Nicaragua, Congress approved a bill that will keep the state water utility Enacal in government hands.

Under the bill, Enacal is seen as a public service provider responsible for guaranteeing the lowest price possible and not a commercial company as it had been defined previously. Paraguay's President Nicanor Duarte vetoed a bill that would have given municipalities and departments the right to manage waterworks, which critics said would have opened the door to possible privatizations (BusinessNews Americas, 2003).

The oil and gas industry

The liberalization of the oil and gas sector has tended to vary from one country to another, depending on the volume of its reserves and the rate of exploration, its market size and dependence on imported supplies, the state-owned companies involved in the sector, the incentives for deregulation and vertical disintegration, and the fiscal pressures that encourage asset sales. The sector, under state control for decades, started opening up more in the later half of the 1990s, and led to international investors establishing a growing presence in activities such as exploration, extraction, processing, distribution and marketing. The various countries of Latin America, however, have pursued different routes to privatization. At one extreme lies Argentina, which completely privatized its formerly state-owned petroleum company, Yacimientos Petrolíferos Fiscales (YPF), which was acquired in late 1999 by the Spanish Repsol (renamed Repsol-YPF after the acquisition). At the other end of the spectrum lies Mexico, which has largely maintained its state-owned petroleum monopoly, Pemex, although allowing it to raise money from local and foreign investors (it sold close to US$7 billion worth of bonds at home and abroad in 2003). The top three oil companies in the region – the Venezuelan PDVSA, the Mexican Pemex, and the Brazilian Petrobras – continue to be majority state-owned. Nevertheless, there have been substantial foreign investments. In Venezuela, ChevronTexaco and Statoil successfully bid in 2003 for blocks two and four respectively of the US$4 billion Deltana LNG project. In Peru, US oil company Hunt was leading the consortium that will export Camisea gas to Lima and Callao as LNG. In Mexico, Belgium's Tractebel was awarded a regasification terminal at Lázaro Cardenas (BusinessNews Americas, 2003).

In general, privatization has allowed Latin American companies more freedom to pursue joint ventures with foreign companies. It has also led to an upswing in overall Latin American petroleum investment and may have encouraged the acquisition of some Latin American petroleum companies by foreign firms, as well as the acquisition of foreign companies by some Latin American firms. The general trend, however, has been to maintain a regulated system of contractual participation in upstream segments of the industry (exploration and extraction) complemented by deregulation of downstream segments (transportation, refining, storage, wholesale marketing and national distribution). Governments have auctioned off secondary reserves, allowed joint ventures to be set up in certain key activities and, in some cases, privatized the entire sub-sector.

The impact of privatization

The overall impact of privatization has been a matter of extensive debate and argument. Public opinion and policy makers in Latin America have turned against privatization, and a major political backlash against privatization has been brewing for some time. Labor retrenchment, for instance, has been a significant component of the privatization experience in Latin America, as privatized firms reduced a substantial percentage of their workforce in almost all countries. In some cases, excessive costs have come to be levied on a society. In Mexico, for example, the bailouts granted to keep banks and highways from going bankrupt increased public debt from less than 25 percent of GDP to over 50 percent (López-Calva, 2003). Bayliss (2002) points to examples of botched privatizations in Puerto Rico and Trinidad and Tobago where water privatization led to price hikes and no apparent improvement in provision. Similarly, the privatization of the electric sector in the Dominican Republic was claimed to have led to more blackouts and higher utility prices, culminating in civil unrest and the deaths of several demonstrators. As mentioned earlier, the government re-nationalized the recently privatized electricity company: which had been bought in the privatization by the Spanish company Unión Fenosa. Concerns have also been raised about the distributional impacts of the gains of privatization, as they may not be reaching the poorest sectors of society. Birdsall and Nellis (2002) have argued that privatization maybe accompanied by worse income distribution despite improvements in efficiency and profitability.

On the other hand, several detailed studies seem to suggest that while failures did occur, they were not the norm. Gains in profitability have been seen after privatization in Latin America, brought about by improved operating efficiency (Inter-American Development Bank, 2002). Galal *et al.* (1994) analyzed 12 privatization cases in Chile, Malaysia, Mexico and the United Kingdom; their results indicate that privatization led to welfare gains of about 25 percent of the pre-privatization sales in 11 of the 12 cases. With regard to telecommunications and railroad infrastructure, Ramamurti (1996) concludes that privatization has had a positive effect in Latin America because it has led to a technological overhaul of the sector and increased both access to and the quality of the services. Early work on the privatization experience in Argentina (Carbajo and Estache, 1996) also shows significant gains in access to services such as water, power and port infrastructure. There are many examples of improvements in access to water, electricity, telecommunications and other services throughout the region that have created benefits beyond lower prices.

Analysts have ascribed most instances of failure to three broad factors – opaque processes with heavy state involvement opening the door to corruption and opportunistic behavior; poor contract design and regulatory capture linked to a lack of deregulation and inadequate re-regulation; and deficient corporate governance institutions raising the cost of capital, hampering restructuring efforts and throwing firms back into the hands of the state (Chong and Lopez, 2003).

Increased political stability

The developments in deregulation and privatization discussed above were in no small measure aided by the democratization process in the region that began in the 1980s and was consolidated in the 1990s. There were just five democratic governments in Latin America in 1930, seven in 1948, and a mere three in 1976. All countries except Cuba now have democratically elected governments, most with strong presidencies. Although this process was stimulated and reinforced by changes occurring globally, it was essentially the product of the region's own development. At its core were the painful lessons drawn from past conflicts that had shattered the political system and destroyed mechanisms to solve social and political conflicts in an orderly way, in some cases degenerating into entrenched military dictatorships and, in others, to civil war and systematic violence. As a result, the thinking of political, social and economic actors matured profoundly, and the resultant shift in the political and cultural climate made it possible to reach a basic consensus about the need to resolve conflicts through negotiation and compromise and to forestall violence and the logic of war. All of this resulted in a reassessment of democratic rules, institutions and procedures.

A series of major reforms were undertaken in the 1990s to strengthen democratic institutions. These included constitutional reforms, changes in the administration of justice, and modernization of the public sector aimed at improving the transparency of governance and the public service. Efforts have also been made to improve electoral systems, modernize parliaments and generate local autonomy.

The democratization movement has tended to facilitate economic stability and help make the region a more sound prospect for investment. Although democracy is well established and there is little risk of a return to military rule, confidence in institutions and the political class is low. Economic underperformance and falling living standards have fuelled instability in several countries, most recently Bolivia and Ecuador. In Venezuela political polarization has reached dangerous extremes, while Colombia remains in the grip of a decades-long guerrilla conflict (EIU Viewswire, 2003). A worrying confirmation that the democratization process is far from consolidated comes from the fact that since 1999 six elected leaders in Latin America have been ousted before the end of their respective terms, the latest being Jean-Bertrand Aristide of Haiti in early 2004. These failings call into question the sustainability of the development process and are detrimental to the thorough exercise of democracy and citizenship in the region. They also help to explain the results of surveys used to assess people's perceptions of democracy in the region. The 2004 *Latinobarómetro*[2] survey found that about two-thirds of those surveyed in 17 countries of the region were dissatisfied with the results of democracy and felt that their country had not benefited from privatization.

Trade agreements: NAFTA, Mercosur, FTAA

While the democratic movement was still maturing in the region, a number of concrete initiatives were taken by Latin American countries to strengthen the region's trade and investment links. In 1994 Mexico joined the North American Free Trade Agreement (NAFTA), which also includes the United States and Canada. The European Union has been the preferred choice of Latin American governments for the establishment of free trade agreements. In 2000 Mexico entered into an agreement with Mercosur (Southern Common Market, see below) making progress in the same direction. Asia was another area of growing interest to Latin American governments, the preference for Latin American countries being to join the Asia Pacific Economic Cooperation (APEC). Mexico was admitted in 1993, while Chile and Peru have participated as full members since 1997 and 1998 respectively. Some Asian countries have also shown interest in strengthening bilateral ties with Latin American countries, as demonstrated by the opening of negotiations for the establishment of a free trade agreement between Chile and the Republic of Korea, and the free trade negotiations between Mexico and Japan.

The agreements signed in 1986 between Argentina and Brazil for the establishment of a preferential trade zone marked the revival of integration. In 1991, with the accession of Paraguay and Uruguay, this bilateral agreement became the Treaty of Asunción, under which the Southern Common Market (Mercosur) was formed. Mercosur is essentially a partial customs union among Argentina, Brazil, Paraguay and Uruguay, with Chile and Bolivia as associated members. In late 1994, Mercosur was converted into a free trade area, with a few exceptions, and the member countries undertook to establish a common external tariff, which should be fully operational by the year 2006. Frischtak (2003) states that Mercosur has played an important role in attracting automotive sector MNCs that established "a new platform and joint operations for the sub region".

Throughout the 1990s the governments of Latin America and the Caribbean combined unilateral liberalization with active participation in multilateral negotiations in the framework of WTO, and with bilateral, plurilateral and interregional free trade agreements. Liberalization of trade and of the regulatory framework for investment in their economies made it possible for imports and exports to expand. The United States has show support for free trade agreements since the 1980s. Mexico has been the key beneficiary of NAFTA – in 2000 Mexican–US trade reached a historic US$263 billion (down to US$235 billion in 2003), more than three times the 1993 pre-NAFTA levels. Mexico consolidated itself as the United States' second-largest trading partner. From 1993 to 2000 US–Mexican trade grew at an annual average rate of 16 percent, faster than the average growth rate of US trade with any other major partner, including China, Germany, Korea and the United Kingdom (Maquila Portal, 2000).

While NAFTA was being ratified by the legislative bodies of the three countries, the US government began to define its strategy for the rest of Latin America and the Caribbean. Its first step in this direction was the 1990 Enterprise for the Americas Initiative, and the Summit of the Americas Conference in Miami in 1994 resulted in a historic understanding to work toward creating a hemispheric Free Trade Agreement of the Americas (FTAA). The FTAA aims at the expansion of NAFTA to all countries of the Americas, except Cuba. The Organization of American States (OAS) notes that a charter to strengthen and protect the hemisphere's democracies, serious progress toward the FTAA, a modern anti-terrorism convention and specific goals for improving health and education are among the accomplishments of the ongoing Summit of the Americas process since 1994. The Miami Ministerial meeting in November 2003 negotiated only a minimum of common rights and obligations and left individual governments free to decide further commitments. The target date for FTAA finalization was set in 2005.

The key challenge to FTAA finalization in 2005 was the disagreement between the US and Mercosur members. The US position on the common set of obligations advocates that the entire universe of tariff elimination should be subject to negotiation, but does not guarantee that all of these tariffs would be reduced as part of the common set of obligations. Mercosur was looking for a firm guarantee that all tariffs – including those on sensitive agricultural and industrial goods – would be reduced to zero, with longer phase-outs for more sensitive items, and that this would be part of the common set of obligations. While Mercosur was looking for a common tier to eliminate all tariffs, other countries were willing to do so only if Mercosur was willing to make deeper commitments on investment, services, intellectual property rights and government procurement. Brazil has long fought to slow down the pace of FTAA plans, and was among those who wanted no mention of a kick-off date for the zone in the summit's final declaration. At the same time, bilateral trade agreements have grown in the last years, for example, the trade agreement between the United States and Chile signed in 2003. The United States opened free trade talks with Central American Common Market countries (Guatemala, Honduras, El Salvador, and Nicaragua, later joined by Costa Rica), Peru and Colombia, and announced it would start talks with Ecuador and Bolivia as well. There is a shift by the US from bilateral to multilateral accords with the Latin American countries ready to do so.

The business context: ownership and control change hands

As the regional economies integrated both intra-regionally and with the rest of the world, and deregulated sectors hitherto under state control, new opportunities opened up for the local private sector and foreign MNCs. The 1990s saw production in the different Latin American industries change noticeably in terms of the relative share of various economic agents. This restructuring was led by three major categories of firms: subsidiaries of MNCs, large local conglomerates, and locally owned small and medium-sized enterprises. These groups had vastly different access to the markets and played out their strategies accordingly. The most notable shift was that as deregulation and privatization advanced, the role of state-owned companies as suppliers of goods and services diminished greatly. The vacuum left behind by the retreating state sector was filled by large private companies, especially the MNCs.

Multinationals gain power

While the MNCs entered Latin America in droves during the 1990s, their reasons for entry were not the same. Three main objectives can be identified: efficiency seeking, growth seeking and resource seeking (Casanova, 2004). Efficiency-seeking MNCs aim to reduce costs in their global production process through access to cheaper labor and proximity to destination markets such as the United States. Growth-seeking firms enter Latin American markets to grow and/or acquire new markets. They are by nature more dependent on macroeconomic conditions in local markets for their success. Resource-seeking firms enter Latin America in search of minerals, metals, and hydrocarbons at a reasonable cost. The following sections look at the different strategies from US, European Union (mainly Spanish) and Japanese firms.

The United States

As the source of 39 percent of the FDI flows to Latin America in the latter half of the 1990s, the United States remains the single largest investor in the region (Vodusek, 2001). US FDI has been concentrated in the manufacturing sector and the exploitation of raw materials. After the debt crisis of the 1980s, US investments shifted from market-seeking[3] to efficiency-seeking objectives, mainly in Mexico and the Caribbean Basin. Such investments leveraged local advantages, e.g., proximity to the United States, cheap labor, and privileged access to US markets with low transportation costs. In this way, US firms boosted their competitiveness at home, and were able to face competition from other countries, notably from Asia. General Motors and Ford are examples of firms that were better able to withstand Asian competition from Japan and Korea due to their manufacturing presence in the *maquila*[4] (in-bound assembly plants for re-export to the US) in Mexico. Between 1990 and 2000, US FDI to the region increased from US$4.2 billion to US$10.4 billion, with a high of US$17.9 billion in 1997 (Vodusek, 2001). Eighty-six percent of US FDI from 1996 to 2000 was concentrated in five countries: Mexico, Brazil, Venezuela, Chile and Colombia (in order of FDI investment in 2000). The United States contributed 67 percent of the US$118 billion of FDI in Mexico between 1994 and June 2003. The Mexican economy was further integrated with the US through US tourism in Mexico (US$9.6 billion/year) and labor remittances to Mexico (US$13 billion in 2003).[5] US investment in manufacturing has decreased from 57.6 percent of FDI in 1990 to 31.4 percent in 2000.[6]

New European arrivals: Spanish investments

The European Union as a whole leads as the regional source of FDI with 58 percent of the FDI inflows. An analysis of the consolidated sales of the 100 largest MNCs in the region also shows European firms to be in the forefront. In 1999, firms from the European Union accounted for 50 percent of regional MNC sales, those from the United States generated 43 percent of sales, Swiss companies had a 5 percent share, and the rest was divided up among Japanese, Australian and Canadian firms.

Since 1994 Latin America has been the prime investment destination in the globalization strategies of major Spanish firms (Casanova, 2002). In the 1990s Spain was the second most important player in the region, with 25 percent of the FDI, representing about US$80 billion until 1999. More recent figures show the volume of the Spanish investments augmented to 104.2 billion until the end of 2002. The levels of Spanish FDI inflow increased sharply after 1994 to reach a total of US$58.52 billion in 1999 (Arahuetes, 2002). One notes that the services sector has benefited from 74 percent of the Spanish FDI, the primary sector has 23 percent, and the manufacturing sector has only 3 percent. Argentina, Brazil and Chile were the three leading recipients of Spanish FDI until then. Mexico has also become a very important destination since 2000.

This phenomenon was of particular interest because, in the space of just a few years (1996–2000 mainly), Spain's energy, banking and telecommunications groups became the leading multinationals in their sectors in Latin America. Moreover, this shift was being led by a small group of large firms (no more than 10), most of which, interestingly enough, have recently been privatized in Spain. Awash with cash during the 1990s, Spain's big companies and banks – Telefónica, Endesa and Iberdrola (electricity), Repsol and Gas Natural (oil and gas), Dragados (construction), Santander Central Hispano and Banco Bilbao Vizcaya Argentaria (banking) – went on a buying spree in Latin America. The biggest investor in Latin America has been Repsol, which in 1999 acquired Argentina's YPF for US$14.9 billion. The acquisition of YPF transformed Repsol, the dominant energy company in Spain, into the largest non government-controlled producer of oil and gas in Latin America. Iberia, the Spanish flag carrier, has 300 weekly flights between Europe and Latin America to 22 destinations, more than any other airline. It claims 15 percent of the traffic from Latin America to Europe. The one notable area where Spain lacked a multinational of significant size was the media, despite a Hispanic market of more than 350 million people in Latin America and the United States. This was partly because of restrictions on foreign ownership of media in most Latin American countries.

In addition to the big Spanish companies, more than 50 other companies have invested in the region. In 2001 earnings from Latin America represented almost one-third of the total of these companies and were generated on investments made mainly over the past five years amounting to US$102 billion. The main reasons for investing were cultural and linguistic similarities (86 percent of respondents) and the belief that Spain was the best platform for entering the Latin American market (83 percent). Other important factors were previous business relationships in the region (60 percent) and supplying Spanish companies already present in the region (30 percent).

The subsidiaries of multinationals in Spain are also investing in Latin America. According to a study by KPMG, 62 Spanish companies controlled by foreign capital invested in Latin America between 1993 and 1999.

There are several pull factors that have spurred Spanish investment in Latin America. Two of these are purely economic: liberalization and privatization have opened up sectors of the Latin American economy that were hitherto off limits, and, after Spain joined the European Union in 1986, the strategic focus of large companies, in particular, gradually changed from one of defending their relatively mature home market to aggressively expanding abroad. Two others are cultural: the first is the common language (apart from Portuguese-speaking Brazil, although Spanish is increasingly being taught in Brazilian schools and the two languages, Spanish and Portuguese, are quite similar), and the second relates to the similarities throughout the upper strata of society. Spanish managers considered Latin America as their "natural market". "Natural markets" (Casanova, 2004), defined as those markets sharing a common history, religion, language or geographical proximity, give Spanish investments a competitive advantage. Spain has also forged closer economic links with Latin America by establishing at the Madrid Stock Exchange the largest in the Spanish-speaking world and the fourth biggest in Europe in terms of trading volume a market in euros for blue chip Latin American securities (Latibex). For Latin American companies, Latibex raises their profile in Europe and opens the door to funding in euros.

Japanese maquilas

Asian investments in the region remain relatively modest, Japan being the leading Asian investor with 2.9 percent of the FDI in Latin America. However, a closer look shows that Japan is the second largest foreign investor in Mexico and the third biggest investor in Brazil. Most Asian firms have focused on efficiency-seeking objectives (e.g., maquilas in Mexico) and resource-seeking objectives (e.g., Japanese stakes in major steel companies in Brazil). Asian firms have also proven to be versatile in overcoming the limitations of non-natural markets to seek organic growth in the region (e.g., Japanese companies utilizing the Japanese immigrant community in Brazil). However, Asian MNCs can do much more in the region and certainly draw upon useful lessons from the experiences of their American/European counterparts and also of successful Asian MNCs.

A number of MNCs have invested in Latin America seeking cheap labor for their manufacturing facilities (efficiency seeking). An excellent example of this is the Maquila Program[7] of Mexico, in which many US and Japanese (through their US subsidiaries) companies in the automotive and electronics sectors have invested significantly. MNCs' investments in the Maquila Program increased following strong devaluations of the peso (in 1982 and 1994), and the signing of the NAFTA trade agreement.

Japanese investment in Mexico began in the late 1970s and early 1980s as a consequence of the increasing manufacturing wages in Japan. In an attempt to maintain price competitiveness in the US market, Japanese companies took advantage of NAFTA by establishing maquilas through their US subsidiaries. By the early 1980s eight of the largest Japanese manufacturers had footholds in Mexico. Japanese FDI was 97 percent in manufacturing, of which 86 percent was in the automotive sector. The automotive and electronics industries took a front seat in terms of Japanese manufacturing priorities.

Japanese manufacturers have become an essential part of the maquila economy with over 100 Japanese-owned maquilas employing over 50,000 workers in 2003 (Maquila Portal, 2003). Indeed, the second and third largest maquila employers in Mexico are respectively Alcoa Fugikura Ltd. and Yazaki Corporation, both Japanese automotive parts manufacturers. Alcoa employs almost 30,000 people in 22 maquila plants throughout the country; Yazaki has 12 maquila plants and around 14,500 employees.

Local business conglomerates adjust to the global economy

Large locally owned companies have adjusted to the new world economic order with different strategies, depending on the conditions presented by the domestic market. The arrival of large volumes of FDI reflected the growing importance of MNCs. If we look at the sales data of the 500 largest companies in Latin America, MNCs accounted for 25 percent of total sales in 1990 while in 1999 their share peaked at 43 percent. With the decline of FDI, the sales of MNCs went down to 36 percent. The sales of local business surpassed the sales of MNCs in 2002 to represent 40 percent of the total. Looking across the region, it can be seen that the larger and more open an economy, the more likely that a Latin American corporation will have specialized (InfoAmericas, 2001).

Specialization enables enormous economies of scale in production, marketing, and industry knowledge, which are especially advantageous in a large market. Brazil, for example, is home to a number of highly focused industrial groups such as Bunge and Born (agri-food), Gerdau (metals), Pão de Açucar (retail), and Safra (financial services). In contrast, in the smaller markets companies tend to either develop international operations and exports, or diversify into different industries to achieve growth. Chile is a good example – it was dominated by highly diversified holding companies such as *Luksic*. In a small economy where a few dozen families control most of the power, Chilean industrialists have found it easier to diversify locally than venture abroad, by using their political connections. However, Chilean entrepreneurs who did not enjoy such power have resorted aggressively to exports. Mexico was a unique mixture of both models – where both specialized giants (e.g., the multinational Cemex) and diversified conglomerates (e.g., Grupo Carso – Carlos Slim's empire of telecom, retail, restaurants, tobacco, electronics, and banking companies) co-exist.

There has been a continuing debate in the boardrooms of Latin American companies: diversify and stay local, or specialize and go global? So far, Argentina and Mexico have been the most successful in grooming their industrial groups for expansion abroad, aided by the faster pace of liberalization there, and the fact that the size of their economies gave them early opportunities to learn and focus. When Latin American economies opened to foreign investment and global competition, the more dynamic groups adapted quickly, exporting and expanding overseas. Indeed, the region's most successful global players – Cemex, the logistics and transportation company TMM, the food and candy group Arcor, the food-processing Bimbo, the agrotechnology and real estate Savia, the leading maker of seamless steel pipes Techint – are from Argentina or Mexico. Cemex of Mexico is now the world's second largest cement producer. The company operates in 30 countries and derives 52.7 percent of its revenues outside Mexico, and 31.7 percent outside Latin America. Other examples of companies that have successfully ventured abroad are Cisneros Group (media) from Venezuela, Durman Esquivel (piping) from Costa Rica, SQM (chemicals) from Chile, Grupo Minera (mining) from Mexico, Grupo Bimbo (bakery) from Mexico, and Telmex (telecom) from Mexico. In contrast, most of Brazil's specialized powerhouses (notable exceptions being Bunge and Borne) have stayed home until now, partly because the slower pace of liberalization there has limited foreign competition, and partly because of the growth opportunities in the large domestic market. However, this has been changing in the last few years, as the economy opens and local growth opportunities become scarcer. Brazilian steel producer Gerdau acquired Ameristeel Corp. in 1999 from Kyoei Steel of Japan, for US$265 million.

Venturing abroad, particularly to the US and Europe, has also had its risks. Grupo Geo, one of the most successful and sophisticated low-income house-builders in the world, recently pulled out after failing to succeed in the US market. While in Mexico and Chile the company has been hugely successful by tapping into government low-income housing credit programs to virtually eliminate credit risk, the absence of a comparable facility in the United States led the company to rely on the credit-worthiness of its low-income Americans, many of whom defaulted.

State-owned companies

State-owned companies represented 32 percent of the total sales of the 500 largest companies in Latin America in 1990. Their share has declined steadily, reaching 25 percent in 2002. The state-owned companies are mainly in the natural resources sector, primarily in oil.

The oil sector

The biggest Latin American companies are in the oil sector and the top three are state owned: Petróleos de Venezuela SA (PDVSA), the Mexican Petróleos Mexicanos (Pemex) and Petróleo Brasileiro SA (Petrobras).

By contrast with the electricity industry, where the share of state-owned enterprises has shrunk considerably, in the oil industry the public sector has continued to invest and to develop new corporate strategies. This has not been the case in Argentina, Bolivia and Peru, which opted to privatize the industry. State-owned enterprises adopted three major new strategies in the 1990s. One of these was internationalization through strategic alliances, as in the case of Pemex, which bought 3 percent of Repsol of Spain and 50 percent of the Deer Park refinery in Texas (United States) from Shell. The second strategy was one of internationalization in upstream segments through operations abroad, as in the cases of Petrobras and Empresa Nacional del Petróleo de Chile (Enap). The third was to conclude regional strategic alliances, such as the one between Repsol–YPF (Spain–Argentina), Petrobras (Brazil) and PDVSA (Venezuela). These new strategies are in addition to the existing one of combining internationalization with vertical integration through the development of activities in downstream segments of the industry abroad, as in the case of PDVSA, which was involved in fuel refining and distribution in the United States market (CITGO Petroleum Co., Unocal and UNO-VEN).

Some countries have introduced major institutional changes in the management of upstream segments by separating the commercial and contractual functions that state-owned corporations used to combine. For instance, Perupetro in Peru and the Agência Nacional do Petróleo in Brazil were established to take responsibility for negotiating and signing contracts with private investors. In most countries in the region with oil-producing potential, however, state-owned enterprises still retain responsibility for contractual functions.

Almost all the countries in the region now allow private-sector participation in the downstream segments of the industry. Apart from the removal of barriers to entry and the widespread dismantling of state-owned monopolies, the most noteworthy feature of downstream activities has been the elimination of price controls and subsidies, although these still persist in a few countries. Brazil saw a remarkable shift in liberalization policy that resulted from its 1995 constitutional reform. Many countries in the region have largely deregulated retail distribution, thus seeing major investments come in. The main aim of the reforms has been to ensure that domestic prices reflect international prices. Some countries such as Chile, Colombia and Venezuela have established oil price stabilization funds to reduce volatility in domestic prices, while some others have resorted to direct price controls.

The refining segment, however, is essentially an oligopoly in structure, while in transport and storage monopolies are the rule, owing to economies of scale. The feasibility of vertical disintegration has been determined by market size, since in practice this option has been viable only in larger markets. In the cases of transport and storage, which in most instances are natural monopolies, a system of open access was applied on the basis of companies' installed capacity and the commitments they had entered into.

The reforms adopted in the energy sector have unleashed a strong corporate dynamic driven by the new actors that emerged from the privatization process and by a renewed flow of foreign investment. In some cases, privatization of the energy sector has also helped to boost regional stock exchanges both through the issuing of new instruments and through a considerable increase in transaction volumes. Un-privatized state enterprises, especially those in the oil industry, have also shown renewed vigor.

Structural changes in labor policies

The reforms undertaken through the 1990s, and the increasing influence of the private sector and multinationals in the regional economies, led to several important changes in the structure, quality, participation, and policies governing workers. These changes, in turn, have profound implications for human resource managers for firms operating in or entering Latin America.

In the 1990s, public-sector employment stagnated, owing to privatization and restrictive fiscal policies, while paid employment in the private sector grew more rapidly (ILO, 1999). Studies by the Economic Commission for Latin America and the Caribbean (ECLAC) have indicated a shift of skilled workers into informal or small-scale activities because of the restructuring of the public sector and the streamlining of production and administrative procedures in large corporations. As the SOEs shrank, managers and workers had to move from a "civil servant" culture to a private company culture. As policies came to favor more flexible labor markets, there was a move towards greater use of short-term contracts (temporary, seasonal, or part-time), the grounds on which contracts could be terminated were extended and redundancy payments were reduced.

The clear trend in favour of higher education meant that there has been a general decline in labor force participation among the population aged below 20, particularly men. As the skill differential between those with university education and those without increased, the pay gap between higher-skilled workers and lower-skilled ones has also been widening. Human resources (HR) managers need to be cognizant of this differential and to design their recruitment and compensation policies accordingly.

In most countries, a combination of the economic crisis of the 1980s, the social movement spearheaded by women and by international organizations, and the establishment of government agencies for the advancement of women, led to a substantial influx of women into the labor market. Between 1991 and 1999, the male participation rate remained stable at about 73 percent, while the female rate rose by 4 percentage points to over 41 percent. The rate at the end of the 1990s exceeded 70 percent among women with 13 or more years of schooling in Argentina, Brazil, Colombia, Ecuador, Guatemala and Panama. It is noteworthy that the proportion of women working was substantially lower in poorer households than in richer ones. Furthermore, progress in women's education was reflected in a greater number of years of schooling, with more girls reaching the middle and higher stages of education. This holds positive implications for HR managers, who can expect an increased quantity and quality of women in the labor force.

The reform in pension systems has had a direct impact on remuneration, structure of employees, and retirement policies. Many countries in the region have reformed their pension systems. This has generally involved the creation of individual funding systems with savings accounts that allow benefits to be linked directly to the contributions of each subscriber. The savings go into pension funds managed by private administrators. Under this system, benefits (pension payments) in each individual case are based on the amount saved and the financial yields obtained during the contribution period. The state is responsible for regulating and supervising the private system.

Challenges ahead

There are a number of challenges and opportunities that the region faces in the new millennium. On including the increasing role of China in the global economy, and, on the other, the lingering effects of Argentina's crisis in 2001. The region is looking for a more pragmatic set of economic policies that will allow Latin America to have stronger and more stable economic growth with equity.

Building bridges with 'China'

China's surfacing as a global trade power is having a big impact in Latin America. On the one hand, it has become a formidable competitor to Latin American manufacturers in low value-added sectors such as shoes, toys and textiles. This is detrimental to countries such as Mexico, but helps others such as Brazil and Argentina. On the other hand, the region has become important to China for the following reasons. First of all, China and Latin America have common trade interests vis-á-vis of the developed countries, as shown at the Cancun meeting of the World Trade Organization in November 2003 when Brazil, China and India led the demands of the G20 developing countries. Second, China is looking for new markets such as Latin America in order to decrease its trade dependence on the United States, Japan and Europe. China perceives Latin America as a more equal, manageable partner. Third and most important, China needs access to stable sources of natural resources that Latin America owns.

In the 1990s China's two-way trade with Latin America rose eight-fold to almost US$26.8 billion in 2003. This figure represents a 50.4 percent increase with respect to 2002. China's trade deficit with Latin America became a trade surplus of US$3.04 billion in 2003. Brazil, Mexico, Chile and Argentina are the countries that trade the most with China, and they represent 73 percent of the total trade between China and Latin America. In that year, the two-way was for Brazil (US$7.9 billion), Mexico (US$4.9 billion), Chile (US$3.5 billion), and Argentina (almost US$3.1 billion). China exports to Latin America are high value-added, mainly machinery (tractors, machine tools, engines, ships, hydroelectric generators, etc.), electronics (TV sets, refrigerators and other household appliances), textiles, clothing, medical products, cosmetics, and light industrial products. China imports from Latin America primary products such as iron, copper, petroleum, paper pulp, leather and wool; metals such as steel; agricultural products such as fish-meal, edible oil and sugar; and machinery.

This trade can only increase because of the complementarities of their needs, as mentioned above. There are, however, major hurdles to this trade because of the distance and also lack of knowledge of Latin America in China beyond soccer, samba and tango. More FDI will help increase the links between the two. However, investment links are in the early stages of growth. By the end of the 1990s, major Chinese investments in Latin America included an iron ore mine in Peru, oilfields in Venezuela, Mexico and Peru, agriculture and textiles in Mexico, timber in Brazil, fish meal and timber products in Chile, fisheries and TV sets in Argentina, motorcycles in Colombia, shrimp farming in Ecuador and gas production in Venezuela and Peru.

Brazil, China's main trade partner in Latin America, considers China an opportunity and its investment links with China are increasing dramatically. Some 50 Chinese firms have direct investments in Brazil in forestry, food processing, transportation and light industry. There is also close cooperation in the technology sector between Brazil and China as shown in the launching of the first earth resources satellite in 1999, built jointly. Brazil and China formed the company International Satellite Communication (INSCOM), an alliance between the China Great Wall Industrial Corporation and the Brazilian company AVIBRAS. The Commission of Science, Technology and Industry for National Defence of China has a close association with Brasilsat. And in 2002 the two countries announced a joint venture between Embraer, the Brazilian aircraft manufacturer, and the China Aviation Industry Corporation II. The world's largest producer of iron ore, the Brazilian Companhia Vale do Rio Doce (CVRD), signed a contract in April 2004 with China Steel Corporation (CSC), one of the largest Asian steelmakers, to supply 600,000 tons of pellets per year from 2005 to 2011. CVRD and Baosteel Shanghai Group Corporation (Baosteel), the largest Chinese steelmaker, formed a joint venture to build and operate an integrated steel plant in São Luís, to produce about 3.7 million tons per year of steel slabs. The slab plant will be the largest investment in the Brazilian steel industry in many years.

Mexico, on the other hand, sees China as a "threat" in a number of dimensions. In the first semester of 2003, China overtook Mexico as the second biggest trade partner (after Canada) of the United States. The access of Chinese firms' products to US markets has been strongly facilitated by China's entry into the WTO in December 2001. Between 2001 and 2003, the number of Mexican maquilas that closed operations rose to 500 (mainly apparel and textiles). The closures cost 240,000 Mexican jobs or 20 percent of industry employment. A number of companies de-localized their production facilities to Asia. Although the overall mood is down, the automotive and computer parts sector are optimistic because of the industry's integration with the US supply chain, where time-to-market is essential. Chinese products are also flooding the Mexican market.

China represents both a challenge and an opportunity for Latin America. The region needs to improve competitiveness in the sectors in which it does not compete with China. The manufacturing of low-end, high-volume goods is going to Asia, not only China but Vietnam and other countries where the cost of labor is lower than in Latin America. Currently Mexican hourly labor costs are four times higher than in China. Sectors such as agriculture, energy, mining, fishing (and tourism) represent an opportunity for Latin America and are complementary to China's needs. Latin America needs to increase the value added in all of these activities in order to become more competitive and counterbalance China's effect in the manufacturing sector.

After the crisis in Argentina

Four years of recession in Argentina led to the un-pegging of the Argentine peso from the US dollar in December 2001. Riots followed the freezing of bank accounts, and the peso was devalued by almost 400 percent in the following months in 2002. Political contagion soon reached Uruguay, and citizens throughout Latin America started questioning the economic policies implemented in the region during the past decade. The election of a new left-wing president, Luiz Ignacio "Lula" da Silva in Brazil, led to a downward spiral of the Brazilian currency in the second half of 2002. Central banks intervened in order to defend the currencies by raising interest rates[8] and, as a consequence, hard currency reserves were depleted.

In parallel, the US demand for Latin American products diminished as the US economy slowed down. Latin American factories are facing competitive pressures from Asian and most importantly Chinese manufacturers. Conditions in 2003 were significantly different in Latin America from those prevailing a decade earlier, when FDI inflow to the continent was steadily increasing. Privatization opportunities have peaked, and the perspective of industrial growth is being negated by economic woes.

Disinvestments of multinationals

Firms seeking efficiency within the framework of NAFTA have been hit by factors external to the region such as the slump in US demand, and by the rise of China as a competitor following its accession to the WTO. In general, firms seeking efficiency thrive when currencies are devalued. This is currently not the case, as China has emerged as an important alternative for efficiency seeking MNCs. Firms most badly hit are those dependent on low-cost labor as a primary input in sectors such as footwear, textiles and clothing, furniture and certain electrical products. According to ECLAC, firms have reacted to the crisis by layoffs (33 percent) and closures (11 percent). For firms assembling technologically more complex products, the effect is much more limited with 6.6 percent firm closures (ECLAC, 2002).[9] According to a survey conducted by the Japanese Maquila Association (JMA), nine companies out of 45 say that the company may withdraw from Mexico, and 14 companies out of 45 are trying to reduce business. While efficiency-seeking firms operating in the region are indeed in pain, the access to US markets continues to attract MNCs. Some firms are adopting defensive strategies by scaling down their production and waiting for the upturn to come.

MNCs coming into the region with growth-seeking objectives, such as the automotive manufacturing firms, were faced with numerous constraints after the Argentinian crisis of December 2001. For one, the industry was dependent on a portion of the components being imported, while revenues from local sales are in, (sometimes), devalued currencies. Additionally, local demand was limited due to consumer prudence in the face of recession. Finally, high interest rates made the financing of transactions prohibitively expensive. This particularly affected the Mercosur countries. The Argentine crisis forced firms to re-orient their strategy towards extra-regional exports. As a consequence, firm success was based on the flexibility of the MNCs to re-orient their strategy from growth-seeking to efficiency-seeking (taking advantage of diminishing labor costs) goals.

MNCs in the service industry, on the other hand, faced different challenges to those in the manufacturing sector. The privatization process slowed down considerably, and worsening economic conditions did not encourage service sector MNCs to invest. These companies suffered in several ways in addition to the limited growth of markets stemming from recession. For one, investors penalized service sector companies with great exposure to Latin America, such as Spanish companies. As of the end of 2002, investors valued Endesa's investments in Latin America at zero. Second MNCs in the region found financing for their investments in the capital-intensive service sector, such as energy or telecommunications, increasingly scarce and expensive due to their perceived risk profile. Third, governments tend to freeze tariffs for regulated services in times of crisis. This created additional difficulties for the operators. Finally, in these trying circumstances, since MNCs were unable to invest in infrastructure, local governments and consumers questioned the value proposition of foreign firms, as services did not improve.

A number of MNCs slowed their expansion plans, froze investments and exited the continent. In Argentina, for example, parent companies from developed countries stopped supporting their local subsidiaries, and numerous firms went into the red. In telecom, firms such as AT&T, France Telecom and MCI either quit the region or announced intentions to quit. In banking, France's Crédit Agricole quit the region in 2002, while Italy's Entesa and the UK's Lloyds quit in 2003. Even heavyweights like Spanish groups Banco Santander Central Hispano and Banco Bilbao Vizcaya Argentaria scaled back operations, choosing to focus more on core markets (BusinessNews Americas, 2003). In some cases, foreign companies had to exit due to the dynamics and conditions of the industry in their home markets.

Companies entering the continent in search of raw materials were the least affected by the regional crisis. Their FDI was for extractive activities targeting overseas markets. They were least exposed to the demand of the local markets, and to macroeconomic conditions. According to ECLAC, in 2002, FDI aimed at raw materials extraction stayed at about the same level as in the preceding year.

It must be said that Argentina's crisis created problems for companies that had to service foreign currency debts, such as Pérez Companc of Argentina, a company that was unable to maintain its independence, being absorbed by Brazil's state-owned Petrobras.

Political instability can also be a cause of concern for investments in countries such as Venezuela because changes of policy may delay projects and reverse privatizations.

Looking for sustainable growth

With economic sluggishness prevailing in many parts of the world, money has trickled back into Latin America. Taken as a whole, the region's economy grew by 1.3 percent in 2003 and should expand by close to 4 percent in 2004, according to the World Bank. Even Argentina, after a four-year slump, is growing again, although debt repayment negotiations with international lenders remain inconclusive.

However, the IMF and the World Bank warn that, despite an improved short-term outlook, Latin America faces deep-rooted obstacles before it can achieve high and sustained growth. Latin America's recent travails caused the region's GDP to shrink by 0.6 percent in 2002, after growth of just 0.4 percent in 2001. Income per person in Latin America now stands at 2 percent below the level of 1997, according to ECLAC. Progress in reducing poverty has halted. This amounts to a "lost half-decade" (1999–2002), says ECLAC, evoking the "lost decade" unleashed by Mexico's 1982 debt default.

The negation of some of the gains of the 1990s by the recessions and financial crises of the last few years has prompted much soul-searching as to what has gone wrong. Governments are debating and looking for a more pragmatic set of economic policies that bring stable and sustainable growth to the region. Many Latin Americans conclude that the "neo-liberal" reforms and the "Washington Consensus" policies are to blame. These are held not only to have failed to deliver sustained growth, but to have made the region more vulnerable, and to have increased unemployment, poverty and inequality. Privatization in particular has become deeply unpopular: privatizations of a water firm in Bolivia in 2000 and of an electricity generator in Peru in 2002 were scrapped after riots. As a result of all this, some political pundits asserted that Latin America was sinking back into populism and/or anti-market leftist nationalism. And they wondered whether the reform process would survive political change.

Other observers maintained that there were other factors at play, most related to long-standing Latin American weaknesses. First, there was the region's chronic vulnerability to balance-of-payments crises. Second, the basic macroeconomic reforms were not fully implemented as most governments failed to save in good times and piled up debts. Third, it was quickly accepted that if macroeconomic reforms were to produce higher investment and thus more jobs, they needed to be complemented by "second-generation" or institutional reforms. These ranged from improving education to bankruptcy proceedings. They were easy to list but hard to implement. And fourth, some reformers, as well as critics, argued that in a region of deep income inequality, growth alone would not swiftly reduce poverty.

The single most important failing was the region's dependence on volatile capital flows. Growth before 1997 coincided with record capital inflows, some attracted by privatization. As a result, currencies became overvalued, hurting exports and local producers, and leading to big current-account deficits. A first hiccup came in 1994–1995 with Mexico's devaluation. Then, in mid-1998, emerging-market investors suffered big losses when Russia defaulted. For South America that triggered what Guillermo Calvo, the chief economist at the Inter-American Development Bank, has called a "sudden stop" in capital flows. To compensate, governments had to adjust the real exchange rate (i.e., either devaluing the currency or making output cheaper through price deflation). Since most countries had beaten inflation by pegging their exchange rates, that was difficult (especially so for Argentina, which had fixed its peso by law). In many countries, most savings and debts were in dollars, so devaluation risked financial chaos. To make matters worse, government debts became more expensive to service, so they had to cut other spending, exacerbating recession.

Looking ahead, analysts and advisors have recommended a slew of reforms in order to achieve long-term sustainability in growth. A new book by a group of (mainly Latin American) economic reformers, co-edited by John Williamson (author of "Washington Consensus") and the Peruvian Minister of Finance, Pedro-Pablo Kuczynski, proposes several "crisis-proofing" measures for the economies of the region.

First, and perhaps most important, is fiscal policy. Governments have begun to write fiscal discipline into law, but many are poor at restraining spending in good times. A more effective fiscal policy would involve surpluses when growth was high, and borrowing only to finance public investment. It also requires reforms of tax and provincial finance. In many countries, local governments depend not on local taxes but on transfers from the center, which rise along with government revenues. But as Enrique Iglesias, president of the Inter-American Development Bank, notes, there was much resistance to counter-cyclical fiscal policies, stemming from a political perception that they help the next government.

Second, exports, which are absolutely vital to the region. Mexico and Chile were the only two of the region's larger countries to register double-digit annual increases in the volume of exports throughout the 1990s. Not coincidentally they escaped the worst of the turmoil of 1998–2002. So further trade opening would help. But the United States is offering less generous terms in the talks on a 34-country Free Trade Agreement of the Americas than it did to Mexico in NAFTA.

Third is currency exchange rate management. In the 1990s the IMF pushed strongly for Latin American countries to lift all capital controls. Many academics now think this should have been done more gradually. It is now believed that what brought Argentina down was the combination of its fixed exchange rate, which made its currency uncompetitive, with persistent fiscal deficits. Another advantage of a competitive currency is that it promotes growth in exports. Most Latin countries have competitive exchange rates, and are likely to stick to floating exchange rates. The challenge here is to develop institutions and mechanisms to allow the orderly transfer of capital from north to south. One answer would be a central bank for emerging markets, to ease adjustment by providing liquidity, given enough political will.

Apart from "crisis-proofing", Messrs. Kuczynski and Williamson make recommendations on three other sets of issues. The first is completing "first generation" reforms. They note that the least progress has been made in the labor market. Across the region, unemployment and "informal" jobs both grew during the 1990s. They propose reforms to severance pay and ancillary benefits, to reduce payroll taxes.

The second item is institutional reform. Many development economists now argue that institutions are crucial for growth. Here, the reform agenda is a diffused one, including a career civil service, better banking supervision, bankruptcy laws that allow banks to collect loan guarantees, and what Williamson calls "industrial policy's modern relative" – a national innovation system for new technology.

Third, the "new Washington Consensus" includes some policies designed to reduce inequality. Recent research suggests that inequality in developing countries itself tends to reduce growth: savings and investment become the preserve of a small rich elite. While warning of the potential cost to economic efficiency of actions to improve income distribution, Williamson concludes that "in a highly unequal region such as Latin America, opportunities for making large distributive gains for modest efficiency costs deserve to be seized". To that end, he suggests more effort to collect income tax, and higher property taxes. But more emphasis is placed on helping the poor gain assets, such as education and property titles, through land reform and micro-credit programs.

The way forward, Mr. Williamson concludes, is to "complete, correct, and complement the reforms of a decade ago", not to reverse them. The challenge is to form a consensus for reform. However cautious, references to selective capital controls, the role of the state, and income distribution, all point to the reform agenda moving toward the center. Nevertheless, there are signs that the region's new center-left governments, such as that of Brazil, might agree with much of this new agenda. President Lula's government in Brazil has not only tightened monetary and fiscal policy, it is pursuing the structural reforms espoused by its predecessor. This is not simply tactical, insists a member of Mr. da Silva's inner circle of advisers. The government's targets include doubling the efficiency of existing social spending in four years, and raising exports by 10 percent a year.

But there is still plenty of room for disagreement. Perhaps the biggest issue is the role of the state. "We don't want to renationalize anything, nor strengthen the state in a traditional sense, but we do want a state that plans things that are fundamental for a development project," said José Genoino, the president of

Lula's Workers' Party. That position is echoed by José Antonio Ocampo, ECLAC's head. "The 'Washington Consensus' wanted to think that growth would be automatic, but it needs active public policies," he says. He argues that while open trade has made some firms very competitive, these have become enclaves, with few links to the rest of the economy. He wants governments to adopt "technology policies", "strategic visions" for different economic sectors, and to help small and medium firms. He notes that Chile, the reformers' darling, employed such policies. He adds that two ways of doing all this would be through government procurement and state-owned banks – both an anathema to the reformers. Two other areas of controversy are labor reforms and further trade opening.

Few argue for turning the clock back to the 1970s, but there is a risk of re-regulation by a thousand obscure decrees and of incremental government handouts in the name of industrial policy, aggravating the low productivity and lack of competitiveness that dog the region. On the other hand, by grounding its recommendations more clearly in the region's economic history and institutional realities, the "new Washington Consensus" has moved closer to becoming a Latin American product. It remains to be seen how much of a consensus it will command, and whether it will guide the region back to growth.

An end to inequalities and poverty?

According to the United Nations' Economic Commission for Latin America and the Caribbean, while in 1980 the number of poor people in the region was 135 million, in 1990 the figure increased to 200 million and reached 204 million in 1999 (Human Globalization, 2003). It is now estimated that in the three years from 2000 to 2002, 13 million more people became poor as a result of the crisis that began in the closing years of the decade (Ocampo and Martin, 2003).

With respect to income distribution, no significant progress was made in the region over the decade. Economic recovery, lower inflation and increased public social spending were not sufficient to produce any substantial improvement in this indicator (Ocampo and Martin, 2003). Of a sample of 13 countries, only five (Colombia, Honduras, Nicaragua, Panama and Uruguay) showed progress in terms of income distribution. In the remaining countries (Argentina, Brazil, Chile, Costa Rica, Ecuador, Guatemala, Mexico and Venezuela), income distribution remained unchanged or actually deteriorated by varying degrees. Among the most striking cases were those of Brazil, where deterioration in the pattern of distribution coincided with substantial progress in poverty alleviation; Chile, which displayed poor results despite vigorous economic growth and a sharp increase in social spending during the period; and Argentina, where economic expansion was accompanied by deterioration in income distribution. In Venezuela, the country with the worst economic performance, income concentration increased markedly.

The causes of the persistent income concentration seen in the 1990s have been the subject of much debate, since they involve the whole complex mix of factors that determines how the benefits of economic growth are appropriated. Among the main factors in the region are, first, a poor record of job creation, due in part to inadequate economic growth and also to a production structure that is unfavorable to sectors making intensive use of direct labor; and, secondly, the persistent concentration of human capital, particularly in terms of education and assets. The poor distribution of income and opportunities also reflects major problems of social stratification and exclusion, which continue to be transmitted from one generation to the next, and which the current development model has no more been able to resolve than those which preceded it. An analysis of the trends of the 1990s gives important insights into what is required to reduce poverty and income inequalities in the region.

In the 1990s, in all countries where the unemployment rate among the poor declined, there was also a decrease in poverty. Three countries – Chile, Colombia and Panama – achieved favorable situations, with falling poverty and unemployment and rising or stable labor force participation among the poor.

Another development during the 1990s was that inflation was brought under control. Since high inflation affects those on lower incomes disproportionately, this had an extremely favorable impact on poverty. The most striking case was that of Brazil, where control of inflation combined with monetary transfer programs to help bring about a 12 percentage point reduction in poverty between 1990 and 1996; similar processes occurred, although to a lesser degree, in Argentina and Peru.

If rural and urban living standards are ever to become more equal, one essential requirement will be for agricultural and non-agricultural productivity levels to converge. Such convergence, however, may be the result of either positive factors (narrowing of the technology gap) or negative ones (more informal employment in urban areas due to immigration from the countryside) (Ocampo and Martin, 2003). If agricultural output per economically active person is taken as an indicator of labor productivity, productivity in the sector grew at an average annual rate of 2.4 percent from 1990 to 2000, to reach US$3,866 at 1990 prices.[10] Average labor productivity in the non-agricultural sectors of the region's countries, while considerably higher (US$8,278 in 2000), grew at an annual rate of −0.02 percent during this period. In the great majority of cases, productivity grew faster in the agricultural sector than in the rest of the economy.

Latin America and the Caribbean have a history of highly concentrated land ownership and tenure. By contrast with other regions of the world, this issue is still actively on the agenda in most of the countries, despite agrarian reform programs undertaken in the 1960s and early 1970s. The fact is that the sectors affected by these programs put up such strong resistance that they eventually succeed in neutralizing and even reversing them. With the exceptions of Brazil, Colombia, Costa Rica and, more recently, Venezuela, there are currently no initiatives to redistribute land. In the 1990s, large expanses of land remained unproductive even as highly unequal structures of land distribution persisted, a situation that was incompatible with the objectives of equity and efficiency implicit in sustainable development.

From the point of view of distribution, the favorable effects of raising workers' average educational levels, which was achieved by widening the coverage of education systems and access to secondary and university education, were counteracted by the widening of wage differentials between different skill levels. This combination of factors helped to perpetuate widespread, structural inequality in income distribution. The pay gap widened between higher-skilled workers and lower-skilled ones, in particular between those with university education and those without. This was reflected in a very sharp and generalized increase in pay differentials between professional/technical workers and other workers, in both the formal and the informal sectors.

Since it was in the informal sector that most new jobs were created, this contributed to the worsening distributional situation. The increase in this differential reflects both productivity factors and the lack of organization and bargaining power (with respect to wages and working conditions) of workers in this sector.

Public spending trends of the last decade show that some of the above problems have been identified and are being acted upon. For Latin America as a whole it is estimated that public social spending had increased from 10.4 percent of GDP in 1990–1991 to 13.1 percent in 1998–1999, with more significant increases in those countries whose per capita social spending was lower at the beginning of the 1990s. In a number of countries the increases were particularly substantial: 7 percent of GDP in Colombia, 6 percent in Uruguay, 4.3 percent in Paraguay and 3.5 percent in Peru. In 1998–1999, Argentina, Bolivia, Brazil, Chile, Colombia, Costa Rica, Panama and Uruguay had public social spending levels of between 15 and 23 percent of GDP, values very close to, and in some cases higher than, those of several developed countries.

The composition of extra public social spending between 1990–1991 and 1998–1999 reveals clear shifts in priorities. Forty-eight percent of all extra spending went on education and health (37 and 11 percent respectively), items where spending has a relatively progressive effects, and 45 percent on social security, whose implications for equity are less clear. The emphasis on the health and education sectors was more pronounced in countries with medium and low levels of relative spending, since in both cases 61 percent of the increase went to these areas. In countries with lower per capita incomes, the rise in spending on human capital was higher in relative terms, whereas extra spending on social security was more substantial, on average, in countries with higher per capita incomes, although there were wide variations among them. Between 1990–1991 and 1998–1999, spending on education increased from 2.9 percent to 3.9 percent of GDP, which represented growth of almost 35 percent in absolute terms. This substantial increase in public spending on the sector was largely geared toward supporting the efforts being made by a number of governments to narrow the gap between teachers' salaries and those of other skilled workers in the public sector. Thus, in the 1990s teachers' salaries increased by between 3 and 9 percent a year, depending on the country, this growth accounting for between 70 and 80 percent of the additional education spending.

In the 1990s, on the whole, the public spending which had the most progressive effects, i.e., whose benefits went in the largest proportion to the lowest-income households, was that allocated to primary and secondary education and to health and nutrition.

Most of the reforms are relatively recent and are likely to take time to develop their full potential; nevertheless, important lessons can be learned, as long as it is recognized that there is still a long way to go. The reforms implemented hold out the promise of substantial efficiency gains in social services provision, as they have created the conditions for better resource management in the public and private spheres, closer links between resource allocation and performance criteria, and the creation of quasi-market mechanisms in public sector structures. It has generally been recognized that coverage, which in some social sectors is still insufficient in most of the countries, needs to be expanded. The objective is to move toward universal systems that can protect poor households and those whose income comes from informal work. Consequently, it has been essential to create alternative mechanisms to ensure that paid employment is not a precondition for continuity of access to services and safety nets and that these are not suspended when earnings temporarily cease.

Subsidy and beneficiary selection policies have become more effective in achieving the aims of progressiveness and equity in access to social services, and are now perceived as more reliable and credible, although it has to be recognized that they have not always been commensurate with the scale of programs and the level of supply, information and transparency required.

In order to protect their populations in times of crisis, countries have had to develop mechanisms, plans and resources capable of being deployed rapidly in response to unforeseen circumstances. There is clearly a need for them to develop forecasting, response and saving mechanisms that enhance their ability to deal with such situations. Regulatory systems also need to be strengthened to ensure that private participation does not result in the exclusion of those who are on low incomes, work in the informal sector, or have higher levels of risk.

Given the scale and diversity of the lessons and challenges emerging from the 1990s, continued reform will require a renewed, broadly based consensus embracing the great majority of economic, political and social actors in each country, so that basic agreement can be reached on the main elements in the social agenda. This consensus has not come easily in the countries of the region, but in the last few years progress has been made, albeit slowly and falteringly. If citizens are committed to a new social development strategy they are more likely to participate actively in solving problems and attaining objectives, and they will value their social services all the more as the fruit of their own efforts.

Notes

1. John Williamson is a senior research fellow at the Institute of International Economics, a non-profit organization headquartered in Washington, DC, devoted to the study of international economic policy. The term "Washington Consensus" was later widely used by the author in his numerous works that followed on Latin America. See: http://www.iie.com/jwilliamson.htm
2. Since the mid-1990s Latinobarómetro, a Chilean organization, has polled political and social attitudes in 18 Latin American countries.
3. After the Second World War, Latin American countries pursued an import substitution-based economic policy. In order to gain access to local markets, companies had to invest in local manufacturing facilities.
4. *Maquila* or *maquiladora* is derived from the Spanish word *maquilar*, which historically referred to the milling of wheat into flour, for which the farmer would compensate the miller with a portion of the wheat, the miller's compensation being referred to as *maquila*.
5. Remittances represent 2 percent of Mexican GDP. As a source of foreign currency they are second to oil exports (US$4.9 billion) and the maquila profits (US$4.57 billion) (Banco de México, 2003).
6. The latter half of the 1990s saw increasing participation from the United States in the service sectors, such as energy, telecommunications, and banking.
7. The Maquila Program of Mexico started in 1964 and permitted US firms to temporarily export parts manufactured in the United States for assembly in Mexico. Re-exports to the United States were made with a tariff on the overseas value added component.
8. As of 21 May 2003, Brazil's benchmark interest rate was at 26.5 percent.
9. And figures from the Mexican Instituto Nacional de Estadística, Geografía e Informática (INEGI).
10. These figures were calculated from official data from the Food and Agriculture Organization of the United Nations (FAO) on the economically active population and ECLAC information on agricultural sector output.

References

Arahuetes, A. (2002) *Las inversiones directas de las empresas españolas en América Latina desde 2001: ¿retirada o replique?* [Spanish firms direct investment in Latin America since 2001: Withdraw or rejoin?], Madrid: Real Instituto Elcano de Estudios Internacionales y Estratégicos.

Banco de México (2003) See: http://www.banxico.org.mx/

Barth, J., Phumiwasana, T., and Yago, G. (2002) *The foreign conquest of Latin American banking: What's happening and why?* Policy Briefs, No. 32, Santa Monica, CA: Milken Institute.

Bayliss, K. (2002) "Privatization and poverty: The distributional impact of utility privatization," *Annals of Public and Cooperative Economics* 73: 603–625.

Birdsall, N. and Nellis, J. (2002) *Winners and losers: Assessing the distributional impact of privatization*, Working Paper, Washington, DC: Center for Global Development.

BusinessNews Americas (2003) See: http://www.bnamericas.com/

Carbajo, J. and Estache, A. (1996) "Competing private ports: Lessons from Argentina," *Viewpoint* December, note 100.

Casanova, L. (2002) "Lazos de familia" [Family relations], *Foreign Affairs en Español* 2 (2): 67–85.

—— (2004) "East Asian, European, and North American multinational firm strategies in Latin America," *Business and Politics* 6 (1), Article 6.

Chong, A. and Lopez, F. (2003) *The truth about privatization in Latin America*, Research Network Working Paper No. R-486, Washington, DC: Inter-American Development Bank.

Economic Commission for Latin America and the Caribbean (ECLAC) (2001) *Latin America and the Caribbean in the world economy*, Santiago, Chile: United Nations.

—— (2002) *Foreign direct investment in Latin America*, Santiago, Chile: United Nations.

EIU (Economist Intelligence Unit) Viewswire (2003) See: http://www.viewswire.com

Frischtak, C.R. (2003) *Multinational's response to integration of Latin American markets*, paper presented at the LAEBA Conference, Tokyo: Inter-American Development Bank and Asian Development Institute.

Galal, A., Jones, L., Tandon, P., and Vogelsand, I. (1994) *Welfare consequences of selling public enterprises*, Oxford: Oxford University Press.

Haque, M.S. (2000) "Privatization in Latin America: The other side of the story," *International Journal of Public Administration* 23 (5–8): 753–790.

Human Globalization (2003) "Globalization in Latin America: Why are people so disappointed?" retrieved 17 September 2004 from: http://humanglobalization.org/latinams/pdf/GlobLatAmLA.pdf

InfoAmericas (2001) See: http://www.infoamericas.com

Institute of International Economics (1990) See: www.iie.com

Inter-American Development Bank (2002) *Beyond borders: The new regionalism in Latin America*, Washington, DC: Inter-American Development Bank.

International Labor Organization (ILO) (1999) See: http://www.ilo.org

López-Calva, L. (2003) *Presentation and comments. Privatization in Latin America: What is the true record?* Santiago, Chile: LACEA.

Maquila Portal (2000, 2003) See: http://www.maquilaportal.com

Ocampo, J.A. and Martin, J. (2003) *A decade of light and shadow. Latin America and the Caribbean in the 1990s*, ECLAC, Santiago, Chile: United Nations.

Ramamurti, R. (1996) *Privatizing monopolies: Lessons from the telecommunications and transport sectors in Latin America*, Baltimore, MD: Johns Hopkins University Press.

Smith, W.R. (2002) "Privatization in Latin America: How did it work and what difference did it make?" *Latin American Politics and Society* 44 (4): 153–168.

Vodusek, Z. (ed.) (2001) *Foreign direct investment in Latin America. The role of European investors*, Washington, DC: Inter-American Development Bank.

3 Managing HR to build social capital in Latin America within MNCs

CAROLINA GOMEZ AND JUAN I. SANCHEZ

The management of human resources (HR) in multinational companies (MNCs) is a delicate balancing act of globalization and localization forces. Indeed, MNCs' success depends not only on their global presence, but also on their successful adaptation to a variety of local environments (Ghoshal and Bartlett, 1989; Ronen, 1990). Localization of HR practices goes hand-in-hand with globalization of the MNC, and the resulting tension between these two opposing forces creates a complex field. Unlike readily imitable, tangible assets such as technology and capital, there is no clearly delineated roadmap describing how to adapt intangible assets such as HR practices to local environments (Sparrow *et al.*, 1994).

MNCs operating in Latin America struggle to adapt to the local environment while preserving their strategic mission. Across Latin America, there is sufficient evidence, some of which is presented in this book, illustrating how the significant differences that exist between local environments affect HR practices in MNCs. Some countries have very specific laws that mandate certain cash payments and benefits. For instance, whereas a one-time separation (i.e. "*cesantía*") payment is an accepted practice in voluntary turnover in the Dominican Republic, a 10 percent reduction in wages is a mandatory, intermediate step in the process towards employee termination in Ecuador. In contrast to these local factors, many companies are imitating "best HR practices" throughout their Latin American subsidiaries. For example, Newell Rubbermaid recently revamped its compensation system by introducing a global job-leveling approach that applied the same seven compensable factors across their Latin American subsidiaries. Newell Rubbermaid reported improvements in corporate governance and transparency, turnover reduction, and talent mobility as a result of adopting this global, uniform job-level practice.

A side effect of globalization is that the known, positive consequences of "best HRM practices" across the board have led many organizations to implement such practices (Huselid *et al.*, 1997). The available evidence suggests that some degree of convergence in HR practices is occurring across MNCs (Sparrow *et al.*, 1994). In this chapter, we propose a new view of HR as a potential buffer between globalization and localization forces. This line of thinking acknowledges that even though practices are bound to differ among countries, strategically speaking, companies will want to keep some practice commonalities across their subsidiaries. The key question is how to balance these two seemingly incompatible goals, respecting and understanding country differences while implementing practices that are strategically aligned with the organization's mission. We argue that HR plays a central role in the process of balancing local and global forces. That is, HR can help MNCs deal with local differences while helping the company preserve practices that are mission-critical for its global strategy. Specifically, we maintain that HR plays a key role in developing social capital, which in turn provides the necessary "substitutes" for formal control that would otherwise be necessary. In a way, our argument is similar to that of Evans (1993), who advanced a view of HR as the "glue" that holds the organizational elements together. This notion is also analogous to the "community" or "relationship building" view of HR, which suggests that HR plays a key role in fostering the kind of organizational culture that facilitates organizational learning and innovation (Rousseau and Arthur, 1999). Our contribution lies primarily in outlining how this new role of creating human capital confers on HR the task of filtering mission-critical practices through a "localization mesh" that ensures success. In other words, HR takes a purely nomothetic mandate from headquarters and transforms it into a set of ideographic practices that take unique and nonrecurring local forces into account.

Social capital is defined as the intangible resources embedded in the network of existing company relationships that assist in the accomplishment of necessary tasks (Snell, 1999). Social capital serves as an informal mechanism that allows MNCs to coordinate and integrate activities, which becomes critical when MNCs are trying to be both locally responsive and cost efficient through globalization. As noted by others (Caves, 1982; Kostova and Roth, 2003), the assumption is that the dispersion of activities across national boundaries has to create a competitive advantage for the firm. A smart and efficient integration of such activities becomes pivotal in achieving such an advantage. Serving as an informal coordination mechanism, social capital can relieve the organization from having to use formal controls. Kerr and Jermier (1978) wrote about how some factors serve as substitutes for leadership. Social capital could potentially be a substitute for leadership in much the same way as the qualifications of the individual or a self-managed work team substitute for a leader. Through a strong organizational culture that builds social capital, organizational members become self-controlling and the activities of MNCs become integrated. By freeing the MNC from policing the subsidiary through a fixed set of controls, HR may also gain the autonomy needed to implement the unique ways of conducting business demanded by the local nuances.

How do HR practices help in the creation of social capital? Some point to a link between high commitment HR practices and an increase in common bonds, trust, and common codes of language (Clark, 2003). We argue here that HR practices can create social capital in locally adaptive ways, and in turn this capital can help in the localization of strategic practices. Specifically, we maintain that HR is strongly affected by national dynamics, institutional factors, culture, and local norms. However, HR does not have to be a mirror-image of these local forces. In fact, HR can act as a mediator between the desired company management strategies and localization forces, thereby channeling the effects of strategy on the localization of HR practices in a manner that is both culturally sensitive and strategically fit.

In this chapter, we adopt a holistic perspective of both the global and local factors through a country's institutional vantage point and strategic perspective. We will consider the impact of the country's environment as well as the MNCs' strategy on HR practices. Then, we will discuss the role of HR as a factor that helps companies implement their strategic practices while modifying them to be culturally acceptable. Finally, we will discuss how MNCs can build social capital through HR practices by taking into account the inherent values in the Latin American culture.

The role of HR in the MNC context

HR practices as a response to institutional forces

A country's institutional environment is comprised of relatively stable rules and norms that direct the economic activity. The institutional environment defines the courses of action open to firms by specifying the conditions to achieve environmental legitimacy (Kostova, 1999; Meyer and Rowan, 1977; North, 1990). Firms often adopt practices similar to those practiced by others to gain institutional legitimacy. This process may be more likely to occur when practices are intangible or difficult to measure, as is the case with HR practices. Institutional theorists would argue that the MNCs' practices depend on the degree to which a subsidiary relies on the MNC versus the local environment; this reflects where or with whom they need to achieve legitimacy. A subsidiary that relies heavily on local managerial, technical resources or local suppliers will be driven to imitate local companies. In this way, institutionalism can be a localization force for subsidiaries.

As noted by Aguilera and Jackson (2003) in their analysis of institutional differences that impact corporate governance, nationally distinct institutions provide different sets of isomorphic pressures. In some countries, such as Germany, strong representation rights lead to internal employee participation in decision making. The institutionally accepted rights make participation an expected component of the job. A firm that wants to obtain legitimacy in Germany would need to allow its employees internal control or participation. This is an example of a localization force that needs to be balanced with the need for global coordination in the MNC.

It would be a mistake to take a deterministic position; although the imitation process is partly determined by the MNC and partly determined by local forces, recent research argues that subsidiaries can change their role while trying to strike a balance between globalization and localization forces (Birkinshaw and Hood, 1998; Ferner and Quintanilla, 1998). In addition, a significant part of a MNC's competitive advantage comes from its ability to utilize its organizational capabilities on a global basis (Kostova and Roth, 2002). Therefore, MNCs often try to implement organizational practices that are well-aligned with their strategic intent (Kostova, 1999), such as total quality management or self-managed work teams. As noted by Kostova (1999), companies transfer organizational practices that reflect their core competencies. Kostova proposes a look at a country's institutional framework, which incorporates the values related toward a specific practice, say, the normative institutions, in addition to regulatory institutions such as laws, and cognitive aspects such as skill sets. A country's institutional framework may either impede or aid the successful implementation of strategic practices (Kostova, 1999).

Rosenzweig and Nohria (1994) used institutional theory to study the HR practices of subsidiaries. They found that the method of founding, dependence on local inputs, presence of expatriates, and extent of communication with the parent significantly affected the degree of similarity to local HR practices. What this research shows is that subsidiary practices reflect an interplay between the country and its values, the dependence of the subsidiary on the local environment versus the MNC, and the MNC's strategic use of common practices.

The effect of regulatory institutions: the legal environment in Mexico

Different countries have different laws that affect many HR practices in distinct ways. A country's laws can affect how a company recruits and selects employees, the pay and benefits offered, and even the dismissal of employees. One need only look at Mexico, one of the United States' largest trading partners, to see how country factors can affect the HR practices of a subsidiary. Certainly, both countries have similarities within their labor laws (Posthuma et al., 2000). The United States and Mexico legally prohibit discrimination based on factors such as gender and age, even though the enforcement may differ considerably between the two countries. Both countries allow organized labor, although administrative or supervisory employees are not allowed to join unions. Still, Mexico has some distinct labor laws. For example, in the United States, employment relationships are generally "at will" such that they can be terminated at any time or for any reason assuming no statutes and federal laws are violated; in Mexico, the assumption is that contracts of employment have an indefinite length. There are a number of situations that would allow a company to hire employees on a temporary basis, but a subsidiary in Mexico should understand the implication if an employee is not specifically hired on a temporary basis. Additionally, in Mexico, an employee not covered under a collective bargaining agreement must have an individual written contract of employment. One of the obvious differences between the two countries is found in the pay and benefits area. When managers assess the hourly wage comparisons between the two countries, they need to understand that the Mexican government requires many benefits that are not required in the United States. As an example, in Mexico, the government requires a yearly bonus referred to as the "aguinaldo", which is equivalent to 15 paid days. A second instance is the vacation premium in Mexico, which requires employers to pay their employees an additional 25 percent above the regular pay during their vacation. A third interesting difference between the labor laws in the two countries is Mexico's required profit-sharing plan for workers.

While Mexican law mandates some of the differences, others occur despite similarities in the law, perhaps indicating more of a cultural history or an institutional failure to enact the laws. While the law in both countries prohibits discrimination, many companies operating in Mexico choose to specify the gender and age of the employees they are seeking. In summary, HR practices are heavily driven by local laws as well as traditions and social customs.

The effect of cognitive and normative institutions

HR practices are heavily influenced by the cognitive and normative institutions in a given country. As noted by Kostova and Roth (2002), the implementation of a quality management program is heavily influenced by the degree to which a skill set related to quality management is present in that country. Certainly, in the HR area, some countries have developed more programs and therefore a more extensive skill set. One such program, specifically the use of performance evaluations, varies among countries (Milliman *et al.*, 2002). In the United States, performance appraisals are used extensively for a range of purposes such as documentation, subordinate expression, and administrative purposes including pay (Milliman *et al.*, 2002). In contrast, the use of performance appraisals is not as common in organizations in Mexico. Companies that use them usually do so for different purposes than those in the United States (Milliman *et al.*, 2002). MNCs may certainly find that the number of people with HR training differs among countries. Such differences reflect the diversity in the cognitive skills available to MNCs as they expand to different countries.

Kostova (1999) also states that normative institutions project a set of values that affect the receptivity toward a practice. Within this umbrella of "normative institutions" falls the effect of cultural values. HR practices have to be adapted due to the influence that cultural values have on employee attitudes and behaviors. Research has shown that collectivists act quite differently from individualists when working in teams. Earley (1989) found that social loafing did not occur in groups with collectivistic beliefs (i.e. Chinese managers). Subsequently, Earley's (1993) research indicated that the performance of collectivists is highest when working within their "in-group". Research has shown that collectivists and individualists may have different reward allocation norms when working in teams. Specifically, collectivists appear to evaluate "in-group" (rather than "out-group") members far more generously than individualists (Gomez et al., 2000). Further, collectivists value maintenance contributions more than individualists, while individualists place higher value on task contributions than collectivists (Gomez et al., 2000). Practices such as self-managing work teams, which are being used increasingly worldwide, may need alterations since evaluations can be affected by value differences.

Research has also shown that individuals are more likely to respond unfavorably to low levels of voice in low power distance cultures than in high power distance cultures (Brockner et al., 2001). Hence, power distance may impact the degree to which participation is well received by employees. Cultural values such as collectivism and power distance have been shown to impact the degree to which individuals resisted the move to self-managed work teams (Kirkman and Shapiro, 2001). Moreover, Lawrence and Yeh (1994) found major differences between the Mexican and Japanese cultures that would appear to make the implementation of Japanese manufacturing techniques such as self-managed work teams more difficult in Mexico.

MNCs have taken these cultural values into account when designing their HR practices for Latin America. Many have argued that by understanding the culture of Mexico, companies can design practices that are congruent with cultural values. Such benefits should increase the performance of employees. A majority of employers use a punctuality bonus that provides employees an extra pay incentive for perfect attendance (Flynn, 1994). Many companies offer additional benefits to deal with the tight employment market. As noted by Posthuma et al. (2000), many plants in Mexico offer at least some of the following benefits: hiring bonuses; free or subsidized cafeterias; coupons for local grocery stores; free or subsidized transportation to and from work; bonuses for recruiting other workers; paid leave to attend family events; tuition reimbursement; company picnics; in-plant medical care; sports facilities; clothing; and protective equipment. Companies can choose HR practices that are culturally congruent above and beyond those mandated by the law.

Despite the significant influence of cultural values and institutions on employee attitudes and behaviors, companies still need to transfer those HR strategic practices that give them a competitive advantage. There are accounts of companies that have successfully implemented such techniques in Mexico (Gomez, 2004; Gowan *et al.*, 1996), suggesting that there are culturally sensitive ways to implement such practices. We now turn to the role that HR can play in implementing and, perhaps more importantly, adapting company-specific practices.

HR as a critical balancing act

HR as a strategic mediator

As indicated, part of MNCs' competitive advantage is their unique company knowledge that is to be transferred to their subsidiaries around the world (Kostova, 1999). There is evidence that foreign MNCs are utilizing different approaches to international human resource management (IHRM) in Mexico. These range from a mechanistic control approach to a developmental approach (Teagarden and Paik, 1993). Compared to other maquilas, those in the United States and Japan appear to implement a more developmental approach focused on control through employee development and socialization.

IHRM proposes that HR practices be used to align MNC goals and objectives with host-country affiliate dynamics (Teagarden *et al.*, 1992). That is, the human resource function has the important task of tweaking strategic practices so that they adequately deal with the challenges provided by the local environment in a culturally-sensitive manner. Despite the MNCs' overriding human resource philosophy and strategic mandate, subsidiaries must adapt these to fit their cultural imperative. In adapting HR practices to local factors, MNCs need to first consider the focal cultural values on which such practices would impinge. Then, MNCs should consider whether the employee behaviors or outcomes that are promoted by those HR practices are consistent or conflictive with cultural prescriptions. MNCs should analyze whether their global HR practices suppress employee behaviors or outcomes that are highly valued in the subsidiary's cultural context. HR practices should be modified accordingly to produce culturally consistent employee behaviors and outcomes. In making these determinations, it is important to remember that the same cultural "construct" might have different behavioral manifestations in each culture (Sanchez *et al.*, 2000). For instance, an internal locus of control may be expressed assertively in the United States, but with more subtlety in Mexico, where assertiveness is seen as rude, arrogant, inappropriate, and ineffective. In this case, HR practices that foster public self-promotion and self-enhancement may make Mexican employees uncomfortable. This balancing act of differentiation and integration is noted as a critical component of IHRM (Schuler *et al.*, 2002; Sparrow *et al.*, 1994).

To obtain a clearer picture of how organizations may strike a balance between localization and globalization, consider the case of a US subsidiary in Mexico.

This subsidiary appeared to have three types of HR practices supporting the strategic mandate to implement an organizational learning approach with self-managed work teams (Gomez, 2004). The first set of standard HR practices included training, goals, a reward structure aligned with the strategic goals, and a team structure. A second set of HR practices seemed to be culture-specific or implemented to deal with the host-country-specific dynamics. In Mexico, some of the culture-specific issues included a cultural history of authoritarian management with which most employees were accustomed, as well as a relatively low educational level in the local workforce. To deal with these host-country dynamics, the company hired high-school graduates and offered them 30 days of training. A third set of HR practices appeared to involve an *ad hoc* cultural "translation" of the MNC's US practices to fit the Mexican culture. One such instance where subsidiary managers "translated" the MNC's HR practices was in the area of self-managed work teams. In order to deal with the potential conflict between family and work teams when implementing the self-managed work teams, the HR manager decided to build team camaraderie in a manner that incorporated the families of the workers due to the nature of the family-oriented, collectivistic culture. Events such as soccer games and bowling championships were organized in which the teams competed against each other, but, importantly, the families were invited to participate in the events. This design allowed the teams to begin to think of their work team members as part of their in-group (e.g. family, workgroup, or collective of importance), which was previously comprised of only family and close friends. In addition, the importance of the team seemed to allow individuals to transfer their loyalty, typically reserved for the supervisor, to the entire team. Each of these types of HR practices contributed to the success of the implementation of self-managed work teams in this subsidiary. However, the importance of this case rests on its forceful illustration of how critical it is to translate work practices into culturally congruent propositions.

The HR control and coordination mechanisms that the MNC chooses in managing its subsidiaries are a key component of the delicate balance between localization and globalization. The control and integration roles of HR are reviewed next.

HR's role in control and integration

We have been discussing the role of HR management in MNC–subsidiary dyads as a tough balancing act of localization and globalization concerns. Not all MNCs require the same level of coordination in their practices. MNCs follow different strategies that emphasize local responsiveness and/or cost efficiencies through globalization (Bartlett and Ghoshal, 1989). Each strategy dictates a different kind of relationship between the MNC and its subsidiaries which is then reflected in the level and type of interdependence among affiliates within the MNC (Kostova and Roth, 2003). An MNC pursuing a local responsiveness strategy tends to provide a high degree of autonomy to its subsidiaries because local responsiveness is the number one priority and does not typically require the integration of activities. In contrast, a major focus for those MNCs following a globalization strategy, in addition to or in place of a localization strategy, lies in controlling and integrating the activities of subsidiaries across many national borders.

Companies have traditionally used formal mechanisms such as centralization, standardization, planning, and output control (Martinez and Jarillo, 1991). Today, many companies are turning to informal mechanisms such as participation, teams, and, more broadly, an organizational culture of shared norms and values (Jaeger, 1983; Martinez and Jarillo, 1991). In fact, Martinez and Jarillo (1989) identified a move away from structural, formal subsidiary controls toward subtler, informal controls such as norms and values. One such informal mechanism of coordination/integration that has recently gained a great deal of attention is social capital. As an informal mechanism, social capital also allows the flexibility needed to provide rapid responses to local forces.

Social capital as a control and integration mechanism

Social capital represents a subtle source of informal control and integration within a company. The need for social capital is greater in MNCs that have a great deal of subsidiary interdependence, and therefore have to coordinate their activities (Kostova and Roth, 2003). Kostova and Roth (2003) argue that the complex interdependence in many MNCs necessitates more flexible mechanisms of control and coordination. The imperative for informal control such as can be created through social capital becomes even more critical in Latin American countries, where government regulations, cultural traditions, and cultural values may make formal controls an ineffective means of managing the subsidiary. Wilkins and Ouchi (1983) note the importance of cultural or clan control when behaviors and outcomes are not easily defined. Social capital, with its embedded set of relational networks, seems ideally suited to serve the purpose of informal control.

Given its potential role in the control and integration of subsidiaries, it is critical to understand how an MNC can build social capital through strategically-aligned HR practices. Increasingly, research on HR has noted that there is a relationship between human resources practices and social capital. Clark (2003) reviewed research showing that high commitment, relationship-based practices tend to create bonds and trust, which in turn feed social capital. Snell (1999) also indicated that practices such as employee development, an egalitarian environment with empowerment and flat wage structures, cross-functional interaction, 360-degree feedback, group incentives, and other practices differentiate firms with high levels of social capital from those with low levels.

Many of these practices seem more appropriate for certain cultural contexts than for others. Cultures that are low in power distance and low uncertainty avoidance lend themselves to participatory management. Therefore, we argue that in building social capital, MNCs must take into account the cultural context in which they operate. The same HR practices that build trust in the United States may fail to do so in the Latin American context. In essence, the regional values inherent in the Latin American culture[1] should be considered when deciding how HR practices can be adapted to generate social capital.

Building social capital in Latin America

It is interesting that the concept of social capital has parallels in constructs that have characterized many cultures around the world. The importance of relationships is valued to such a degree in many Asian cultures that they have their own words to describe the phenomenon: *guanxi* in China; *kankei* in Japan; and *immak* in Korea (Hitt *et al.*, 2002). Not surprisingly, these cultures all highly value collectivism (Hofstede, 1980). Similarly, the cultures of Latin America, also highly collectivist, have been characterized by their emphasis on relationships. Given the importance of relationships to building social capital, the Latin American context appears to be ideally suited to funnel the collectivistic mentality in ways that support the organization's strategy. However, some aspects of the collectivist culture of Latin America speak against its cultural readiness for HR practices that stimulate the creation of social capital. MNCs would consider favoritism toward in-group members such as friends and family to be negative. Nevertheless, the collectivist orientation may make the process of building social capital easier if the MNC understands how to funnel the collectivist mentality toward the organization. The process of building social capital in Latin America will no doubt differ from building social capital in organizations in the United States. This is because of the dominance of collectivist values, and differences in economic development as well as a number of other important cultural values. A discussion of how MNCs may build social capital in Latin America requires a review of some of the key values of this pan-regional culture.

Latin American regional values, attitudes, and behaviors

As mentioned, most Latin American cultures tend to lean toward a collectivistic orientation with an emphasis on family and close friends. The emphasis or attachment to the family has been studied within the US Hispanic community and defined as familism (Sabogal *et al.*, 1987). Latin American cultures also tend to be high on power distance, meaning that employees tend to feel comfortable with differences in power and therefore seldom disagree with their supervisors (Hofstede, 1980). In addition, there is a great tendency toward uncertainty avoidance, wherein individuals avoid uncertain situations (Hofstede, 1980). Thus, a preference for rules and procedures exists. In terms of communication, Latin American cultures tend to be high context, meaning that individuals need to take into account the context surrounding the words, like relationships and body language, to get at the intended meaning. In other words, individuals must "read between the lines" (Hall and Hall, 1997).

Value orientations undoubtedly affect individual attitudes. In the United States, few concepts are valued more than equality. Yet in Mexico, as Condon (1985) explains, the notion of all men being equal is almost an insult. In Mexican society, each individual is unique and different from everyone else. As noted by Harris and Moran (1991), reality is not just objective but interpersonal for Mexicans. These value differences in individualism/collectivism are reflected in the respective human resource management practices. Staffing and recruitment decisions in the United States are typically based on merit and qualifications, and aim at being objective, legal, fair, and job-centered (Arvey *et al.*, 1991). On the other hand, selection and recruitment processes in Latin American countries such as Peru and Mexico are often unsystematic and not necessarily job-related, usually focusing on who the person is, and on his/her social class (Arvey *et al.*, 1991). In contrast to anti-nepotism sentiments in the United States, family ties are seen as legitimate reasons for preferential employment in Mexico, and relatives are often given jobs or contracts because their relation to employees makes them trustworthy (de Forest, 1994).

Recent research has found that the focus on interpersonal issues in Mexico impacts theories such as organizational justice and the influence that justice may have on employee commitment (Gomez and Kirkman, working paper). Distributive justice, the fairness of the distribution of outcomes, and interactive justice, perceived interpersonal treatment received during the enactment of organizational procedures, predicted affective commitment or the emotional attachment felt by employees. Conversely, US findings show that procedural justice (the perceived fairness of the policies and procedures) seems to be a better predictor of employee commitment than other forms of justice such as interactive and distributive justice. This focus on the form of interpersonal treatment is also consistent with the emphasis that Latin American cultures place on "face", or ensuring that individuals do not lose their dignity and the respect of others (Hall and Hall, 1997). In the United States, ensuring that fair procedures are in place is essential to gain employee commitment; in Mexico, it is more important to ensure that the treatment of the employee is of a "high-contact", personalized nature. Since organizational commitment has been linked to the level of social capital in organizations (Clark, 2003), these findings suggest that extra care should be put into the "form" of individual treatment of any HR practice in Latin America.

Building social capital in Latin American subsidiaries through HR practices

The distinction between private and public social capital is an important element of social capital that should be taken into account when assessing the cultural fit of HR practices (Kostova and Roth, 2003). Social capital can be seen primarily as a "private" good that benefits an individual or it can be seen as a public good if it is available to members of the individual's group. On the surface, one might expect collectivist cultures to make social capital more of a public good, yet this perspective would ignore the importance of understanding the members of a particular culture's "in-group", the strong, cohesive group in which the individual is embedded (Triandis *et al.*, 1988). In a culture such as Japan, where the in-group tends to be the work group (Lawrence and Yeh, 1994), it would seem logical to expect social capital to become public. Conversely, in the Latin American culture, the in-group typically involves only the family and close friends; therefore, private social capital may be extended to their benefit, but not automatically to the benefit of the entire work group. Maintaining sight of who forms the true "in-group" is critical when attempting to build social capital in Latin America.

To build social capital in Latin American subsidiaries, MNCs need to think about how their HR practices can be modified in a way that fosters a sense of family, which is the essence of this collectivist context. We are not advocating that MNCs entirely change their management and HR practices, but that they examine their practices and ensure that their implementation is congruent with the cultural values of Latin America. There are certain criteria that any HR practice must abide by in Latin America in order to build social capital. First of all, the employee's in-group must be included among the beneficiaries of HR practices. Secondly, HR practices must focus on the interpersonal aspect, with particular attention to the form of exchanges and communications between the organization and individual employees. A third major criterion is to manage the practices in such a way that the employee views the organization as part of his/her in-group. Obviously, these recommendations are interrelated. Targeting the employee's in-group may well lead the employee to view the organization as part of his/her extended family. Next, we look at different HR practices and discuss how these criteria can be incorporated into each practice.

While a MNC's strategic mandate may include an objective mechanism to assess applicant qualifications, we would argue that MNCs assess the possibility of modifying this mechanism by allowing current employees to play a part in the process. While many Latin American countries have been criticized for "nepotism", we believe that current employees may, through their relationships, provide a more culturally adept assessment of the true qualifications of an applicant. Research has shown that having the right personal connections is a top hiring factor in Mexico (Huo *et al.*, 2002). US MNCs should consider potential candidates who enjoy "in-group" ties, albeit indirect ones, with current employees. Such ties would help build social capital, but additionally, considering these candidates shows that the MNC looks after the employee's in-group, which hopefully will be expanded to include the organization in its entirety.

Many MNCs have a strong socialization process. Socialization is critical when getting the employee to think of the organization and its members as part of his/ her in-group. Socialization should focus on making the employee proud of being part of the organizational family. It should also allow for plenty of time to interact among employees and managers so that they can be perceived as in-group members. However, given a relatively high power distance, managers and employees may not feel immediately comfortable interacting with each other. In our work with Latin American managers, we have often been asked for advice regarding how to solicit feedback from subordinates, which is sometimes seen as a sign of weakness or incompetence in high-power distance cultures. For this reason, providing structure and coaching to guide these interactions seems advisable.

Training and development programs can build social capital if they show a genuine, long-term interest/investment orientation in the employee as an individual, just as *bona fide* members of the in-group would. Research by Drost *et al.* (2002) shows that managers in Mexico and Latin America overwhelmingly believe in training as a reward as well as a chance to develop technical and interpersonal skills. From the MNCs' perspective, training on basic skills may help overcome shortcomings in the workforce; communication skills may help deal with ingrained cultural values towards the traditional hierarchical, authoritarian organizational practices. The benefits unit should emphasize that the MNC is investing in its employees for their long-term benefit because employees are part of the organizational family. Employees should be proud of being sent to training, because it signifies that they have been embraced as true in-group members in whose long-term development the organization is genuinely interested. Although such a long-term perspective can contribute to the sense of family that develops social capital in Latin America, organizations should be cautioned about betraying employee expectations. Such betrayals are likely to be seen as infamies analogous to the betrayals of well-trusted in-group members, and therefore employees will react accordingly. MNCs must make it clear that the future is uncertain in today's rapidly moving business environment and that, despite their long-term investment in employees, employment-for-life is no longer a suitable promise. On the other hand, MNCs should note that if their employment ceases, employees will walk away with the fruits of the organization's investment in their professional development, which would give them an edge in a possibly tight job market.

While performance appraisals are not typically a formal process in many Latin American companies, we believe an MNC can gain significantly from implementing this mechanism of feedback. Nevertheless, it is critical that managers in MNCs understand the importance of saving face in a collectivist culture (Sully de Luque and Sommer, 2000). Providing public feedback must be done carefully. Even in private, feedback must not be given in such a way that the employee feels that s/he is losing face. As already mentioned, the interpersonal or interactive justice component will be as important if not more important than the procedural or distributive components of evaluations. The manager must be interpersonally sensitive and deliver feedback with care. Sometimes this may require a less direct, non-confrontational approach that puts individual respect at the forefront of all interactions.

Perhaps one of the most important areas in building a family-oriented culture capable of producing social capital is rewards and compensation. Employees must sense that the organization is really taking care of them. This does not necessarily mean direct, monetary remuneration. In Latin America, symbolic rewards show that an employee is respected and are highly appreciated. Some MNCs in Mexico help employees to deal with local transportation, health, or inflation problems. Depending on the employee's level, food coupons, health care, and transportation may be benefits that communicate a sense of family and a feeling of being embedded in the in-group. Company-sponsored social events may help build this perception. When these events occur, MNCs should ensure the inclusion of employees' families; this will truly enhance the probability that the company will start to be seen as an extension of the in-group.

MNCs in Mexico have been successful at building progressive company cultures that use self-managed work teams and empower employees. Such empowerment is more typical of egalitarian cultures. Egalitarian cultures can work on a long-term basis, but it is important that MNCs provide defined roles for employees and supervisors/individuals who can guide them. The style of leadership will play an important role. The typical leadership behaviors of initiating structure versus consideration apply to Latin America as well (Drost and Von Glinow, 1998). Leaders will be expected to engage in task-related activities such as organizing, setting goals, meeting deadlines, and giving directions, as well as establishing trust, rapport, and communication with subordinates. US theories focus on when one is more appropriate than the other. In Latin cultures, the orthogonality of these two types of behaviors does not seem to hold; behaviors of consideration become important even when providing task/structure initiation.

We can summarize the suggestions made above by delineating how the dimensions or criteria noted at the beginning of this section are met with each HR practice (see Table 3.1). By meeting these criteria, the practices will be culturally congruent and more readily accepted by Latin American employees. Such acceptance will result in a solid foundation of social capital. Cultural values are changing in countries such as Mexico (Maznevski et al., 2002), so companies must realize that individual attitudes toward HR practices may change accordingly. Some cultural "deviance" in HR practices may represent a competitive advantage as workers may enjoy HR practices that represent a departure from the old

Table 3.1 Building social capital through HR practices in Latin America

HR practice	Target: Ingroup	Process: Interpersonal	Desired outcome: Identification with company
Recruitment/selection	✓		✓
Socialization/training			✓
Performance appraisal		✓	✓
Rewards/compensation	✓		✓
Employee empowerment/leadership		✓	✓

system. Employees working for foreign MNCs are often proud to be working for well-known foreign companies that are associated with progress and change.

An MNC in Latin America should generally focus on managing the HR practice in such a way that employees will eventually identify with the company as if it were part of their in-group. It typically benefits the MNC to emphasize the interpersonal aspect more so than it has in the US culture. The form of HR practices should always be respectful. The beneficiaries of HR practices should be expanded to include close in-group members so that the organization becomes an extension of the in-group. Each HR practice that the MNC is thinking of implementing should be filtered through a "localization mesh" that identifies possible clashes with local values and simultaneously allows for modifications that will make the practice fit culturally and efficiently build social capital.

Notes

1. Although many researchers argue that each country in Latin America should be dealt with separately, much research has shown commonalities in values with the region. Based on Hofstede's (1980) research, Latin American countries tend to be collectivist, high on power distance, as well as high on uncertainty avoidance. In addition, most Latin American countries are considered high-context in their communication style.

References

Aguilera, R.V. and Jackson, G. (2003) "The cross-national diversity of corporate governance: Dimensions and determinants," *Academy of Management Review* 28: 447–465.

Arvey, R., Bhagat, R., and Salas, E. (1991) "Cross-cultural and cross-national issues in personnel and human resources management: Where do we go from here?" *Research in Personnel and Human Resources Management* 9: 367–407.

Bartlett, C.A. and Ghoshal, S. (1989) *Managing across borders: The transnational solution*, Boston: Harvard Business School Press.

Birkinshaw, J. and Hood, N. (1998) "Multinational subsidiary evolution: Capability and charter change in foreign-owned subsidiary companies," *Academy of Management Review* 23: 773–795.

Brockner, J., Ackerman, G., Greenberg, J., Gelfand, M.J., Francesco, A.M., Chen, Z.X., Leung, K., Bierbrauer, G., Gomez, C., Kirkman, B.L., and Shapiro, D.L. (2001) "Culture and procedural justice: The moderating influence of power distance on reactions to voice," *Journal of Experimental Social Psychology* 37: 300–315.

Caves, R. (1982) *Multinational enterprise and economic analysis*, Cambridge: Cambridge University Press.

Clark, M.M. (2003) "Academics tout 'social capital' as latest thing in strategic HR," *HR Magazine* 48 (2): 38.

Condon, J. (1985) *Good neighbors*, Yarmouth, ME, USA: Intercultural Press.

de Forest, M. (1994) "Thinking of a plant in Mexico?" *The Academy of Management Executive* 8: 33–40.

Drost, E.A. and Von Glinow, M.A. (1998) "Leadership behavior in Mexico: Etic philosophies – emic practices," *Research in International Business and International Relations* 7: 3–28.

Drost, E.A., Frayne, C.A., Lowe, K.B., and Geringer, J.M. (2002) "Benchmarking training and development practices: A multi-country comparative analysis," *Human Resource Management* 41 (1): 6–86.

Earley, P.C. (1989) "Social loafing and collectivism: A comparison of the United States and the People's Republic of China," *Administrative Science Quarterly* 34: 565–581.

—— (1993) "East meets West meets Mideast: Further explorations of collectivistic and individualistic work groups," *Academy of Management Journal* 36: 319–348.

Evans, P. (1993) "Dosing the glue: Applying human resource technology to build the global organization," in B. Shaw and P. Kirkbride (eds) *Research in Personnel and Human Resource Management*, Vol. 3, Greenwich, CT: JAI Press.

Ferner, A. and Quintanilla, J. (1998) "Multinationals, national business systems, and HRM: The enduring influence of national identity or a process of 'Anglo-Saxonization'," *International Journal of Human Resource Management* 9 (4): 710–731.

Flynn, G. (1994) "HR in Mexico: What you should know," *Personnel Journal* (August): 34–44.

Ghoshal, S. and Bartlett, C.A. (1989) "The multinational corporation as an interorganizational network," *Academy of Management Review* 15 (4): 603–625.

Gomez, C. (2004) "The influence of environmental, organizational, and HRM factors on employee behaviors in subsidiaries: A Mexican case study of organizational learning," *Journal of World Business* 39: 1–11.

Gomez, C. and Kirkman, B.L. (working paper) *Organizational justice: Its applicability and predictive power on employee commitment in Mexico*, Working Paper, Florida International University.

Gomez, C., Kirkman, B.L., and Shapiro, D.L. (2000) "The impact of collectivism and ingroup/outgroup membership on evaluation generosity," *Academy of Management Journal* 43: 1097–2007.

Gowan, M., Ibarreche, S. and Lackey, C. (1996) "Doing the right things in Mexico," *Academy of Management Executive* 10: 74–81.

Hall, E.T. and Hall, M.R. (1997) "Key concepts: Underlying structures of culture," in H.W. Lane, J.J. DiStefano, and M.L. Maznevski (eds) *International Management Behavior*, 3rd edn, Cambridge, MA: Blackwell.

Harris, P.R. and Moran, R.T. (1991) *Managing cultural differences*, Houston, TX: Gulf Publishing Company.

Hitt, M.A., Lee, H., and Yucel, E. (2002) "The importance of social capital to the management of multinational enterprises: Relational networks among Asian and Western firms," *Asia Pacific Journal of Management* 19: 353–372.

Hofstede, G. (1980) *Culture's consequences*, Beverly Hills: Sage.

Huo, Y.P., Huang, H.J., and Napier, N.K. (2002) "Divergence or convergence: A cross-national comparison of personnel selection practices," *Human Resource Management* 41 (1): 31–44.

Huselid, M.A., Jackson, S.E., and Schuler, R.S. (1997) "Technical and strategic human resource management effectiveness as determinants of firm performance," *Academy of Management Journal* 40 (1): 171–188.

Jaeger, A. (1983) "The transfer of organizational culture overseas: An approach to control in the multinational corporation," *Journal of International Business Studies* 14: 91–114.

Kerr, S. and Jermier, J.M. (1978) "Substitutes for leadership: Their meaning and measurement," *Organizational Behavior and Human Performance* 22 (3): 375–403.

Kirkman, B.L. and Shapiro, D.L. (2001) "The impact of cultural values on job satisfaction and organizational commitment in self-managing work teams: The mediating role of employee resistance," *Academy of Management Journal* 44 (3): 557–569.

Kostova, T. (1999) "Transnational transfer of strategic organizational practices: A contextual perspective," *Academy of Management Review* 24: 308–324.

Kostova, T. and Roth, K. (2002) "Adoption of an organizational practice by the subsidiaries of the MNC: Institutional and relational effects," *Academy of Management Journal* 45 (1): 215–233.

—— (2003) "Social capital in multinational organizations and a micro–macro model of its formation," *Academy of Management Review* 28 (2): 297–317.

Lawrence, J.J. and Yeh, R. (1994) "The influence of Mexican culture on the use of Japanese manufacturing techniques in Mexico," *Management International Review* 34: 49–66.

Martinez, J.I. and Jarillo, J.C. (1989) "The evolution of research on coordination mechanisms in multinational corporations," *Journal of International Business Studies* 19: 489–514.

—— (1991) "Coordination demands of international strategies," *Journal of International Business Studies* 21: 429–444.

Maznevski, M., DiStefano, J., Gomez, C., Noorderhaven, N., and Wu, P. (2002) "Cultural dimensions at the individual level of analysis: The cultural orientations framework," *International Journal of Cross Cultural Management* 2 (3): 275–296.

Meyer, J.W. and Rowan, B. (1977) "Institutionalized organizations: Formal structure as myth and ceremony," *American Journal of Sociology* 83: 340–363.

Milliman, J., Nason, S., Zhu, C., and De Cieri, H. (2002) "An exploratory assessment of the purposes of performance appraisals in North and Central America, and the Pacific Rim," *Human Resource Management* 41 (1): 87–102.

North, D.C. (1990) *Institutions, institutional change and economic performance*, London: Cambridge University Press.

Posthuma, R.A., Dworkin, J., Torres, V., and Bustillos, D. (2000) "Labor and employment laws in the United States and Mexico: An international comparison," *Labor Law Journal* 51: 95–111.

Ronen, S. (1990) "Human resource management in France," in R. Pieper (ed.) *Human resource management: An international comparison*, Berlin: de Gruyter.

Rosenzweig, P.M. and Nohria, N. (1994) "Influences on human resources management practices in multinational corporations," *Journal of International Business Studies* 25: 229–251.

Rousseau, D.M. and Arthur, M.B. (1999) "The boundaryless human resource function: Building agency and community in the new economic era," *Organizational Dynamics* 27 (4): 7–18.

Sabogal, F., Marín, G., Otero-Sabogal, R., Marín, B., and Perez-Stable, E. (1987) "Hispanic familism and acculturation: What changes and what doesn't?" *Hispanic Journal of Behavioral Sciences* 9: 397–412.

Sanchez, J.I., Spector, P.E., and Cooper, C.L. (2000) "Adapting to a boundaryless world: A developmental expatriate model," *Academy of Management Executive* 14 (2): 96–106.

Schuler, R.S., Budwar, P.S., and Florkowski, G.W. (2002) "International human resource management: Review and critique," *International Journal of Management Review* 4: 41–70.

Snell, S.A. (1999) "Social capital and strategic HRM: It's who you know," *Human Resource Planning* 22: 62–65.

Sparrow, P., Schuler, R.S., and Jackson, S.E. (1994) "Convergence or divergence: Human resource practices and policies for competitive advantage worldwide," *International Journal of Human Resource Management* 5 (2): 267–299.

Sully de Luque, M.F. and Sommer, S.M. (2000) "The impact of culture on feedback-seeking behavior: An integrated model and propositions," *Academy of Management Review* 25: 829–849.

Teagarden, M.B. and Paik, Y. (1993) "Strategic implications of maquiladora human resource management system design: A comparison of Japanese, Korean and US practices," *Business Association of Latin American Studies Proceedings*, pp. 295–302.

Teagarden, M.B., Butler, M.C., and Von Glinow, M.A. (1992) "Mexico's maquiladora industry: Where strategic human resource management makes a difference," *Organizational Dynamics*, Winter Issue, 20 (3): 34–47.

Triandis, H.C., Bontempo, R., Villareal, M.J., Asai, M., and Lucca, N. (1988) "Individualism and collectivism: Cross-cultural perspectives on self-in-group relationships," *Journal of Personality and Social Psychology* 54: 323–338.

Wilkins, A.L. and Ouchi, W.G. (1983) "Efficient cultures: Exploring the relationship between culture and organizational performance," *Administrative Science Quarterly* 28 (3): 468–492.

Paternalism as a positive form of leadership in the Latin American context: leader benevolence, decision-making control and human resource management practices

PATRICIA G. MARTÍNEZ

Some of them come to see us as protectors ... whether moral or psychological. ... If it is in my reach to help ... I will.

(Andrés, Owner, Mexican Border City maquiladora)

They have loyalty towards the patrón. They see that he has human qualities. ... These things you return in your service, this is how he has gained our loyalty.

(Ivette, Clothing Contractor Supervisor in Mexican Border City)

Although the Western scholarly literature would define this exchange, as well as others detailed in this study, as "paternalism", this Mexican business owner and supervisor were merely describing the relationship between the *patrón* (boss) and his employees. Paternalism is an approach to managing or leading individuals that combines elements of benevolence with control of decision making (e.g. Archard, 1991; Kerfoot and Knights, 1993). Particular leadership behaviors are associated with specific cultures, and so the impact of these behaviors will vary across cultures (Dorfman, 1996). This potential cultural variation may be associated with opposing views of paternalism, such that one culture's values, norms, and other contextual factors suggest that this type of leadership is positive, while in another culture it may be viewed negatively. Uhl-Bien *et al.* (1990: 420) note that "Americans typically perceive paternalism negatively ... as making them dependent upon and subservient."

While this negative view may partly explain why paternalism has received little attention within the Western organizational literature, paternalism as a form of leadership may prove particularly valuable for examining human resource management practices within the Latin American context for several reasons. First, in Latin America, the precursor to modern forms of organizations, the hacienda or great estate, is regarded as a social community that existed in a culture of paternalism and included kinship between the landlord and the workers (Guerra, 1988). Second, studies across multiple disciplines suggest that a key feature of paternalism is a set of benevolent management practices that provide for employees' welfare. Although the term human resource management (HRM) originated in the late twentieth century, during earlier centuries, organizations adopted practices to manage and reward employees, and thus these paternalistic management practices may be viewed as early forms of more contemporary HRM practices. Finally, an analysis of paternalism within the Latin American context may provide insights into how paternalism may be positively related to employee job attitudes and performance, a prediction that would be contrary to those developed from the human relations tradition and research in participation and decision making.

The objective of this chapter is to examine the contributions of paternalism for analyses of leadership and HRM practices in the Latin American context. In previous research (Martinez, 2003) I conducted a literature review and an initial analysis of semi-structured interviews of Latin American organizational leaders to develop an organization-based definition of paternalism. Here, I specifically examine how paternalism, Latin American studies, and the interview data illustrate the historical and cultural influences upon HRM practices.

Some researchers have proposed that paternalism continues as a style of a management in contemporary Mexico (e.g. Morris and Pavett, 1992). According to Boyer (2000), paternalism has been a strong force on workers because it is derived from traditional, gendered family roles and established Catholic precepts that cast employers as the caretakers and family of their workers. As a result, for this analysis I have selected the context of Mexican-owned organizations that are based in Mexico or that are owned by Mexican immigrants in the United States and employ only first-generation, Spanish-speaking Mexican immigrants. While the results of this analysis cannot be generalized across all Latin American countries, it provides a starting point for examining paternalistic leadership within the Mexican cultural context.

Defining paternalism

The majority of studies that define paternalism are conducted in sociology, political science, philosophy, and history. They employ qualitative methods and they are based on historical data. Paternalism is any action that benefits a person independently of his wishes and that intends to provide good or to protect

(Kultgen, 1992); and the usurpation of one's choice of good by another, which decreases an individual's ability to choose (Archard, 1991). In an organizational context, paternalism is a way of controlling employees through family imagery. The manager acts as a caring and protective head of the industrial household (Kerfoot and Knights, 1993). Although paternalists are presumed to possess benevolent intent and an understanding of subordinates' best interests, their acts decrease subordinates' decision-making ability. This control is exhibited by the degree to which the paternalist has control over an individual's decision-making ability in personal and job-related matters.

Paternalism studies suggest that significant contextual factors include: industrial reform movements of the late nineteenth and early twentieth century; and cultural values, including those of Mexico (Morris and Pavett, 1992) and Japan (Uhl-Bien *et al.*, 1990). The key theme among these studies is that paternalism is congruent with and fits the cultural or societal values of these contexts. In the Latin American context, hacienda studies provide unique insights into how historical and cultural factors fit with paternalism.

Paternalism and the hacienda

While Mexico and Peru were two crucial and central geographic areas for haciendas (Lockhart, 1969), Latin American scholars have studied haciendas in other Latin and Pan American areas including Brazil, Peru, Colombia, Bolivia, Ecuador, Puerto Rico, and the Caribbean region. Although Latin American hacienda studies do not examine paternalism *per se*, in scrutinizing the evolution of this agricultural model into a commercial model, they inevitably address the management style of the *hacendados*, who are commonly regarded as paternalistic (e.g. Diaz-Saenz and Witherspoon, 2000; Guerra, 1988).

Diaz-Saenz and Witherspoon (2000) note that during the late nineteenth century, Mexico's agricultural economy began the process of industrialization. During this period, the textile industry developed production systems that were widely adopted throughout Mexico, with many factories established in the haciendas in rural Mexico. Although the hacienda system, the basis of the agrarian sector of contemporary Latin America, began its decline during the nineteenth century, it continued well into the twentieth century before readily disappearing in country after country.

According to Miller (1990: 229), the orthodox position on the nineteenth-century Mexican hacienda is to regard it as a feudal system and as "vast seigniorial properties on a New World scale, dwarfing the equivalents in Europe." Haciendas were considered feudal because of their antiquated methods and autocratic management. However, both Miller (1990) and Gibson (1964) argue that haciendas did not possess a uniform feudal character. While earlier studies argued that relationships between feudal lords and their subjects included clear obligations, more recent studies have highlighted haciendas as a hybrid between feudalism and free enterprise. During the nineteenth century, haciendas began to include elements of free enterprise and capitalism, where workers typically had rights, freedom, compensation, and perquisites.

Frequent labor shortages throughout Latin American haciendas, where hacendados experienced significant problems in recruiting workers, are a primary example. This condition could not occur under feudal arrangements where workers were captive subjects. Hacendados resorted to various incentives and inducements in order to deal with these shortages. The "*enganche*" system was a system of labor recruitment where cash advances were offered to attract workers; it originated in Peruvian haciendas and spread to other Latin American and Mexican haciendas (Knight, 1986).

Worker compensation included various fringe benefits. Some estates commonly offered workers rights to food rations, a company store, credit and cash advances, and access to land. In many cases, only permanent workers received these benefits while temporary and sharecropping workers might have been provided the opportunity to purchase food rations at discounts. Peasants lived on haciendas because they received employment or land for rent, as well as food, clothing, and household goods. In some systems, workers had the freedom to come and go easily; they often chose to work for the hacienda with the best overall compensation (Miller, 1990).

According to Knight (1986: 44), haciendas often had a "quasi monastic deference and religiosity" where hacendados pursued "deft economic paternalism." Workers were often rewarded for tasks such as chasing criminals or putting out fires. Knight also notes that Mexican case studies are replicated in the study of late nineteenth- and early twentieth-century haciendas throughout Latin America. Graham (1990: 110) notes that Brazilian landlords found peasants to be united with them through a "force of habit that resulted from ancient customs, ties of gratitude, displaying just and reverential respect toward the landlords."

Many of the late nineteenth-century textile mills were established in haciendas and, as a result, paternalistic relations between mill owners and employees had deep roots (Boyer, 2000). Mill owners throughout Mexico continued to provide workers with many of the perquisites that were typical of the haciendas. Many owners also took responsibility for the moral development of their workers, providing them a modest education and building local churches. As Mexico's hacienda agricultural model began to evolve, it was evident that a number of the paternalistic practices continued. These "benevolent" practices provided for a number of basic needs for workers and, often, their families.

Paternalism in contemporary organizations

In a contemporary context, Morris and Pavett's (1992) empirical findings support the view that Mexican management is a benevolent authoritarian system with limited employee freedom and defined interaction, communication, and decision making, which the authors define as paternalistic. In comparing the productivity and management styles of a Mexican *maquiladora* and its US parent plant, the Mexican plant's management is significantly more authoritarian than the US plant's, but their productivity does not differ. The researchers argue from a contingency view and propose that their findings support that efficient management depends on the fit between culture and management. In this case, the benevolent authoritarian style fits the Mexican cultural values of respect, hierarchical relations, family, and personal relationships.

Adaptation to contemporary context

Contextual factors may also provide insights into how cultural factors may contribute to the persistence of paternalism. Weber (1947) predicted that as organizations increasingly relied upon rules, hierarchy, and the protection of individual rights, the rational–legal model of bureaucracy would replace traditional forms of control, such as paternalism. However, the varied contexts of paternalism studies reveal that rather than becoming extinct, paternalistic practices have adapted to competitive pressures. For example, in agrarian or early industrial settings, relationships were severely unbalanced since subordinates relied upon patriarchs for basic life necessities. In the context of contemporary organizations (e.g. Morris and Pavett, 1992; Padavic and Earnest, 1994), paternalistic relationships display mutual obligations that are based upon employment benefits and perquisites. These benefits and perquisites, or HRM practices, are described as common characteristics of these employment relationships.

An organization-based definition

Paternalism combines control with benevolence, where the paternalist manages or governs by partially assuming the subordinate's decision-making capacity. The relationship often exhibits mutual caring and affect as the paternalist seeks to protect or to promote another's good or benefit. Thus, paternalism is a system or a practice of managing individuals that combines control, authority, and decision-making power with benevolence; it seeks to promote the good or to benefit another as a means of achieving the goals of the enterprise (Martinez, 2003).

In the following sections, I first link paternalism to a leadership framework, arguing for its value in an analysis of paternalism. Second, I discuss a set of qualitative field data and how these reinforce and provide further insights into paternalistic leadership and its related HRM practices.

Leadership and social exchange as frameworks for paternalism

Most definitions of leadership share the characteristics of the ability to influence, providing direction over a group and the use of goals (Bass, 1985), characteristics that closely resemble paternalism. Despite these parallels, only a limited number of leadership theorists have examined paternalism as a form of leadership. In examining the national and cultural differences in forms of leadership, Bass (1990) proposes that when paternalism exists in a culture, authoritarian leadership is accepted. In Dorfman and Howell's (1988) study of cross-cultural samples of employee data from Taiwan, Mexico, and the United States, employees rated Hofstede's (1980) factors of cultural dimensions. The authors' analysis yielded an additional factor that they identified as paternalism. When paternalism was high, employees expected job security, and they expected their company to look after them as a person, not just as a worker.

Leadership research is generally categorized according to the trait, behavioral, contingency, and the new or emerging approaches to leadership. While these approaches differ on the dimensions of leader behaviors or attributes they examine, most of these approaches include dimensions that are comparable to paternalists' benevolence and decision-making control. The behavioral approach identified task-oriented (decision-making control) and relationship-oriented (benevolence) behaviors as components of leadership (Yukl, 1994).

The new or emerging leadership theories include transformational and transactional models of leadership. Transactional models view leadership as a two-way influence relationship and ascribe followers a crucial role (Hollander and Julian, 1969). Transactional leadership offers contingent rewards, using positional and organizational resources to compensate for services rendered under an employment contract (Bass, 1985). In transactional models, exchanges are defined in terms of costs and benefits that consider the economic and social value of these exchanges. With economic exchange, followers' performance is motivated by self-interest, and they do not undertake behavior outside of the employment contract. With social exchange, individuals offer esteem and social approval for valuable services (Homans, 1961). It also promotes feelings of personal obligation, gratitude, and trust as well as facilitating the acceptance of role requests beyond those specified in the employment contract (Blau, 1964).

Social exchange is exhibited in leader–member exchange (LMX) theory (Dansereau *et al.*, 1975), or the quality of the leader–follower relationship. Leader–member exchange is judged according to the extent to which interaction and exchange between the leader and follower exceeds the formal employment contract. It is also judged by the degree of mutual trust, loyalty, and respect in the relationship. Research suggests that high-quality exchange relationships are related with increased subordinate performance and job satisfaction. However, the detailed LMX processes involved in exchanges and relationship formation are an area of this theory that has received limited attention (Duchon *et al.*, 1986). Bass (1990) proposed that in Latin American cultures, LMX may be manifested in the development of a paternalistic relationship between the leader and the subordinate. By examining the HRM practices related to paternalistic leadership, this study provides insights into these exchanges.

Paternalism and HRM practices in contemporary organizations

Given that a qualitative, grounded-theory approach is useful for rarely explored constructs, this project incorporates semi-structured interviews of organizational leaders that describe the phenomena of paternalism and its related HRM practices.

Sample, data collection, and qualitative analysis

Conducting extended interviews of organizational leaders enabled a greater understanding of their perceptions of their leadership and direction for their employees as well as the procedures and policies of their organizations. The interview questions were based upon the paternalism and hacienda studies literature review. Here, I focus on the interview questions related to the categories of: (a) supervisor–employee relationships; (b) culture and climate; and (c) employment practices. These interview questions included:

1. What do you perceive as motivating your employees?
2. What kind of respect and trust exists between employees and your management?
3. What kind of employment terms do your employees expect?
4. If your employees were to draw an analogy, how would they describe the company?
5. How do you establish employee loyalty?
6. How do you recruit for open positions?

The paternalism studies reviewed here suggest that paternalistic leaders have close and frequent contact with their subordinates. In small organizations with less than 100 employees, workers at all hierarchical levels may have direct contact with the owner-manager or chief operating officer of the firm, and this individual may directly supervise numerous employees. Consequently, this sample primarily includes small organizations. However, in order to allow a contrast for organizational size, one medium and one large organization are also included. Furthermore, owner-managers are primarily selected as interviewees, as they are responsible for the supervision of several employees and they have the final authority for employment matters.

Mexican labor laws dictate a significant employer responsibility for the conduct and improvement of workers' lives. The Mexican Revolution ended the old *patrón* system of haciendas and peasants in 1922, and Mexican labor law sought to modernize this formerly feudal relationship by establishing the mutual obligations of employers and employees (de Forest, 1994). In order to contrast the potential effects of contextual variables such as labor laws and labor market conditions, the sample includes four leaders in organizations that are based in Mexico and three Mexican leaders of United States-based organizations with employee workforces of primarily Mexican immigrants. The three US interviews were conducted in organizations based in Southern California, whose management and employees share many Mexican cultural dimensions such as language, work ethic, value for respect and hierarchy, and value for personal relationships. Table 4.1 details the interviewees and their respective organizations.

The semi-structured field interviews followed the long interview method (McCracken, 1988), a sharply focused, rapid, highly intensive interview process that is used when total immersion in the studied scene is impractical or impossible. Five interviews were taped and transcribed. Data for the remaining two interviews were collected using detailed interview notes that were expanded immediately after the interviews were conducted. The interviews that were conducted in Mexico were conducted in Spanish and translated during the transcription process. In some of the English interviews in the United States, leaders used specific phrases or expressions in Spanish to emphasize a point. Although these words were translated, the original Spanish words were retained and noted in parentheses or italics.

For this qualitative analysis, I rely upon Strauss and Corbin's (1990) technique of grounded theory-building. It is an iterative process of thematic coding and comparison of emerging categories and their associations, and it assists in the identification of contextual factors, antecedents, behavioral components, and outcomes.

Contextual factors

The interview data suggest that labor market conditions and production context are two significant contextual factors. Several of the leaders' organizations operate in tight labor markets and recruitment costs are key concerns for Angelo, Ivette, and J.C. As detailed below, leaders view paternalistic actions rationally as retention strategies. The leaders' factories or offices exhibit unpredictable orders or high-pressure project schedules, which can lead to shortened workdays or work weeks or, in contrast, overtime in work hours.

Table 4.1 Interview sample

Industry/sector	Organization size	Interviewee[3]	Title/position	Description of employee population
Maquiladora, assembles electronic products to customer specifications (e.g., plates for integrated circuits)[1]	45 employees	Angelo	Owner	The majority of employees occupy various low-skilled assembly positions; a few employees occupy first-line supervisory, quality control, and administrative positions
Office of the State District Attorney[1]	Office has 25 employees	Mark	Assistant District Attorney	Office employees include attorneys and clerical support
Clothing contractor, assembles cut clothing pieces into finished garments[1]	50 employees in company's clothing contracting shop	Ivette	Purchasing/Operations Manager	Sewing machine operators
Satellite branch of a major Mexican retail and commercial bank[1]	Two employees in branch, over 2,000 organization-wide	Ray	Manager	Branch is staffed by interviewee and a cashier/clerk
Clothing cutting service[2]	45 employees at main location	JC	Owner/Operations Manager	The entire workforce are Mexican immigrants and Spanish is their first language
Mexican specialty foods[2]	100 employees	Juan	Owner	Nearly all of the production workers are Mexican immigrants or Mexican-American
Property management and real estate design and construction firm[2]	9 employees	Marcelo	Owner	Three clerical support staff, six are professional staff (i.e., engineers, accountants, finance professionals)

Notes
[1] Organization is based in Mexican border city.
[2] Organization is based in Southern California.
[3] Pseudonyms are used for all interviewees.

Antecedents

Antecedents can include elements of time, culture, economics, technology, history, and individual attributes. In this case, leaders discuss respect and social hierarchy, personal relationships, organizational culture and climate, supervision and formalized rules, personal values, and employees' personal, family, and economic situations.

Respect and social hierarchy

Leaders perceive employee relations from a position of power and knowledge, describing delineation of and respect for formal lines of authority. Social stratification is clear in their descriptions of positional differences. Many leaders refer to the position of "*patrón*", the Spanish word that denotes the position of a boss that commands authority and respect.

Personal relationships

Personal relationships are highly valued within Mexican society and this is exhibited in Angelo and Ivette's descriptions of employees' expectations for frequent contact. According to Ivette, a lack of personal greetings is interpreted negatively: "They expect you to greet them and to take the time to talk. If you don't, they think you're conceited or something is wrong. They require very special treatment."

Organizational climate

All leaders describe the climate and culture of their organizations in positive terms, relating warm, friendly relations among employees, supervisors, and themselves. Ray, Angelo, Ivette, Mark, and J.C. are very aware of their organizations' climate and culture, and they discuss managing it. J.C., Angelo, and Marcelo describe joking and light-hearted "playing around" with employees. Juan proudly described the remarks of a magazine reporter who was writing an article that featured the organization: "He couldn't get over how happy our employees are. He said that he visits small companies ... but that he really doesn't see employees as happy and comfortable as ours."

Supervision and formalized rules, policies and procedures

With the exception of Ray's bank and Mark's district attorney's office, most organizations have few formalized rules. Angelo's organization operates under strict maquiladora employment regulations, which include mandated benefits and minimum wage levels. Wage and compensation policies, however, are not formalized at Angelo's maquiladora. Juan's Mexican food company has an employee policy manual, yet it does not provide great detail for a number of policies and procedures. Ivette, J.C., and Marcelo's organizations do not have employee handbooks or policy manuals. A lack of formalized rules and procedures appears to facilitate situational-based employment decisions. This affords the leaders greater control over rewards and recognition as well as greater flexibility in responding to employee needs and requests.

Leader attitudes and values

The qualitative data support the characteristics of a paternalist identified in the literature review: benevolent intent, interest in subordinates, a preference for long-term employment, and a presumed understanding of their needs. The data also reveal leaders' empathy and belief in a responsibility to assist subordinates. Angelo, Marcelo, Ivette, and Mark describe a genuine interest in their employees as individuals. According to Angelo, "You have the opportunity to know them not only as workers but also as persons." Marcelo stated: "We take an interest in them ... we get to know them." This analysis also reveals empathy toward subordinates. J.C. explains: "Sometimes they'll tell me, 'I know that you have a lot of work, but my wife is in the hospital, can I leave early to go see her?' I try to put myself in their position." J.C.'s father asked him to give a long-time employee a full week's work schedule, despite insufficient work; "My dad said, '*El tiene necesidad.* He has the need and obligations; you're not married, and you don't know what it's like.' "

Angelo describes this personal interest driving other expectations: "They feel that you have their interests as persons in mind and that because you know them ... you will try to help them." He also describes one of the most striking roles: "I honestly believe that they come to see us as protectors, in any aspect, whether moral or psychological." Yet he admits that these motivations are based on good business sense. "If it is in my reach to help the person, morally or economically, I will. The problem could be emotional, or if it is a matter of money and I can help, I do. Many times we do this for the convenience of the company ... it is a business situation ... and in the long term it helps me."

Juan believes that he is aware of his employees' best interests. He expects a mastery of English for long-term tenure: "We require them to learn English because they need to realize that if they are going to stay and succeed in this country, they will need [it]."

Employee personal situation

Employees' personal situations affect their need for flexibility in their work schedules and assistance. Ivette's employees may have childcare problems and J.C.'s and Angelo's employees request time off for hospital or medical visits. Angelo's employees' financial problems may trouble them or affect work attendance.

Human resource management practices and leader behaviors

Strauss and Corbin's framework allows for identifying behavioral components that are purposeful and goal-oriented. In these data, they are manifestations of benevolence and control. Leaders exercise control through employees' felt obligation to exhibit flexibility in work schedules. Control is also exhibited in leaders' control of most work decisions. Yet the key findings, which have not been addressed by previous research, are the dual components of benevolence: provisions of employee welfare as well as supportiveness and positive regard for employees. Provisions of employee welfare include actions that provide for employees' job-based, personal, and family needs, within and outside of the organization.

Hiring, compensation and benefits policies

Interviewees reveal details of personalization and situational criteria. J.C., Ivette, and Angelo prefer to hire through personal, family, or employee ties. Angelo also expressed a preference for rehiring former employees with whom "trust is established." The majority of organizations in this sample provide wage levels and benefits that are average or slightly above average. At the maquiladora, Angelo pays his employees fairly well, but not top dollar. J.C.'s policy of a week of paid vacation is unusual within small clothing cutters. None of his direct competitors offer this benefit. A number of the organizational leaders perceived that employees were satisfied with an average level of pay because they received other benefits, security, and a positive environment.

Promotions, development opportunities, and recognition

Leaders recognize employees through a variety of practices. Ivette, J.C., and Ray offer employee dinners; Marcelo treats staff to drinks and dinner when projects are completed. Angelo recognizes employees through an employee-of-the-month program. Leaders generally offer promotions and developmental opportunities based on merit and to reward commitment and loyalty. J.C., Angelo, and Juan proudly described their efforts to develop committed employees.

Employee disciplinary actions

Discipline is handled through a variety of strategies. Angelo must follow the progressive discipline mandated by Mexican labor laws. In contrast, J.C.'s father's approach to discipline is strict and unstructured. J.C. described his father's strategy for tardiness: "If you aren't going to get here on time ... go home and come back tomorrow when you can get here early; you have a responsibility." Leaders also interact with employees from a position of authority with different degrees of control. Despite his familiar interaction with employees,

Marcelo maintains direction and control: "When it's necessary I still treat them firm[ly], with discipline ... I'll bark at them."

Supportiveness

Leader supportiveness is displayed through personal attention and support, flexibility in employment terms, and assistance in personal matters. They maintain frequent and close contact with employees through constant inquiries into family and personal matters. Angelo states: "I have a bad habit or a good habit that some applaud or criticize, but I do not enter into my own office until I say hello to all of [our] people." Employees have contact with a leader who interacts with them on the shop floor, during meal times, and at social gatherings. This attention is also demonstrated through listening, empathy, and comprehension. Ivette believes that "employees respond well to comprehension." According to Angelo: "They look the most to the supervisor ... and they know that they have not only a supervisor but ... a friend, someone who will support them." Ivette believes: "Employees take a connection with supervisors much into consideration. Letting them see that you understand them."

Leaders describe offering coaching and feedback in a variety of manners. For J.C.: "They get thrilled by the fact ... that you say something nice and call it to their attention. ... But it's just little comments, day after day." Angelo views feedback as a motivational tool: "Recognizing, congratulating them and not only rebuking or calling things to their attention ... but also saying things when they are doing well."

An additional type of supportiveness is schedule flexibility, such as release time for family illness, childcare issues, or transportation problems. In Ivette's organization, senior employees are paid a full day's base salary even if they miss a few hours due to childcare issues. According to J.C., his family-run business is more responsive to the needs of his employees because it is small and "for them it's much easier to ask to leave earlier ... than if they were working at McDonald's, where they don't care about your family."

Personal assistance

In Angelo's case, personal assistance has translated into personal loans. As mentioned earlier, J.C. described his father's assistance to a long-term employee by ensuring that he was given a full work week, despite low demand. Ivette's company reported an employee accident as occurring on the job so that health insurance would cover the injury. As mentioned, Angelo perceives that one of his roles is to assist his employees.

Potential outcomes and the dynamics of exchange

In this qualitative analysis, interactions between paternalistic leaders and subordinates parallel theorists' conception of social exchange: esteem and social approval are offered as rewards for services. The exchanges described are often open-ended and unspecified in their nature of the discharge of existing or future obligations; these interactions promote feelings of personal obligation, gratitude, and trust.

These exchanges link contextual factors, antecedents, and paternalistic actions with the perceived outcomes that are described by the leaders: employee flexibility, loyalty and trust, long-term tenure and low turnover, and friendship. They are similar to and expand upon researchers' proposed outcomes: obedience, compliance, trust, employee flexibility, career investment, satisfaction, and loyalty. This final section details these outcomes within the social exchange dynamics described by leaders.

Employee flexibility

Employee flexibility is demonstrated in their adaptability to fluctuations in work schedules and over time. J.C. and Angelo's businesses often face high fluctuations in orders and production demand, which translates into weeks with under- or over-capacity production. In J.C.'s case, if he is low on orders, he will send employees home after they work their legally required four hours. If he is uncertain of the following day's work, he will ask employees to call in the morning once he has determined their starting time. When receiving large orders, workers are asked to work overtime; if one of the factories needs extra employees, J.C. will send workers from one location to another.

Ray describes reciprocal giving and expectations for flexibility: "You give and I give. When you have given [flexibility], the employee expects to deliver it when you ask for it. When he asks for the time off, then you know you can ask [him] some day to stay later." He also believes that a climate of respect engenders flexibility: "In having that kind of environment, when it's necessary to work late, they will. ... When it's not there, the person will complain."

Ivette clearly describes social exchange from a cost perspective: "When the person is made to feel important, they respond without charging you for it. They will work extra hours, weekends ... without complaining because they have been made to feel valued." She also believes that the benefits spill over into their performance and quality of work: "When you treat an employee with appreciation for his work, they do better work for you, more work."

As an employee, Mark says, "I never say no when they ask me to work extra hours, but that's because they have given me the flexibility to continue my volunteer coaching job."

Loyalty and trust

One of the greatest gestures of loyalty and trust that Angelo received from his employees occurred during a two-week period where he had to close down operations due to a lack of orders. Mexican labor laws require two weeks severance pay, yet his employees agreed to forego this benefit in return for his commitment to rehiring them and recognizing their seniority when he re-opened his maquiladora several weeks later.

Ivette describes an exchange of loyalty for understanding: "They have loyalty towards the boss. They see that he has human qualities. He realizes that in the case of a family emergency, you will drop everything. ... These things you return in your service, this is how he has gained our loyalty." In addition, Angelo describes the dynamics in terms of mutual valuation: "I have valued them and they have valued me." Similarly, Mark offers commitment for a climate of respect. Yet in his previous job: "It was not a climate of respect, [the boss] was a strict authoritarian and I did not exercise punctuality, but I was not motivated to do so. ... Now in this office, where I see respect, I can see the difference in my motivation to be punctual."

Tenure and turnover

The majority of these leaders describe retaining long-term employees and a low turnover. J.C. reports that the average tenure of his 50 employees is five to seven years. Juan says that ten to twelve years is a common tenure for his employees. Though the United States–Mexico border clothing contracting industry has a high turnover rate, Ivette's organization has many long-term employees. The average turnover rate in Angelo's industry is 18 percent, but his turnover is 3 percent. The leaders perceive that employees forego employment opportunities elsewhere. For Angelo, stability is the motivation: "Many feel that their salary could be better, that it could be higher ... but because ... they can resolve more personal problems ... they feel more stable."

Summary

This analysis has revealed that leaders describe various forms of HRM practices such as employee recognition efforts, employment benefits and perquisites, promotional benefits, and developmental opportunities. They also describe employee-centered attitudes as elements of social exchange with employees. In turn, leaders perceive that their employees exchange flexibility and adaptation to fluctuating work schedules and responsiveness to overtime. These outcomes support social exchange research that suggests that an organization's positive actions, which benefit employees and create high-quality exchanges, create obligations for employees to reciprocate in positive ways. This sense of indebtedness creates an imbalance that employees reduce through reciprocation. Although paternalism studies have focused on leaders' benevolence, this qualitative analysis suggests that benevolence exhibits two dimensions: leader supportiveness and welfare provision for employees' job-related, personal, and family needs.

Discussion

The primary objective of this project was to examine paternalism as a form of leadership and its related HRM practices within the Latin American context. A contribution of the study is to highlight a form of leadership whose value in the study of contemporary organizations has generally been discounted. The paternalism literature and qualitative analysis identified that leader benevolence exhibits the dimensions of leader supportiveness and welfare provision. Welfare provision includes attention to employees' job as well as personal needs outside of their organizations. Furthermore, the qualitative data suggest that a number of the elements of leader–subordinate relations and management practices remain strikingly similar to those described in hacienda studies. Knight's (1986) description of "deft economic paternalism", where hacendados rewarded workers for actions that benefited the hacienda, is echoed in Angelo's explanation that he helps employees because "it is a business situation ... and in the longer term it helps me." Hacendados believed that they understood workers' best interests and felt responsible for their welfare and moral development. In requiring that his employees learn English so that they may "succeed in this country", Juan feels he is helping his employees; Angelo believes that employees "see us as protectors ... whether moral or psychological." Marcelo, Ivette, and Mark also described a genuine interest in their employees and a belief in a responsibility to assist them.

In the context of the haciendas and these small contemporary organizations, benevolent practices provide for the needs of employees and their families. Furthermore, organizational leaders continue to provide personal economic assistance through cash advances or employee loans to help them manage financial difficulties. Finally, while hacienda workers generally received average to below-average wages, many haciendas provided various perquisites to their permanent workers in order to reward and recognize their loyalty. Leaders of these contemporary organizations often perceived that employees were satisfied with average pay because this was supplemented with job security, perquisites, and a positive work environment. While HRM practices may not provide for workers' basic needs and subsistence, these practices are related to perceptions of leaders' responsibility to care for and assist workers.

The contextual, antecedent, behavioral, and outcome variables identified in this analysis appear within a set of leader–subordinate exchanges that hold both economic and social value. Viewing these exchanges from a social exchange perspective may provide valuable insights into how employees who possess a limited amount of job discretion and decision-making ability can simultaneously hold positive job attitudes. The value that employees place upon these practices might potentially outweigh or suppress the otherwise negative attitudinal effects of employees' limited decision-making ability.

The context of this field research contains cultural factors that potentially impact receptiveness to paternalism. As a result, leadership that combines decision-making control with benevolence may be associated with positive employee job attitudes and behaviors. Yet the similar results across US and Mexican-based organizations suggest the need to examine individual cultural values rather than associating particular values with a given country. Given the globalization of business and the diversification of the US workforce, it is more likely that Western-owned firms will employ individuals with varying cultural values and might respond differently to particular leadership styles.

A limitation of this study is its primary reliance on a sample of leaders and managers and the absence of first-line employees. While three of these manager interviewees expressed their opinions as employees of the organization as well as managers, their opinions may not necessarily reflect those of first-line employees. Future study of paternalistic leadership can easily address this limitation by expanding the sample to include subordinates. Additionally, expanding the sample to larger-sized organizations that consist of a given set of formalized HRM practices would allow further differentiation between paternalism as a style of leadership and a form of employment relationship.

Perhaps the most surprising find is the clear conceptualization of paternalism within a context of social exchange, where leaders and subordinates calculate costs, benefits, and expected reciprocations. Leaders' descriptions of their actions may represent what scholars have defined as paternalism, but these leaders believed that they were describing positive employment relations between a leader and subordinates.

This contrast leads to a final idea of this study: research conducted in a Western, democratic, and highly individualistic cultural context might develop a linguistic label for a phenomenon that in another culture may not be recognized as such. Paternalism undoubtedly needs to be informed by linguistics-based research, but here it will serve as a closing remark that is based upon this researcher's experience in pursuing this topic.

Culture exists in a taken-for-granted state, where individuals can have difficulty articulating common, everyday phenomena and events, norms, and rules for interaction. When crossing cultural boundaries, researchers are well served to recall that the linguistic label for an organizational phenomenon in one culture may not exist or be used in another. When first developing interest in this topic of paternalism, it was my belief that the noun "paternalism" might not easily translate into Spanish and that this concept might not be readily recognized in a Latin American context. While five out of six Spanish–English dictionaries consulted did not contain a translation for paternalism, conversations with at least a dozen Mexicans and Colombians were more revealing. These individuals, who continue to live and work in their respective countries, interpreted this researcher's description of paternalism as merely a description of relations between leaders and subordinates. Such differences in viewpoints and interpretation of concepts such as "paternalism" suggest an avenue for international and cross-cultural organizational research.

References

Archard, D. (1991) *Paternalism defined. Analysis*, Cambridge, MA: Basil Blackwell.

Bass, B.M. (1985) *Leadership and performance beyond expectations*, New York: Free Press.

—— (1990) *Bass and Stogdill's handbook of leadership, theory and research and managerial application*, New York: Free Press.

Blau, P.M. (1964) *Exchange and power in social life*, New York: Wiley.

Boyer, C. (2000) "The threads of class at La Virgen: Misrepresentation and identity at a Mexican textile mill, 1918–1935," *American Historical Review* 105: 1576–1598.

Dansereau, F., Graen, G., and Haga, W.J. (1975) "A vertical dyad linkage approach to leadership within formal organizations: A longitudinal investigation of the role making process," *Organizational Behavior and Human Performance* 13: 46–78.

de Forest, M.E. (1994) "Thinking of a plant in Mexico?" *Academy of Management Executive* 8 (1): 33–40.

Diaz-Saenz, H.R. and Witherspoon, P.D. (2000) "Psychological contracts in Mexico," in D.M. Rousseau, and R. Schalk (eds) *Psychological contracts in employment: Cross-national perspectives*, Thousand Oaks, CA: Sage, pp. 158–175.

Dorfman, P. (1996) "International and cross-cultural leadership research," in B.J. Punnett, and O. Shenkar (eds) *Handbook for international management research*, Cambridge, MA: Blackwell.

Dorfman, P. and Howell, J.P. (1988) "Dimensions of national culture and effective leadership patterns," *Advances in International Comparative Management* 3: 127–150.

Duchon, D., Green, S.G., and Taber, T.D. (1986) "Vertical dyad linkage: A longitudinal assessment of antecedents, measures and consequences," *Journal of Applied Psychology* 71: 56–60.

Gibson, C. (1964) *The Aztecs under Spanish rule*, Stanford, CA: Stanford University Press.

Graham, R. (1990) *Patronage and politics in nineteenth century Brazil*, Stanford, CA: Stanford University Press.

Guerra, F.X. (1988) *México: Del antiguo régimen a la revolución* [Mexico: From the old regimen to the revolution], Vol. 1, Mexico: Fondo de Cultura Económica.

Hofstede, G. (1980) *Culture's consequences: International differences in work related values*, Beverly Hills, CA: Sage.

Hollander, E.P. and Julian, J.W. (1969) "Contemporary trends in the analysis of leadership processes," *Psychological Bulletin* 71: 387–397.

Homans, G.C. (1961) *Social behavior: Its elementary forms*, New York: Harcourt, Brace and World.

Kerfoot, D. and Knights, D. (1993) "Management, masculinity and manipulation: From paternalism to corporate strategy in financial services in Britain," *Journal of Management Studies* 30: 659–677.

Knight, A. (1986) "Mexican peonage: What was it and why was it?" *Journal of Latin American Studies* 18 (1): 41–74.

Kultgen, J. (1992) "Consent and the justification of paternalism," *The Southern Journal of Philosophy* 3 (3): 89–113.

Lockhart, J. (1969) "Encomienda and hacienda: The evolution of the great estate in the Spanish Indies," *The Hispanic American Historical Review* 49 (3): 411–429.

McCracken, G. (1988) *The long interview*, Newbury Park, CA: Sage.

Martínez, P.G. (2003) "Paternalism as a positive form of leader–subordinate exchange: Evidence from Mexico," *Management Research, The Journal of the Iberoamerican Academy of Management* 1: 227–242.

Miller, S. (1990) "Mexican junkers and the capitalist haciendas, 1810–1910: The arable estate and the transition to capitalism between the insurgency and the revolution," *Journal of Latin American Studies* 22: 229–263.

Morris, T. and Pavett, C.M. (1992) "Management style and productivity in two cultures," *Journal of International Business Studies* 23: 169–179.

Padavic, I. and Earnest, W.R. (1994) "Paternalism as a component of managerial strategy," *The Social Science Journal* 31: 389–405.

Strauss, A. and Corbin, J. (1990) *Basics of qualitative research: Grounded theory procedures and techniques*, Newbury Park, CA: Sage.

Uhl-Bien, M., Tierney, P.S., Graen, G.B., and Wakabayashi, M. (1990) "Company paternalism and the hidden investment process," *Group and organization studies* 15: 414–430.

Weber, M. (1947) *The theory of social and economic organization* (trans. A.M. Henderson and T. Parsons), New York: Oxford University Press.

Yukl, G.A. (1994) *Leadership in organizations*, Englewood Cliffs, NJ: Prentice Hall.

Part II

Human resource management in Latin American countries

5 Human resource management in Argentina

RUBÉN A. FIGUEIREDO

Argentina has ventured into the twenty-first century amidst one of the deepest crises in its history, after sailing through a parabola that led to its ranking, at times, among wealthy and promising nations and, at other times, among developing, emerging and even under-developed countries.

Its economy has undergone several stages. Initially a scarcely populated country based on agricultural and beef exports, Argentina started to develop its industrial might by the end of the 1800s. Both cornerstones would remain in place – with some fluctuation – until the late 1980s, largely driven by a protectionist (or semi-protectionist) model encouraging the substitution of imported finished products by local manufacture. The turn of the century and the ensuing globalization enabled Argentina to embark on a long-lasting economic opening experience that favored foreign investment and secured a decade of stability.

The evolution of the "human resources" (HR) area and function (alternatively known as "personnel" and "industrial relations") in Argentinean companies will be analyzed within an international and domestic historical framework, intertwining social, political, and economic factors. These related aspects will provide a better understanding of "talent" creation and management in Argentina, where "human capital" was trained through the state-managed educational system and the corporate contributions of the twentieth century. Accordingly, each analyzed period will include references to these various aspects in order to offer readers a more thorough picture of local realities.

Historical stages

From colonial times until 1930: the onset of local industry

The birth of the nation during the first half of the 1800s was marked by an economy based on agricultural exports which yielded political and economic power along the Rio de la Plata. Cattle breeders and beef processors shared the local wealth with merchants during this pre-industrial stage. The second half of the nineteenth century, shaped by political and economic transformations, featured a broad immigration policy, agricultural development, and a fledgling domestic industry. Among the first companies incorporated in the 1880s were Alpargatas (clothing and shoes) and Bagley (food).

The country started its "industrial revolution" and needed trained individuals to expand, develop, manage, and consolidate it. The National Industrial School (later known as Otto Krause) was created. Probably one of the most relevant events revealing the link between corporate needs and education, its mission was to train students in various specializations required by the initial procedures involved in gross material production.

In the early twentieth century, Argentina's burgeoning industry, coupled with consolidated beef- and grain-exporting patterns, generated employment. Large foreign companies, such as the car-manufacturing Ford, Swift and Armour, a beef company, and many others arrived in Argentina in the early twentieth century and provided employment to thousands of people.

The country benefited from the outcome of the First World War and began to rebuild its economy, which grew steadily from 1917 through the 1929 world crash. During the Depression, the first military *coup d'état* took place in Argentina in 1930. The democratic and constitutional government was overthrown and the nation was cast into a 50-year-long cycle of alternating military and civilian rule.

From 1930 through 1960: the early years of the HR area

Environmental milestones

This period featured great stability in terms of monetary and employment conditions, which in turn fostered savings and long-term planning. Economic development zeroed in on the food industry, followed by textiles and immediate consumption. Most companies were large in size and captured 40 percent of employed labor.

The government was involved in economic regulation and similar activities. The most outstanding example of this pattern developed during President Juan Perón's administration from 1946 to 1955. The agricultural sector became less relevant and a structurally feeble industry emerged under state support, protection, and funding. Renewed nationalist objectives prevailed, such as the nationalization of foreign debt, transportation, communications, as well as the recently developed and strategically significant oil, steel, and finance sectors.

After an initial thrust, the expanding economy began showing signs of recession in 1949. Technical education boomed while higher education experienced a similar growth. The National Labor University (later the National Technological University) was founded in 1953 to offer graduates a degree in "factory engineering". The number of national universities tripled.

By 1955, economic goals were still remote. Social unrest increased and a new coup staged by the military overthrew the Peronist government. After the military regime, a new democratically elected president, Frondizi, took office. In spite of the steps taken by the new administration, 1958 ended with rampant inflation and the announcement of a new stabilization program involving fixed exchange rate and currency devaluation policies. The local deficit led to numerous lay-offs and price increases in transportation and state-run utilities. Credit became stringent and the public works plan shrank.

Early professional associations: labor relations and labor laws

The period from 1930 to 1960 may be viewed as pre-history in the evolution of the HR area. From a combination of several factors including the 1929 world crisis, the global changes brought about by the Second World War, and the local onset of the Peronist movement, immediate and decisive influences shaped the HR task.

The "personnel" function was restricted to administrative and executive tasks; specifically hiring and firing employees. Until the emergence of the Peronist movement, union activities were hardly relevant or influential in the area. Thus, "a rather resolute" profile was required in order to fend off the typical daily confrontations. Except in rare cases, such as railways and foreign oil companies, there were no personnel management policies in place in companies.

When unions became protected and empowered by the government they took on an unprecedented strength. Extensive labor and social legislation ensued disregarding the necessary balance between the sectors. This period saw the development of genuine domestic labor laws. In companies, union representatives secured a leading role. The industrialization process that unfolded in this period fueled the need for a more determined and noticeable role for the HR area. In order to respond to the increased environmental complexity, the area required a more professional profile.

The first institution gathering area professionals was not built until 1948. The Argentinean Personnel Leaders' Institute (IADP)[1] was founded as a result of the evolution of employer–employee relationships and the need to have specialized professionals. Until then, there was no clear "role and function awareness" or "specialty". Efforts to train HR position holders abounded. In 1949 and 1950, the IADP organized two Personnel Management Conferences,[2] attended by international guest representatives. In February 1952, the IADP announced the launch of its "Personnel Management School", with a curriculum that included labor and union relations, labor laws, labor scientific organization, safety, statistics, political economy, and psycho-techniques. The association of gathering personnel professionals changed its name to the Argentinean Industrial Relations Institute (IARI) in 1954. The new name did not entail a change in methodology and goal continuity.

Tools

While most companies only focused on dealing with unions, managing files, and payroll, cutting-edge companies started working on training, hygiene, safety, methods, and time management. Spreading throughout innovative companies was "Training within Industries" (TWI), an interactive training method developed in the United States during the Second World War to allow companies to train large worker populations efficiently. There are records showing that, even in those early years, some organizations had begun to use psychological techniques in their recruiting efforts. The "leading" companies of the time, with their own developments in personnel issues, were mostly of foreign origin (such as ESSO, Shell, and Goodyear) but included a few domestic firms (such as Alpargatas).

Another significant topic surfaced during this period which was to remain at the top of corporate agendas and academic curricula: the need to build teamwork in companies. Other outstanding concerns at the personnel helm were to enhance productivity and curb absenteeism.

From 1960 through 1989: the area's professionalization

Environmental milestones

The political situation eventually led to the military uprising of March 1962, which brought President Frondizi's development to an end. During the 1960s, a succession of democratic and military governments protected the full-employment economy and unknowingly paved the way for the opening of the economy that would unleash during the 1970s. Plagued by political turmoil, the unions overpowered the political scene until 1976, when their attitude seemed more sensible, though it remained basically unchanged. After the death of the movement's leader, the third Peronist administration, besieged by the military, the *guerrillas*, and economic distress, plunged into chaos with a new military coup on 24 March 1976.

The military regime tried to implement some liberal policies during its reign from 1976 to 1983. Until 1979, the country held high employment rates with great labor demand and high personnel turnover. Later, the local industry surrendered to a deep recession while the financial sector grew to unprecedented proportions. The economic and political systems upheld by the military weakened increasingly, which encouraged the country to restore its democracy in December 1983.

The newly elected President, Raul Alfonsín, failed to consolidate economic recovery. The country faced a new round of social unrest and general skepticism. Carlos Menem won the 1989 general election and took the Peronist party back to the presidency.

HR's role

In the 1960s, Argentinean factories ceased to be "bottlenecks" and other areas became more relevant. The personnel or industrial relations function shifted its focus and, still attentive to factory, union, and labor issues, started to expand into other business areas. Notions such as "corporate social responsibility" and "labor humanization" entered and remained on the scene.

In June 1960, the Argentinean Productivity Center began to train executives according to the contributions of OIT experts and, after May 1961, was officially supported by the National Industrial Technology Institute. By then, higher education also reflected these developments: for example, in 1963, the Universidad Argentina de la Empresa (UADE) created the first BA in Industrial Relations program.[3]

The professional association changed its name again in 1960, and in July of 1967, a new professional organization was born: ADPA. The HR agenda was still focused on reviewing the union–labor, salary, and employment market. It also tried to understand the new local social characteristics, such as the gradual reduction of the value of experience as a consequence of the natural obsolescence produced by technological advancement. In those days, a personnel area executive had reached the highest position in a large company, which was a very rare occurrence in Argentinean business: Juan María Courard became the President of top-tier multinational company, Ford Argentina.

Faced with this scenario, HR professionals tried to act as moderators in all interactions potentially involving conflicts of any kind. The environmental changes settled in everyday operations and demanded that the area develop a "new HR management" approach: companies needed new procedures, new options based on updated policies, and, above all, training for people in leading positions. The "old personnel function" gave way to the "HR area" in order to provide richer responses to a more complex reality. Intense activity and a myriad of forums reflected on this change. In 1987, ADPA celebrated its twentieth anniversary, forty years after the remote creation of IADP in 1947.

Labor relations

The union scenario in the early 1980s was marked by political unrest and fights over the control of union funds, which drove traditional unions to engage in more vindicating activities. In 1983, when the government change was imminent and the new administration was to be elected in free elections, strikes swept the country. Companies worked on their relationship with unions, including collective negotiations, supervisors' roles in unions, and flexible work schedules.

Once again, this union stage called for political savvy. The general atmosphere announced the unions' return to the spotlight, since they would provide the setting for the first confrontation. These conditions decisively shaped the role of the personnel area. In the early years of the democratic restitution, the personnel area was plagued by old claims, social scars, recession, plant closings, un- and underemployment, and inflation. Constant salary adjustments and union demands only added more pressure to the area, already immersed in an increasingly complex global world.

Professionalization and updating

The "personnel administration" development was nourished by a broad source of specialties and professions including engineers, attorneys, sociologists, and psychologists. Each contributed a distinct feature: people management was not specific to any one company sector or field of knowledge.

The need to rise to the occasion increasingly called for trained individuals to respond to new social realities and build a more relevant and hierarchical future role in companies. For instance, in 1984, ADPA created its Personnel Administration School where students graduated as "Higher Personnel Administration Technicians". They needed to develop knowledge on several management techniques, as well as prepare for future changes through constant training.

Training activities referred to legal aspects: family allowances, wage and salary payments, and labor situation analysis. There were also constant offerings for topics such as motivation, culture, performance evaluation systems, hygiene, labor medicine, and the new notions imported from Japan. A recurrent subject gathered momentum: leadership.

More and more, the area started working with middle managers, professionals, and employees. In this context, the more modern and mature personnel area rapidly absorbed the notions coming from the United States, France, and the United Kingdom.[4] New horizons called for new abilities while dealing with conflictive daily operations. More time had to be devoted to "softer" issues: psychological evaluations became more comprehensive for recruiting, and several companies (such as Alpargatas, Price Waterhouse, Ipaco, Nobleza Piccardo, Merck Sharp & Dohme, and Johnson & Johnson) were already using them systematically.

The "management by objectives" approach was adopted, and the need to handle HR development adequately and professionally became ingrained in the area. HR development included topics such as performance evaluation, potential, training, development, succession plan, and retribution. Japan became a relevant influence in this quest for elements and techniques contributing to more effective people management with their quality circles, total quality, and *Kaizen*.

From 1989 through 2001: strategic thinking

Environmental milestones

The new democratic government headed by President Menem in 1989 marked the beginning of a new stage that would span little over a decade. This period of inflation-free stability, on the basis of the new "convertibility law" that tied the local currency to the US dollar, also featured a privatization process for state companies and a surge of mergers and acquisitions. Argentina opened up to an already globalized world, while the region sought integration through Mercosur. The need to ensure competitiveness turned "reorganization" into the buzzword of the times, along with "labor flexibility", viewed as a necessary condition to enable the efficiency required by global competition. Unemployment rose,[5] while unions remained calm and inactive.

Core issues

Social changes bring about changes in working people. In this case, in order to speed their responses, companies started looking for increasingly younger professional profiles that could face an unprecedented scenario: stability and opening. Marketing grew like never before in Argentina. The escalating complexity of the situation demanded more training in leadership and cultural change, while it challenged the HR practices used to date. Compensations evolved into more comprehensive and sophisticated systems with new elements, such as variable pay based on group achievements (called "gain sharing") and pay-per-knowledge. The more traditional approaches, like remuneration based on job value and rewards or raises according to individual performance, were enhanced and maintained.

Understanding who HR worked for and what the value added of the function and "intangibles" was turned into critical issues to define the "HR strategy", another notion that found its way into the agenda. Some companies, typically the larger ones, made groundbreaking progress in expanding the area's foci. For example, the multinational Unilever or the domestic Techint created key "breeding grounds" for future expansion. Supported by considerable investments, they trained versatile executives and professionals to enrich their ranks. Their personnel departments went beyond union-oriented activities, industrial security, claims, and conflict resolution. They grew in prestige by adjusting their role to the new business leaders' profile, contributing novel and effective approaches.

The World Congress on Personnel Management was held in Buenos Aires during this period.[6] Lectures dealt with vogue topics of the times, including "HR Management in Crisis", "Company Culture will Call for more Training on Leadership and Cultural Changes Resulting from Mergers and Acquisitions", "Personnel Management Strategic Dimension", "Leadership through Culture", and "Multinational Companies and their Arrival in Developing Countries".

HR was also drawn by the outsourcing trends of the times. "Non-essential" activities were outsourced in order to achieve leaner and more efficient structures. Subsequent merger, acquisition, concession, franchising, and outsourcing processes yielded deep consequences for organizational life, especially for employees involved in these change processes.

The 2001–2002 crisis

Environmental milestones

The policies implemented between 1989 and 2001 led the country to the crises of late 2001, which included the fall of President De La Rúa, the end of stability, currency depreciation, and the nation's default on external debt. A new political and economic scenario set in. Un- and underemployment soared, and, once again, the nation turned to the subject of "social peace". Poverty, which had risen during the last years of the twentieth century, exploded almost lethally in 2002.[7]

HR area

In this situation, companies resorted to the following actions during the crisis and 2002: (a) massive lay-offs; (b) voluntary retirement programs; (c) transference of key personnel to other countries, to preserve their skills; (d) changing criteria in recruiting and lay-offs, sometimes regarding labor and severance costs over performance and potential; (e) actual extension of working hours for employees remaining in the company; (f) salary and benefit reductions; (g) suspensions; (h) variable salaries; (i) training investment reduction; (j) greater short-term focus; and (k) disinvestments.[8]

Specifically in the case of multinationals, some local subsidiaries experienced greater difficulty in contacts with headquarters due sometimes to headquarters' failure to understand domestic conditions and, in other cases, because of a loss of trust. Other companies regionalized their local management and created shared services centers.

The future

Although the Argentinean economy started to grow again in 2003, sketching a more favorable picture of the following years, poverty and unemployment reductions were hardly automatic.[9] The future will largely depend on successful negotiations with the IMF and foreign creditors. Amidst this domestic and international setting, successive turnarounds in most Argentinean companies have scarred their social fabric. People must face new demands after going through the worst of the crisis. In a scenario showing signs of change but straying from past experiences, there are special features. On the one hand, stockholders – particularly international stockholders – and customers increase their claims; on the other hand, rewards are scarce. Motivation and commitment seize the spotlight again. Prior loyalties seem to have vanished or changed. Conflicts, whether explicit or latent, are no longer restricted to the union arena. At the same time, new and potential employees confront the results of current policies: their commitment or "psychological contracts" take new shape. What will be their disposition and motivation for their task and what kind of commitment will they embrace in light of what happened to their elders?

During 2003, some of the main action drivers in HR included providing support for employees through workshops and individual interviews. Additionally, new training initiatives recovered some of their former vigor after their fall during the crisis and promoted social responsibility activities, both for companies and employees on an individual basis. According to research conducted by the Argentinean Human Resources Association (ADRHA) in a sample of 60 companies intent on "increasing training hours without increasing budgets", 68 percent invested an equal or a lower budget in training than the year before, and only 32 percent increased their training budget. Fifty-eight percent resorted to "in-company" training using internal resources, reversing the 1990s trend to train employees through external seminars or courses abroad. Fifty percent of the companies focused their training efforts on middle and top management, especially in the service, marketing, and industrial sectors. The most popular topics included attitudinal training and specialty courses (32 percent each), followed by quality and productivity (18 percent). As to preferred methodologies, 66 percent chose classroom activities, 24 percent preferred on-the-job training (trainee programs and turnover), and only 10 percent resorted to distance learning (e-learning, videos, self-managed manuals).

Corporate initiatives for community aid, social promotion, and solidarity grew throughout the country. The Labor and Social Studies Institute (IDELAS) of the

Universidad de Ciencias Empresariales y Sociales (UCES) granted its
Human Resources Development Award to the Buenos Aires Hilton Hotel in the
category for companies with over 300 employees and to Central Térmica
Güemes in the category for companies with less than 300 employees. Tenaris
Siderca, part of the Techint Group, received a special mention. In all cases,
initiatives involved self-employment projects, local community improvements,
soup kitchens for children, and other related measures. These efforts sought
to reinforce employees' commitment to local communities as well as to
mitigate unemployment and poverty in surrounding areas (*La Nación*,
2003).

Conclusions

The almost constant oscillations in Argentinean political, social, and
economic life have deepened locally the already sharp worldwide changes of
recent decades. The succession of stability, crisis, market opening, "living on our
own production", inflation, and deflation contributes to Argentina's vulnerability
in an already complex world situation. Thus, the domestic repercussions for
companies and people should not come as a surprise. Swinging from employment
and unemployment, attracting and retaining development and growth
opportunities versus cost reductions and layoffs, and open and closed cultures
have almost naturally forced organizations to develop certain abilities closely
related to improvization, agility, and flexibility ("sprint, brake and speed up" and
"spark"), as well as their benefits and inherent risks.

In Argentina, multinational and domestic companies have coexisted since the
very beginning of economic development in industry and service sectors.
Multinationals, evolving locally as small, medium, or large companies, largely
resembled their headquarters in features.[10] Ongoing management system and
techniques development and updating generated by headquarters "imported" for
application always impacted the local reality. Many HR management
advancements resulted from the pioneering initiatives brought in by large
international companies, which adjusted them to local conditions and somehow
transferred them to other domestic companies.

The "imported tool-boxes" were not always adequate, especially when
implemented directly as "closed packages". In some cases, these initiatives failed
because their design did not fit local scenarios. In others, "time and space"
maladjustments resulted from a failure to grasp local realities and a demand to
fully implement applications, regardless of their local inadequacy, for the sake of
global compliance. As to practices, the professionalizing and updating task is
anticipated to be paramount to HR success. "Customized" models and tools will
be designed to respond as accurately as possible to the mentioned local
conditions.

Domestic companies had a more uneven HR development as compared to their multinational counterparts. Their size was instrumental in this regard. In general, "large" companies such as Techint, Alpargatas (until its crisis in the 1990s), the Pérez Companc Group, Cervecería Quilmes, Aluar, and others followed multinationals' evolution quite closely, resembling their features, albeit in a more localized fashion. Small and medium-sized companies were slower to update, and are therefore facing a larger gap in this regard.

Size and origin were not the only factors enabling HR advancement and state-of-the-art practice application. Based on Argentinean history and companies' developmental stage and business type, some firms have been able to plan their future while others have only managed to secure their day-to-day operations. Thus, it is not possible to discuss an "average behavior" in this area, since there is no "average". Local management has varied and will continue to vary due to the aforementioned reasons.

What will HR management be like in the new scenario? What will be its contribution to business results? Which capacities will it require from its professionals? Is it sensible to assume that, in addition to constant attention to labor and union issues, HR areas and professionals will be expected to contribute differential value, more so when faced with deep change processes? To this end, HR professionals should understand external conditions such as globalization, mergers and acquisitions, marketing standards, and customer purchasing criteria, and drive the required cultural transformation in organizations.

In the current unruly environment, traditional advantages are rapidly eroded. Companies' ability to create human organizations bearing different mystiques and talents becomes one of the most significant factors for competition and success in markets. Both literature and practice signal the outstanding role people have come to play. In many cases, the so-called "intangibles" have turned into one of the only true competitive organizational weapons.

It is safe to assume that the HR function in Argentina will maintain and, perhaps, increase the relevance it has built throughout its history by pursuing worldwide HR trends. Although response intensities may differ, overall directions remain the same. In other words, regardless of the different environmental challenges faced by HR areas in each country, turbulence and uncertainty are present across the board, and HR professionals seem to need a common set of competencies to face and add real value to their organizations. The preliminary conclusions drawn from the Research on HR Competencies, Argentinean chapter, conducted in 2002,[11] reveal that short-term differentiating skills will revolve around three core goals: greater strategic contribution, turning change and cultural management into a business priority for criticism and achievements, and aligning HR practices to organizations' desired culture.

Notes

1. Sponsoring firms included: SAIC Fábrica Argentina de Alpargatas, Farmacia Franco Inglesa, Cristalerías Rigolleau, Johnson & Johnson de Argentina SACI, and Manufactura de Tabacos Particular. "Pioneering partners" came from other companies, such as the renowned: Alba (paints), Saint Hermanos, Harrods, Orbis, Industria Metalúrgica, Remington Rand Argentina SEL, Standard Electric Argentina SAIC, Firestone de Argentina, and RCA Víctor Argentina SAIC.

2. In time, new partners joined the IADP, including Atma SAIC, Nobleza de Tabacos, La Cantábrica SAMIyC, Noel y Compañía, Shell Mex Argentina, Neumáticos Goodyear, Gurmendi y Compañía, SAF Cinzano y Compañía, Establecimiento Metalúrgico Santa Rosa, and Cervecería Bieckert.

3. Later, the Universidad del Salvador created the BA in human relations program. In 1998, Argentina had 15 universities offering university programs in labor relations, industrial relations and human resources: 10 in the Capital District and five in the hinterlands (ADPA, October/November 1998).

4. Especially relevant was research into the impact of past experiences, conducted by the Tavistock Institute in London.

5. From 1991 through 1995, the unemployment rate rose rapidly, reaching 18.4 percent in the first half of 1995.

6. It was held from 24 to 28 September 1990, hosted by ADPA and the Inter American Federation of Personnel Administration.

7. The general situation in Argentina regarding employment and income distribution at the time of the crisis may be summarized as follows: (a) launching the convertibility program, along with market opening and public companies' privatization policies, implied a change in the behavior pattern of the local economy. (b) The labor market underwent substantial changes as a result of the above mentioned reforms. The combination of an increase in the number of people actively seeking a job, added to the population growth, increased the labor offer while there was a decrease in labor demand. Unemployment rose, reaching 17 percent in 2001. (c) Another typical phenomenon throughout this period was the increase of work precariousness, one of its expressions being continuous work schedule reductions. (d) Income distribution became regressive, since the household survey for 10 income levels showed a strong income reduction for all categories except the top one. The number of people affected by poverty reached an average of 2.5 million by 2001. In practical terms, this share of the population had no income whatsoever.

8. Research conducted by the author.

9. Favored by global conditions as well as positive internal expectations for the administration of President Kirchner, there is increasing activity in most sectors. Unemployment rates are also showing signs of improvement.

10. These companies upheld their original characteristics taken from their headquarters, usually in the United States and Europe. More recently, companies from other cultures have arrived in the country, including the Asian Toyota and the Latin American firms of Petrobras, Brahma, and Bimbo.

11. The Human Resources Competency Study (HRCS) is a global research project aimed at identifying and comparing major competencies needed by HR professionals. It also seeks to analyze current trends to spot areas posing improvement opportunities. This research is conducted every four years under the initiative of the University of Michigan Business School. In Argentina, 1,200 HR professionals have been involved in this project.

Further reading

ADRHA (2000–2003) *Recursos Humanos en la Argentina* [Human resources in Argentina], Vols. 1–3, Buenos Aires: ADRHA.

Aldao, C.M. and Hermida, D.H. (eds) (1994–1995) *Relaciones industriales y recursos humanos en América Latina* [Industrial relations and human resources in Latin America], Buenos Aires: FIDAP, ADPA, WFPMA.

Hatum, A. (2002) *Organizational flexibility in an emergent economy*, unpublished doctoral dissertation, Warwick Business School, University of Warwick, UK.

La Nación (2003) "Premios solidarios" [Joint awards], Sección Economía, 134 (47453) (12 December): 5.

Ramallo, J.M. (2002) *Etapas históricas de la educación Argentina* [Historic periods of education in Argentina], 2nd edn, Buenos Aires: Fundación Nuestra Historia.

Sioli, A.L. (2000) *The impact of the focus and roles of HR departments and professionals' competencies on business performance in change contexts*, unpublished doctoral dissertation, IESE, Universidad de Navarra.

Archives

Bulletin, Argentinean Human Resources Association (ADRHA).

Bulletin, Argentinean Personnel Leaders' Institute (IADP).

Bulletin, Argentinean Industrial Relations Institute (IARI).

Personal, Argentinean Personnel Leaders Association (ADPA).

Relaciones del Trabajo, Argentinean Personnel Leaders Institute (IADP).

6 Human resource management in Brazil

BETANIA TANURE

The growth and irreversible opening of markets throughout the world have posed new challenges to companies. These main characteristics of the economic globalization process have been apparent in Brazil, especially since the 1990s. The challenges percolate all organizational sectors, including one of the most strategic of all: people management. In the context of business internationalization, the challenge of people management has crossed borders. In different parts of the world, growing competition and technological commoditization highlight the role of people in corporate performance.

Despite the ubiquity of human resource management (HRM) theories, HRM priorities and main practices carry significant local flavors. It can be said that, in each nation, there is a unique and particular HRM ensemble into which that country's political, economic, social, and cultural peculiarities have been factored. Brazil is no exception. Brazil's GDP is the largest in Latin America; the country is noted for its continental dimensions, branded by the linguistic unity and cultural diversity of its population, which is in excess of 175 million. As of the mid-1990s, business competition increased in Brazil. Following the monetary stabilization process, business ineffectiveness could no longer be hidden in the wake of chronic inflation. This prompted some Brazilian companies – especially those established in the country's south and southeast – to strive for a world-class management sophistication level.

Based on this need to dramatically improve business performance, I shall discuss the main issues relating to people management and the organizational environment that substantially interfere with such a process. Additionally, I will discuss the cultural characteristics of this continental country and their impact upon management.

Among the core roles of HR management, and among the issues approached in this section, is management of the change process. One instance when changes occur most dramatically is in the merger and acquisition process, which is so common in Brazil these days. I carried out an investigation focusing on the HR role in these processes, which generated data for analysis within this text. Other critical success factors for people management in Brazilian companies touched upon in the chapter include: the evolution of capital–labor relations; management of multiple links in a society where outsourcing is growing; the attraction, development, and retention of talent; people management in companies which are or intend to be global; and the great challenge of balancing private life and professional life. An integrated analysis of these different outlooks – including the perception of Brazilian executives in HR areas as well as the perception of their peers and corporate presidents – is offered, encompassing the various concerns with this function as a strategic partner. Finally, a Brazilian case study will be shown, in which HR has truly acted as a strategic partner. Some final considerations will be offered as well.

Characteristics of the Brazilian culture

Following management models often based on American styles, Brazilians seek to implement the different methodologies that appear in the First World. There is no time to reinvent the wheel and, often, shortcuts are needed to recoup lost positions. Attempts to implement many models have not been seen to yield full benefits. Therefore, in this chapter we discuss the characteristics and the specificities of Brazilian culture, resorting to a dynamic cultural action model that articulates around three basic axes: power, personal relations, and flexibility. These aspects result from the research I carried out in 1996 and 2003. The latter included 1,732 Latin American executives, of whom 895 were Brazilian (Barros, 2003a, 2003b; Tanure, 2004a, 2004b).

Data from other sources show a trend toward power concentration in the Brazilian company, though masquerading as more inclusive behaviors, which today correspond to the will of a good part of all Brazilians. One of the investigations I carried out was a replication of the well-known study by Hofstede (1980). Brazil, in particular, ranked 69th in a scale from zero, which denoted countries with a more egalitarian inclination, to 100, which indicated countries with a greater power concentration. After these years, the country remains in the same cluster at the 75th index, and regional variations are notable; São Paulo, the richest Brazilian state, is the one with the lowest index (64), while northeastern states hover at levels above 80. This demonstrates that the basic values of how to handle power did not change, despite the often different observed behavior. Power concentration is no longer explicitly seen, but no one doubts that power remains in the hands of the boss (Barros, 2003a, 2003b; Tanure, 2004a, 2004b).

The spectator stance is the other side of the power concentration coin. Brazilians work as guided by external authority. The transfer of responsibility for decision making is a phenomenon seen at all levels. This process is reinforced by the ambiguity trait, typical of Brazilian society, broaching maneuvering space for those who wield power. This trait appears to be more in tune with the contemporary era, whose hallmark is uncertainty.

The development and exercise of decision-making power, at its different levels, must be based upon the values that a company's leading team practices or wants practiced. It calls for the implementation of mechanisms to favor the change of culture and even the mode of operationalizing values; inertia prompts the individual to act in compliance with the more centralized power structure in force. In order for this entirely possible change to crystallize, however, it is necessary for the HR top to engineer the processes and systems which support the new momentum; it is imperative that the management team be genuinely committed to the process. Some Brazilian companies ran through important cultural change processes while seeking to change this power concentration trait; these companies include Natura, Alpargatas, Banco Real ABN Amro, and BankBoston. The organizations have very different characteristics and dissimilar management strategies but share a common trait: their main leaders share values based on the democratization of power and are endowed with the tenacity and persistence to run this change process. Besides that, the companies have implemented unique human management systems based on these processes.

Personal relations

Another fundamental trait of the Brazilian culture is expressed in the manner and importance of personal relations. This is a society where the bonds among people are strong and shape the structure of relations in different social groups. Brazil is acknowledged by visiting foreigners for its friendliness of relations, hospitality, and the inclusion of the personal dimension in professional relations.

In the interaction of this trait with organizational hierarchy, there is personalism based on the counterpart of the conflict-avoidance inclination. Conflict is not coped with directly in order to avoid jeopardizing relationships, to avoid embarrassment, and to prevent the upsetting of group harmony. Emotional confrontation is avoided especially with those who wield more power.

In Brazil, where hierarchy and personal relations differentiate the citizen, the magnetism of a specific individual is highlighted by his/her relationships. Paternalism sprouts directly from this combination of power concentration and personalism. The counterpoise to paternalism is the fear of erring; the desire to always do well and be recognized by "big power" is one of the origins of this stance. Two remarks are in order *vis-à-vis* the fear of erring. It can be paralyzing and negative to the performance of the organization, or it can be well-handled by the leaders and become encouraging for improvement on the quest for self-actualization.

Social cohesion is subjected to social ethics, which in Brazil is manifested by loyalty, by which the group member values the needs of the leader. Therefore, the interconnection of the different groups of a society is person-centered upon, essentially, the leader. Trust rests upon the leader. This process generates the feeling of belonging, which is a strong cohesion mechanism. He who obtains the loyalty of his group amasses personal capital by the quantity of followers and amount of information accumulated from them. The price of this loyalty is the pressure applied by group members for security.

This trait also maximizes the potential mobilization of people, a characteristic in strong demand in contemporary times. Brazilians are also different from other peoples for being more easily mobilized by their "leader" because of an easily created feeling of belonging. At a time when society discusses how to capture the allegiance of people, how to make people engage more deeply in the "causes" of organizations, this seems to be a facilitating trait and point of leverage for important processes. An interesting example is the restoration of this trait of Brazilian culture in Método Engenharia; their organization changed processes in order to snap the strong hierarchical structure. Using mechanisms to encourage trust building, informality, and friendliness in relationships and by counting on a well-structured process and the explicit sponsorship of the main leaders, a more democratic, personalized mode of handling power was established.

The great articulating trait: flexibility

Building a framework for a dynamic understanding of Brazilian cultural action was one of the great challenges of my research. Depicted in the following chart, these different traits have as their structuring axis the manner of handling power, personal relations, and flexibility. The latter is the major articulator as seen in Figure 6.1.

Flexibility is, in fact, a double-faced category reflecting adaptability and creativity. Adaptability is identified in several situations in the companies, for example in the agility they show in adjusting themselves to the different government economic plans that have been so common in the recent past. Seen from the process side, the adaptability concept does not relate to producing anything new in the purest sense of creation, but it has to do with an adaptive capability exercised within pre-established limits.

The concept of creativity adds an innovating element. It occurs both in situations in which there is *de facto* originality as well as in those where there is *de jure* equality. Even in so-called samba schools, there is that individual who stands out in the group or in the hierarchy braced by personal relationships. This is another hallmark of the Brazilian culture: the flexibility to coexist with hierarchy in a *de facto* egalitarian milieu.

Flexibility is also permeated by one of the outstanding traits of Brazilian culture: affectivity. Brazilians disclose thoughts and feelings through the verbal medium

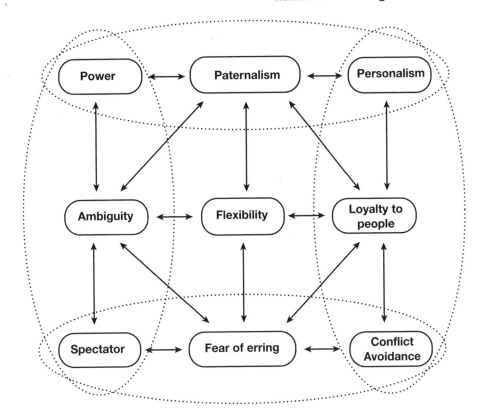

Figure 6.1 Brazilian cultural action system

and in other ways. They are inviting and do not shy away from physical touch; their gesturing and expressions are strong and their talk is fluent and dramatic. The capability to hover in the spaces of leaders and followers or institutional and personal spaces explains a few of the paradoxes of Brazilian society: it is happy and harmonic, even in poverty; it is creative, but with a low level of critique. The manner of handling these apparent paradoxes is what typifies Brazilian culture, and external observers marvel at the Brazilian way of being. Coexisting with opposites is an art typical of the country's culture.

An external force: performance

The unequivocal need to achieve good performance is an external force that acts and interacts with the cultural action system. Brazilians have their own way of managing and need to build a global competitiveness level from it. Also unequivocal is the observation that Brazilians have a natural vocation to commit to objectives submitted by the leader; this vocation can, however, be curtailed by the fear of erring caused by the authoritarian, centralizing behavior of whoever holds power.

Thus, it is necessary to reflect on such attitudes as related to power, such that the relationship of dependence can be changed into a relationship of interdependence for leaders and followers. It is essential that the followers adopt a more active role within their group. Managers, on their part, need to believe in their collaborators' capabilities in an educative attitude to make their group grow in terms of participation and performance. In this way, the HR role is essential to the conduct of processes and changes.

Change management

Among the crucial roles of the human resource field is the role of contributing so that the strategy may in fact happen, and one of the essential ways to do it is via change processes, whether radical or evolutionary. We elected the radical change scenario of mergers and acquisitions (M&A) to discuss management of people and culture.

In Brazil, the M&A theme gained importance in the early 1990s when the number of transactions increased due to the influence of factors such as the reduction of barriers against the entry of foreign capital, the privatization process, and the insertion of the country into the global market.

I investigated the 500 largest Brazilian companies to find the key success factors in their operations.[1] The study identified critical issues for the business perspective, such as mistaken strategic decisions, excessive expectations of synergies, disregard for customer impact, and the inadequate assessment of the technological or market potential.

The most outstanding failure reasons, 62.8 percent of failure reasons based on the study, relate to management of people and culture, themes not normally included in the due diligence processes. Although many companies indicated that they had a capable multidisciplinary team endowed with the expertise to execute this stage of the process, this was not the overall rule. Most commonly, a team was set up to review the financial aspects of the operation. This trend has changed the due diligence process into a focused assessment centered almost exclusively in the quantitative, hard aspects of the business, leaving aside issues such as the profile of people and values in force. In the Brazilian sample, the involvement of HR areas after the due diligence process happened in 20 percent of all cases, a low figure which reveals an enormous opportunity for the HR area to better occupy its own place.

A critical point in the M&A cultural change process is that the relation established between the business strategy and the cultural integration strategy is not always taken into account. The four models of cultural integration should be taken as an orientation to the HR manager who structures the culture and people integration plan at the base of the business strategy. Most companies, or 59 percent of companies based on the study, carry out these operations because of market-linked reasons, followed by those related to scale gains, know-how acquisition, and price. We analyzed four cultural integration models that should be chosen bearing in mind the articulation with business strategy, and run by the top change management team or top people manager partnered with the first manager. They are:

1. *Cultural assimilation*: when the prevailing culture is that of the buying company.
2. *Cultural blend*: when the two cultures coexist without the prevalence of either.
3. *Cultural plurality*: when there is no significant influence of the purchasing company's culture upon the acquired company.
4. *Reverse movement*: characterized by a great change in the corporate culture of the purchasing company and a low-level change at the purchased company.

In Brazil, most cultural integration processes involve assimilation. This desire to swallow the acquired company may contribute in some instances to destroyed value. An example of a process handled in a planned and competent fashion is the acquisition of Banco Francês e Brasileiro (BFB) by Banco Itaú, one of the largest Brazilian banks. The BFB, a subsidiary of Credit Lyonnais, had the knowledge to handle complex corporate operations and dealings with the high-income segment, competences that were not found at the Itaú at the time of the acquisition in 1995. The main reason for the four years of cultural integration strategy employed in this case was plurality, that is, the preservation of the acquired bank's culture until such time as the Itaú thought it had already absorbed all competences acquired. On the other hand, the same bank, Itaú, made countless acquisitions of state-owned banks with the main objective of acquiring market share. In such operations, Itaú opted for an absolutely different cultural integration strategy of assimilation. Very quickly the bank tried to change the processes and the culture of the acquired company, incorporating it to its own standards. This case shows the competence of the change strategy planning, run at the time by the Marketing and Organizational Development VP, José Jacinto Mathias.

When the acquired company is hanging by a thread, from the performance viewpoint, a quick intervention process that will influence the integration strategy is needed. The issue to be highlighted is that 52 percent of presidents report that integration happens naturally, without a clear, rational choice and without managing the process. Some of the remaining 48 percent funnel this action down to the definition of a new organizational structure and strategy with a few integration workshops. These data demonstrate that there is an enormous opportunity for the HR.

This is a period in which a climate of anxiety pervades people in acquired companies. The main uncertainty is job security. Who will be dismissed and who will remain are questions that beg attention first and foremost. The HR team, the great engineer in this process partnered with the integrating team, should be prepared to handle stress typical of the moment in a way that will not negatively interfere with performance.

The analysis of the HR role in the processes of radical changes, as M&A, reveals part of the transformation of the HR role inside Brazilian organizations. Historically, the capital–labor relation has occupied relevant space. It has, however, been decreasing during the last few years. This allocates some place beyond the change management for the attraction, development, talent retention, and management of the balance between personal and professional life. The latter is one of the biggest paradoxes Brazilian managers experience. These issues will be discussed further.

Other critical issues in the people management praxis

Evolution of capital–labor relations and the new multiple-link scenario

The development of the Brazilian capitalist model and the authoritarianism of the 1960s, 1970s, and 1980s branded the government and contributed to positioning the segments of society represented by capital and labor in opposite fields. With a recent history of disputes, these relations ran the gamut of exceedingly significant changes in the past few years, drastically altering the role of trade unions. In a much less combative way, unions are presently directed toward the assurance of employment and are stronger in the categories that work for state-owned enterprises or autarchies. Most private companies have increased their openness and transparency in their relations with employees, which has prompted the unions to review their role.

One of the issues that belong in the current discussion, not only in the scope of the relations between capital and labor, but in a much more general and systemic manner, is the management of people with multiple links. Following a deep outsourcing movement, managing these people became an important issue, especially for large organizations. Fernandes (2003) investigated the 500 largest Brazilian companies (Exame Melhores e Maiores, 2003), who report that building a skilled outsourced team aligned with corporate objectives is a major challenge. Analyzing all this in a stratified manner, private domestic companies have a more acute need to establish relations of trust and commitment with outsourced personnel. Multinational corporations, on their part, prioritize skills, career structuring, and turnover. State-owned companies rank among their special concerns the feeling of injustice yielded by differences in pay standards, stability, and career progress. As is the case with managing their own collaborators, the managers who benefit from the efforts of outsourced personnel but do not feel responsible to manage them are the ones who perceive the most hurdles against a healthy relationship.

The different types of outsourced activities tend to require differentiated forms of people management, making the manager's role more complex in the organizational network. The HR manager is faced with the need to manage the multiplicity of his environment. Since outsourcing is routine, he should harmonize policies, perceptions, and values in this complex scenario of multiple links.

Although in the past three years there has been a perception of improvement in the outsourced personnel management praxis, the distance has increased, in quality terms, between the management of outsourced personnel and collaborators. Most organizations admit that they have not established a new way of managing this great group. There was some evolution in the format of work relations, but policies for this new scenario were not changed in a systematic and organized fashion either from the perspective of companies or from the perspective of the unions. On the other hand, if the central company undertakes any equalizing action, interpreted as a formal labor link and according to laws in force, the companies would be assuming significant risks.

Talent attraction, development, and retention

Despite a recessive market, the process of attraction, development, and retention of employees, especially executive talent, has undergone substantial changes in the past few years. A stable environment in which large companies attracted the blind loyalty of professionals they wanted, assured them stability, and cared for them and their families for life has morphed into an environment of less security and loyalty.

There are major frailties in terms of talent management in Brazilian companies, which begin with the lack of definition of the word "talent" and of its profile characteristics. The frailties are characterized by gaps relating to policies and practices designed specifically for this group. Excessive contributions expected from these professionals, and especially the "indifference" with which the "others" not included in this category are managed, are problematic. Current practices do not present consistent responses to issues linked to the organizational environment quality, quality of living, development, career, and compensation. *Development* is to be understood not only as formal and structured programs, but also as the capability to cope with multiple challenges. A contradiction that begs discussion is that most professionals consider that they are acquiring knowledge and an attractive variable compensation for the main purpose of strengthening the bases for their career construction. This career can be developed in the medium or long term, within or outside that company, or can even be translated into them opening their own businesses. Companies make another assumption:

they see the talents in which they are investing as future organizational leaders, like a group that will yield a president.[2]

The greater strain in the relationship for companies is whether the promises made during the selection process are delivered, but this perception is not held by younger talents. Because of this, they feel frustrated, since they consider one of management's fundamental issues to be at jeopardy: the feeling of justice. Therefore, the great challenge is to adjust and manage expectations on both sides, as well as to harmonically integrate, by people management policies, the talents and the different organizational actors.

HR in global companies

Several Brazilian companies are undergoing an important moment of strategic definition: being local or going global. Some that can be characterized as young multinationals cope with significant challenges relating to HR management. Recent studies have identified their main motivations: growth, a need created by the saturation of the domestic market and by the quest for new opportunities; coming closer to current and potential strategic customers; competing against the best in the world and being among the market leaders; reducing costs through economies of scale in products and processes; reducing risk with a lower cost of capital; and meeting the ambitions of the stockholders.

From the viewpoint of HR management, some of the identified challenges are: having a pool of competent people to act abroad who have a strong command of the language, allowing companies to increase the number of expatriated Brazilian collaborators and have foreigners working in Brazil; and developing and disseminating an international mindset, thereby effectively managing diversity. There is a general perception that along these dimensions are many opportunities for the human resource field to broaden its role.

Imbalance between personal and professional life

Based on an investigation I carried out with 626 Brazilian executives, I could identify three major sources of stress at work: volume maladjustment; competence maladjustment; and values or affinity maladjustment. They can be summed up as follows:

Volume maladjustment

Until recently, the peak workload was related to the development of specific projects or specific times of the year. This has changed dramatically. Peaks no longer exist because the accelerated work pace is constant, averaging 11 working hours each day. Among the executives surveyed, 68 percent regularly work at weekends, and information technology contributes to the increasing pace and stress. The stratification of the research design indicates that the level of dissatisfaction is lower in small companies and among the CEOs of companies of any size. By analyzing the sample by gender, we noted that women are more dissatisfied, especially those who have children younger than 10 and who are held in great demand by their own families.

Competence maladjustment

Changes in requirements and the demands of a job are the most common causes of this type of maladjustment. The old paternalistic relationship is gradually being replaced by clear-cut performance demands. Companies no longer have the same tolerance for lack of results that they had in the past, and previous responses are now worthless. One of the ways in which to seek professional improvement is by participation in training and development programs. We saw the mushrooming of MBA programs in Brazil. This movement, albeit positive, yields an enormous feeling of insatiability in the executives, besides increasing even further the demand on time and energy. This source of stress is present in situations such as job or company changes. A stratified analysis shows that this restlessness is stronger among men and those older than 45. This is explained by the emphasis on younger society and the responsibility borne by men to provide for the family.

Values or affinity maladjustment

This source of stress is related to the individual's pride or lack of pride in the company where he works. Alternatively, individuals may or may not share the organization's purposes and values, or, though they do not ponder these issues, they could relate to the fact that they do not enjoy the type of work they perform; perhaps they do not identify with their work or with the decisive process style. The difference between personal and organizational values yields great stress. Stratified analysis indicates that this source of stress affects women and younger executives more acutely.

Is there a way out?

The great mistake lies in planning only for the professional, when the fundamental issue is caring for different roles, including the professional as well as the parent, child, spouse, and citizen with a physical and spiritual life. A person can only be considered healthy when he is aware of the influence he has in the success of his different roles. In Brazil, we are watching a clear movement for greater individual accountability for holistic individual careers.

A fine example of a company that seems to have found a healthy way to deal with people is Nokia do Brasil. The president, whose great partner is the HR director, reports that one of the innovations he implemented was an internal ombudsman for the purpose of working with the level of employee (dis)satisfaction. He was bothered by the fact that his executives remained at the office until 9 and 10 pm regularly. After the ombudsman service was implemented to support the self-knowledge process it was determined that several people remained at the office because it was more enjoyable than their homes. Decisions were made with HR leading the way in a true partnership between the human resource director, Marcos Combinato, and the company's president, Fernando Terni, who concluded: "This is more than a wager; it is a belief."

The great challenge: how to effectively turn HR into a strategic partner

The matter of strategic partnering has been one of the great concerns of the human resource field in Brazil. Area professionals, in line with international trends, seek to expand their background, deepening the vision of business logic. Much has been achieved in this direction, but much remains to be done.

I carried out an investigation on the perception of effectiveness in the HR area as a strategic partner, and I will discuss a few of the results here. Perhaps the most relevant is the difference between the assessment made by corporate managers and the assessment of area professionals. In a point scale from 1, which indicates that the respondent fully disagrees that HR plays the role of a strategic partner, to 7, which indicates full agreement, professionals generously self-assessed themselves with a result of 6.11 on average. Among fellow executives from other areas and senior managers, the average was 3.9. Most critical are staff executives with an average of 2.78, followed by finance and accounting professionals. Company presidents disagree or do not agree that HR can be a strategic partner: they allocate 4.14 points to this role.

The research disclosed an uncomfortable position for the human resource field. An important discussion to develop is the impact of the investment made by those responsible for HR, especially in the past decade, to better understand the business perspective, a crucial movement that often times left aside the focus on HR-specific expertise.

This can be a trap afflicting Brazilian organizations of which top HR managers may not be fully aware. The relevance of human resources stems from their true contribution to the performance of organizations. As such, it is necessary to manage the apparent paradox between the competence of the business, which should be updated and operational, and the competence and actualization of the technical base, which should also be operating. This discussion is a good challenge and we should not flee from it.

A discussion on the position of the presidents regarding the true importance of people and the weight they carry in the decision-making process cannot be ignored. Undoubtedly, general opinion has it that "people are the best organizational asset". However, the practice shows ambivalence in the position of the CEOs. Following this theme, organizations can be broken down into three major groups:

1. Those that truly seek to increase the consistency between discourse and practice in this theme, with presidents who walk their talk.
2. Those that follow the assumption of the importance of people in the discourse, believe in it but do not follow a consistent practice, which acutely shows the ambivalence previously discussed.
3. Those that have an articulated speech but do not go beyond it.

The second and third groups yield credibility problems. The third group especially acts based on the often unconscious assumption of the human being as a disposable entity.

HR as a strategic partner: Xerox in Brazil

Xerox do Brasil has always been a successful company; the company's position in the Brazilian market and its flexibility in handling unstable economic environments have been the hallmarks of its operations. The Brazilian subsidiary was considered to be the "crown jewel" of the corporate world and enjoyed substantial managerial autonomy.

The company coped with the local crisis entailed by the maxi-devaluation of the dollar by intensely downsizing, and until the third quarter of 2000 its operating results gave a wide berth to the world corporate crisis. In 2000, the company had a well-designed strategic plan and an engaged and committed workforce. Above all, it was extremely self-confident, with assurance amassed over the years. The business base in Brazil was equipment rental with company portfolio financing.

The liquidity crisis of the corporation worldwide surprised the Brazilian operations under a substantial dollar-denominated debt that met constraints to maintain direct customer financing and found no external debt-financing alternatives. Xerox do Brasil counted on a strongly decentralized structure based on a direct sales force present throughout the country. The company amassed extraordinary market share and created a customized customer service. The operating structure unfortunately carried a very high cost, which involved great complexity in the management of business processes and infrastructure. In 2001, the company recorded the first losses in its history.

In this environment, the company implemented the change of its business model: from rental to sale; from market share to profitability; from direct sales force to distribution channels. The high confidence in the company's past success hampered the operation of the new model and prevented the diagnosis of an acute crisis situation. One of the verifications indicated that the process would only be feasible if there were an employee mobilization to understand the situation of the company and willingness to commit with the changed agenda. The agenda showed its ugly face, typical of any turnaround process. The diagnostic was not favorable: the leaders acted so as to maintain the status quo; there was no cumulative experience regarding radical changes since they had never been required; the teams were unprepared to run the new business model; morale was low; and there was much confusion with the sudden change in status from a crown jewel to a sinking company.

Led by the president, Guilherme Bettencourt, and coordinated by the executive director of HR, Priscila Soares, the basic agenda for change was assembled and named "Recreating Xerox: To change or to change". Implementation took place over one year with an exhaustive process of communication with all employees. Many modes were used besides specific and one-way communication: meetings with deep discussions; individual interviews; and formal communications providing for reflection and discussion throughout the process.

Different from more classic processes, in which communication flows through the hierarchy, this process followed another model: it happened by convening a cross-section of the different levels of the organization. Technical project teams were structured based on the diagnostic taken; voluntary committees oriented to mobilize toward the change process. The participants raised issues they considered important, such as the organizational ambience, education and development, all of them having the issue of values at the base. The intended result was an agenda of suggestions to advance the process and the main product was to be the reflection caused by this theme. The organization was deeply impacting and this was a way of draining the negative energy while finding new success symbols and icons, since the previous ones were no longer valid.

The communication and end marketing areas, coordinated by HR, were crucial to support the emotional process of people. Employees read the papers and were constantly asked: "Will the company break? Will the company know how to get off the crisis?" There was no longer pride in saying "I work for Xerox." One of the suggestions from the communication area was a project called *"Xô, Baixo Astral"* (literally, "Shoo, Gloom"). Priscila admits: "At the beginning, I feared being unable to adequately drain off emotions that were very strong." Reflecting on the proposition and with the unequivocal support of the president, who had the assuredness to handle subjective and emotional issues, the project was successfully implemented. These processes were all supported by an open discussion about the problems, the necessary changes, and the timing of problem resolution.

Another outstanding project was "*Coração Xeroquiano*" (literally, the "Xeroxan Heart"), which aimed to rescue the pride in belonging to Xerox, a pride that had been so strong in the past. One of the questions that the HR director asked herself was, "Why did I return to Xerox?" She had worked for the company for many years before joining Citibank, where she remained for a few years before returning to Xerox at a time of critical crises, which did not make much sense from the rational viewpoint. "Why? Because the Xeroxan Heart talked louder." The campaign's symbol was a very sore heart, which encouraged debate about what had to be done for the company to get away from the crisis more quickly and rescue the pride of the Xerox name.

HR's homework

The HR field undertook its responsibility as the conductor and inductor of this radical change process. It touched base in the body of employees, guaranteeing open and candid talk. It took over the task of translating the strategy into work plans, helping the managers to set up their own performance excellence processes (PEP, and their internal BSC) and defined the pathways of people management for the company as a whole. By having a deep knowledge of the business, HR resumed its functional responsibility and met the need of the company and the wish of the employees to rescue Xerox's values.

Throughout the process, the HR department's role was abundantly clear as the conductor that supported the leader and as the articulator with the managerial body to obtain engagement and commitment within the guidelines and change plan. The HR department was an internal mobilization and conflict-handling agent; conflicts were rife, as in any radical change processes. This approach reveals a successful experience in the HR field in the integration of business strategic objectives, processes, and people. The experience of the conductor, with a solid background in human resources enhanced with three years of executive responsibility for the auditing area of Xerox for Latin America, certainly helped shape this process. In the same fashion, the president's leadership, albeit lacking a communication style fit for large audiences, conveyed deep confidence and made people feel genuinely cared for, despite the sour side of change.

There were certainly difficulties, the greatest of them being the mobilization of the managerial body in a growth career and people with long seniority in the company. It was necessary to create mechanisms to host people coming from the market who contributed experience and knowledge that had not been available in the internal body; otherwise, they could potentially be undermined in silence. Another critical point was the difficulty in admitting that the practice did not respond to the challenges as implemented. It was like a denial of the many years of success and it prompted feelings of individual incompetence and the failure of the old model. Actions orchestrated by the HR department were meant to enable people to comprehensively understand that what was done was absolutely correct for that time, but the world required new answers in the present time.

In 2002, the phase was completed, the paving was done, and the worst part of the turnaround process was over. The company was ready to resume growth in 2003, which did happen, and the company resumed positive business results. The housekeeping year is 2004, for the refinement and the consolidation of business processes, infrastructure, and systems. The challenge is to resume the easy ride and maintain a healthy balance after many years of riding the gravy train of growth with positive results and no crises followed by the dramatic moments of the turnaround rough riding (Ghoshal and Tanure, 2004).

Final considerations

There is no doubt that in this global and competitive world human resources professionals must be competent to act to a world-class standard. Being world-class concerning people management, which has its roots in the values of the local culture, means that the particularities of the country's culture and the organization's environment should be considered.

Notes

1. 196 corporate CEOs participated in quantitative research and more than 350 interviews were held in 10 companies that had acquired others at myriad organizational levels. The research was completed with the qualitative part.
2. Reported by Resende, Sarsur, and Sant'Anna in partnership with Companhia de Talentos (2003).

References

Barros, B.T. (2003a) *Fusões e aquisições no Brasil: Entendendo as razões dos sucessos e fracassos* [Mergers and acquisitions in Brazil: Understanding the reasons for the successes and failures], São Paulo: Atlas.
—— (2003b) *Gestão à brasileira* [Brazilian management], São Paulo: Atlas.
Exame Melhores e Maiores (2003) *As 500 maiores empresas do Brasil [The 500 best companies in Brazil]*. São Paulo: Abril.

Fernandes, M.E.R. (2003). *Gestão dos múltiplos vínculos de trabalho: Um estudo sobre a visão dos dirigentes das maiores empresas operando no Brasil* [Multiple working relations management: A study of the vision of the managers of the largest companies operating in Brazil], dissertation, Belo Horizonte: Pontifícia Universidade Católica de Minas Gerais.

Ghoshal, S. and Tanure, B. (2004) *Estratégia e gestão empresarial: Construindo empresas brasileiras de sucesso: estudos de casos* [Strategy and business management: Building successful Brazilian companies: Case studies], Rio de Janeiro: Campus.

Hofstede, G. (1980) *Culture's consequences*, Beverly Hills, CA: Sage.

Sarsur, A.M., Resende, R.P., and Sant'Anna, A. (2003) *Onde estão os talentos? Onde está a gestão de recursos humanos?* [Where can talent be found? Where is HR management?], in ENANPAD, XXVII, 2003, Atibaia [Anais eletrônicos . . .], Rio de Janeiro: Anpad. 1 CD-ROM.

Tanure, B. (2004a) *Fusões e aquisições no Brasil: Entendendo as razões dos sucessos e fracassos* [Mergers and acquisitions in Brazil: Understanding the reasons of the successes and failures], 2nd edn, São Paulo: Atlas.

—— (2004b) *Gestão à brasileira* [Brazilian management], 3rd edn, São Paulo: Atlas.

7 Human resource management in Central America and Panama[1]

ASBJORN OSLAND AND JOYCE S. OSLAND

Central America officially includes the countries south of Mexico and north of Panama: Guatemala, El Salvador, Honduras, Nicaragua, and Costa Rica.[2] Panama, which is not considered part of South America, is also included in our focus. Although these small countries are closely situated, each boasts a unique social, cultural, economic, and political landscape. They have diverse populations with a significant number of Native American residents in all countries except El Salvador and Costa Rica. African Americans can be found along the Caribbean coast, except in El Salvador. Costa Rica has a predominantly European ancestry and an agrarian system characterized by small landowners who did their own work, rather than a "*latifundio*" system comprised of large landowners who depended upon cheap, unskilled labor. This is one reason for Costa Rica's greater income equality, according to the UNDP's Gini Index.[3] Additionally, Costa Rica has a more egalitarian, participative culture, as evidenced in Hofstede's power distance score of 35 for Costa Rica versus 95 for Guatemala and Panama on a scale from 11 to 104 (Hofstede, 1980, 1983). The Gross National Income (GNI) per capita varies from US$710 in Nicaragua to US$4,070 in Costa Rica (World Bank, 2004) and reflects the diversification of their economies, governmental development policies, education systems, natural resources, and political stability. Costa Rica and Panama have the top two economies respectively.[4] The violence of war-torn Guatemala, Nicaragua, and El Salvador in the 1960s and 1970s contrasts starkly with Costa Rica's disbanding of their army in 1948; Costa Rica has a long history of democratic tradition unique in the region (Saint-Germain and Morgan, 1991). Panama's history is also unique given US involvement in the creation of the nation, the Panama Canal, and the 1989 invasion.

Within these countries, we find various combinations of organizational forms, including: small and large family businesses; cooperatives; parastatal organizations; and large multinationals (MNCs). Each organizational type has different traditions and constraints, which result in more or less sophisticated human resource management (HRM) practices. Given all this variety, we should expect differences in HRM practices from country to country and according to organizational types.

There are also similarities in regional HRM practices. These can be traced to relatively similar socio-economic conditions, a common language and Spanish colonial heritage, common agricultural commodities such as coffee and bananas, and the availability of inexpensive labor to attract foreign investments. The countries also share many cultural characteristics, such as the importance of family ties and personal relations. Furthermore, political problems forced some people into exile in neighboring countries, which created closer cross-country ties and familiarity. The presence of large organizations and multinational corporations that set examples, and the influence of INCAE (Central American Institute of Business Administration), Latin America's top-rated business school, also promoted similar HR practices.

In an effort to address both the unique country aspects and regional commonalities, the chapter contains: (a) contextual factors important to HRM; (b) the state of HRM and current practices; (c) a case study of Intel in Costa Rica; (d) the impact of culture; and (e) concluding theoretical remarks.

While there are numerous articles on HRM in Mexico, there are few refered articles (e.g., Snyder *et al.*, 1995) in databases that specifically focus on Central America or its individual countries. There is a study of best HRM practices in Latin America, but it does not separate out the data for Central America (Von Glinow *et al.*, 2002). Therefore, one of the bases for this chapter is an expert panel consisting of two HR managers and an HR professor who all have extensive experience in the region. Rafael Corrales of Intel and Alvaro Gonzales of Chiquita Brands responded to a lengthy survey on regional HRM practices. Dr. Guillermo S. Edelberg taught HR at INCAE from 1974 to 2004 and recently wrote a book about current, general topics in HRM. The chapter is also based on the authors' research on the region and their experiences living and working in Guatemala, Costa Rica, and Panama for almost six years. Asbjorn Osland was country director of a non-profit international development agency he founded in Guatemala and the HR manager for Chiquita Brands in Panama. He interacted frequently with HRM colleagues in Honduras, Guatemala, and Costa Rica, and wrote his dissertation about leadership of a total quality change effort in Central America (Osland, 1994, 1996, 1997). Joyce Osland worked as a researcher, consultant, and department head in Guatemala and taught in INCAE's graduate programs and executive seminars. She was responsible for INCAE's annual seminars on HR and women executives, and carried out several research studies on the region.

Contextual factors

With regard to HRM in Central America and Panama, the most noteworthy contextual factors are explained in the following sections: dependence on agricultural exports, labor force characteristics, and labor relations.

Dependence on agricultural exports

Agriculture still plays a significant factor in regional economies, ranging from 7 percent of GDP in Panama to 30 percent in Nicaragua, as shown in Table 7.1's descriptive statistics.[5]

Even more significant are the percentages of employees in the agricultural sector, ranging from 20 percent in Costa Rica to 50 percent in Guatemala. Historically, coffee and banana exports have been vital to the region. Since there was no shortage of low-wage workers and minimal training was required, there was little impetus to develop innovative HRM practices geared toward non-professional workers in these industries. Uncertainty in the sector came, not from human resources, but from the overwhelming influence of international trends such as problems exporting bananas to the European Union and the collapse of coffee prices due to the excess supply from strong production in Vietnam and Brazil. Despite country variations, the crises in agricultural commodities have been significant and the coffee crisis is still ongoing.

Labor force characteristics

Economic conditions and a demand for jobs that exceeds supply drive Central American migration to more developed countries with labor shortages, usually the United States, via legal or illegal entry. Migrants send remittances home to support their families. According to one survey, approximately 28 percent of adults in El Salvador and 24 percent in Guatemala received remittances (Inter-American Development Bank, 2004). Remittances make it possible for people to marginally improve their living conditions.

Unemployment statistics, shown in Table 7.1, are relatively low in Guatemala (3.1 percent) and Honduras (3.8 percent), but high in Nicaragua (11.2 percent)

Table 7.1 Descriptive statistics for Central America and Panama

Country	GNI per capita, 2002	Agriculture as percentage of GDP	Percentage employed in agriculture sector	Unemployment rate as percentage of labor force	Amount of remittances in 2003 (US$ million)[1]	HDI index	Gini index
Costa Rica	4,070	9%	20%	6.4	$306	42	45.9
El Salvador	2,110	10%	30%	6.2	$2,316	105	50.8
Guatemala	1,670	23%	50%	3.1	$2,106	119	55.8
Honduras	930	14%	34%	3.8	$862	115	59
Nicaragua	710	30%	42%	11.2	$788	121	60.3
Panama	4,020	7%	21%	13.2	$220	59	48.5

Note
[1] Inter-American Development Bank, 27 March 2004.

and Panama (13.2 percent) (World Bank, 2002). These statistics do not allow for the educational background of workers. The oversupply of workers in many Central American countries means that employers hold the upper hand and are less likely to view HRM as a strategic tool in competing for human resources.

The small size of these countries makes it possible for well-educated people to move back and forth easily between the public and private sectors, which exposes them to different HR practices.

Labor relations

A recent International Labour Organization (ILO) study (2003) provides a comprehensive overview of Central American labor laws with the exclusion of Panama. This study, however, failed to examine whether these laws are actually enforced. Latin American legal codes are both idealistic and comprehensive, resulting in a high percentage of laws that are not enforced (Rosenn, 1988) or are randomly enforced. While numerous HR laws fall into this category, for example sexual harassment, a review of existing legislation is useful to understand government intention:

1. All five Central American countries recognize the right to organize, although El Salvador has some limitations for the public sector.
2. Collective bargaining is permitted. In Costa Rica, however, there are also direct pacts with non-unionized workers, and civil servants "with statutory employment status" are not permitted to engage in collective bargaining. The determination of this special status is left to the government.
3. The right to strike exists in all countries.
4. Discrimination is banned. In the case of Guatemala, specific mention in the law is made to race, religion, political conviction, and economic status but not to "colour, sex, national extraction, [or] social origin" (ILO, 2003: 6).
5. The constitutions of all five countries abolish child labor and forced labor.

Free trade zones, which allow duty-free import of inputs and export of products, have had a mixed influence on HRM practices. Some foreign companies employ sophisticated practices while others do not respect national labor legislation. There is anecdotal evidence that some employers in free trade zones abuse workers or deny them their right to organize (Lemoine, 1998). Some *maquilas* employ young women who are more docile and less likely to protest against unfair practices. Since governments rely on free trade zones to resolve their unemployment problem, foreign employers are in a strong position to ignore labor laws and can threaten to move to another low-wage country to escape enforcement.

External pressure groups in the form of non-profit organizations sometimes influence labor practices and report abuse in what are perceived as sweat shops in

Central America and elsewhere. For example, the US-based Workers Rights Consortium (www.workersrights.org) and the Fair Labor Association (www.fairlabor.org) both found the Primo plant, which made clothing for Lands' End in El Salvador, guilty of violations (Workers Rights Consortium, 2003). Lands' End subsequently improved personnel practices and ceased blacklisting job candidates who were union sympathizers at Primo (Stein, 2004; Workers Rights Consortium, 2004).

Specific leaders have also had a tremendous impact on labor relations. General Omar Torrijos, who ruled Panama from 1968 until 1981, was perceived as a populist ruler who established a labor code more favorable to workers (US Library of Congress, 2003). He intervened personally to resolve labor disputes of the largest private employer, the Chiriqui Land Company, a wholly owned subsidiary of Chiquita.

Labor unions and solidarismo

The labor union movement in Latin America was based on left-wing ideology, which meant unions were often viewed as too radical or leftist by industry, government, and the ruling elites. During the conflicts of the 1960s and 1970s, union leaders and sometimes company representatives were aggressively persecuted and killed in Guatemala and El Salvador.

Costa Rica was also plagued by labor unrest in the 1950s and 1960s, resulting in concerns about foreign direct investment and damage to the social fabric of the country.[6] As Robert Rojas, former Minister of the Economy, Industry, and Commerce, stated, "During the 1950s and 1960s, unions were politically part of the communist movement and disruptive to our work environment. Society decided we did not want unions in Costa Rica" (Sheppard, 1993: 4A).

What many see as a win–win solution to this problem is credited to two Costa Ricans. In the late 1940s, Alberto Martén Chavarría began advocating a concept called *solidarismo* that sought a middle ground between the conflicting interests of employer and employees with regard to termination benefits. The idea became even more widespread after a Catholic priest, Claudio Solano, founded an institute in 1963 that taught the principles of *solidarismo*. They astutely interpreted the Costa Rican context, where people are culturally prone to compromise and negotiation, as consistent with *solidarismo*. Its basic premises are that management and labor are interdependent and should share the common goal of making the organization succeed; then both would benefit. Both employers and employees contribute a percentage of employee salaries to their organization's *solidarismo* association fund, which is managed by an elected board of directors. Each association decides how the money will be used to benefit employees and their families with loans, company cafeterias, recreation centers, transportation, education needs, housing assistance, low-cost medical and dental care, or company stock.

The movement has been very successful. Some companies include *solidarismo* membership as a job benefit in their advertisements. As of April 2004, 228,861 of Costa Rica's workers were members (www.solidarismo.com). *Solidarismo* is credited with achieving labor peace and a high level of foreign business investment, both key factors in making Costa Rica's economy the most stable in Central America.

Solidarismo's most vociferous critics are international labor organizations. The ILO claimed that it interferes with trade union activity. In 1994, the AFL-CIO made an unsuccessful request that the United States drop Costa Rica's favorable trading privileges. They argued that *solidarismo* functions like a union and membership is a requirement of employment. Both the ILO and the AFL-CIO urged Costa Rica to provide more protection to workers trying to form trade unions. Nevertheless, *solidarismo* is an innovation uniquely suited to a culture that values democracy and harmony.

There are limited examples of *solidarismo* in other areas of Central America. The owners of Nicaragua's Coca-Cola Bottling Company were exposed to the movement when their firm was expropriated by the Sandinistas and they went into exile in Costa Rica. After the war, when the company was returned to them, Coca-Cola sent several union leaders and workers to Costa Rica to see *solidarismo* in action and invited Costa Ricans to Nicaragua to talk to workers. Since Nicaragua did not have a law concerning *solidarismo*, management organized a legal entity that successfully operates as a *solidarismo* association.

Nicaragua has a legacy of *Sandinismo*, the leftist ideology that inspired the Sandinista revolution that successfully toppled President Anastasio Somoza in 1979. The Sandinistas are still very powerful in Nicaragua, as are some unions. Strikes are common occurrences in Nicaragua and other Central American countries. Although they comprise a very small minority, progressive firms such as Intel offer greater levels of employee involvement and stock options to maintain good relations with personnel without unions.

In summary, the role of unions varies widely from country to country due to history, interventions, and innovations by leaders, and may even vary within countries due to the active discouragement of unions in some free trade zones and union avoidance tactics by some firms.

The state of HRM

Within each country, there are sophisticated local firms, such as Paiz in Guatemala, Taca in El Salvador, Dos Pinos in Costa Rica, and Grupo Pellas in

Nicaragua, with model HRM practices. There are also family-run companies of varying sizes, smaller traditional companies, and subsidiaries of multinational enterprises. HRM varies tremendously from company to company. Some family-owned firms are very progressive and attempt to introduce programs like six-sigma quality improvement or TQM, whereas others are more autocratic and paternalistic. Firms that value HR hire trained professionals, while firms that fail to perceive its value make no effort to put skilled people in charge, relying on accountants or secretaries for basic HR functions.

In the last 25–30 years, there have been tremendous changes in HRM practices in the region. Before, it was not uncommon to find firms with no explicit HR policies or trained personnel. The political arena drove some of the major changes; the civil wars in El Salvador and Guatemala and the Sandinista regime in Nicaragua produced worker reforms. When violence forced their citizens into exile, they were often exposed to different practices in other countries, which they adopted when it was safe to return home. Other factors that contributed to upgrading HR practices include:

1. Improvement in local educational opportunities;
2. The professional development of HR directors and managers;
3. The motivation to be seen as modern; and
4. Management succession in large local firms, when founders turn over the management of the firm to their better educated children.

Multinational enterprises have also influenced HRM, primarily in positive ways, as explained in later sections. Some MNCs are preferred employers due to their enlightened practices. A minority of the firms operating in free trade zones, however, have resorted to regressive "sweat shop" policies such as corporal punishment, union busting, and infringement of employee rights. One garment factory in Managua's free trade zone posted numerous large signs reading, "It is not allowed to talk during working hours."

Current HRM practices[7]

Variance in HRM practices

Where multinational companies have large operations across the region, practices tend to be fairly standard with core programs implemented across the different countries, such as "performance management systems", "management bonus", "management improvement program", "leadership profile", benefits packages, and the development of salary plans and bonuses.

Most local companies tend to be run by families and are closely held. In such companies, HRM practices, beyond legal compliance, depend on the preferences of management. Some owners and managers follow current HRM trends while others adhere to traditional practices. With the exception of some Costa Ricans, local companies are typically led by managers who are authoritarian, which is consistent with the high power distance scores of the region (Hofstede, 1980). Employees are usually risk averse and have difficulty confronting managers when employees perceive that management is incorrect.

Leading firms in Central America

The many prominent, large, local firms include Dos Pinos in Costa Rica and Grupo Pellas in Nicaragua. MNCs with a significant presence in various countries, such as Chiquita, Dole, and Procter & Gamble, are the largest employers. In terms of total compensation and benefits, multinationals are generally seen as good employers, although compensation and benefits vary. Coca-Cola Interamerican Corporation, Nestlé, Esso, Shell, and British–American Tobacco are perceived as good employers in the region. In Costa Rica, Kraft, Chiquita, and H.B. Fuller all pay well, as do management jobs in the financial sector.

HRM innovation and diffusion

MNCs with extensive professional staffs and a strategic view of HRM often have more resources available for innovation than local firms, many of whom are attempting to catch up with the traditional HRM areas such as job descriptions, evaluations, and performance appraisal. Local firms tend to learn and adapt modern technologies and practices developed elsewhere. Among the large local firms known for their efforts to modernize their HR practices are Incesa and Grupo Pellas.

While some MNCs tend to be more progressive, the direction of HR knowledge transfer is also influenced by their approach to international HRM, described in Janssen's (2001) typology.

1. The *adaptive* approach reflects a multi-domestic strategy that is context-specific and reflects differing cultures and legal settings. Its advantage lies in its suitability to local conditions; its disadvantage are fragmentation and duplication of efforts.
2. The *export* approach, consistent with a global strategy, emphasizes generalizability and internationalization. Its advantages are standardization and internal consistency; its disadvantages are potential inflexibility and rejection.
3. The *integrative* approach is based on a global strategy, top managers' belief in sharing knowledge, and encountering good practices in affiliates. Its

advantage is the transfer of best practices; its disadvantage is that such practices may be ill-suited for a particular context.

Most MNCs adopt an exportive approach to the region; they tend to focus more on promoting their HR practices rather than trying to learn from indigenous practices or trying to integrate the two. Both cultural and legal considerations need to be accounted for to contextualize MNC practices to make them suitable. For example, Intel is attempting to export its constructive confrontation approach because they want employees to challenge their supervisors when needed and be less risk averse. Despite years of training, cultural norms prevent many employees from speaking up. Chiquita adopted total quality management in the early 1990s, spending a good deal of time and energy diffusing it throughout its Central American subsidiaries. Despite some gains and successful implementation, the formal program was abandoned several years later; the move from a strong-man leadership style to participative TQM did not fit the culture of the company or the banana industry.

Diffusion occurs in many ways: via local HRM training, university programs, and MNC corporate universities, as well as via individuals who share knowledge – local employees hired away from more progressive firms, MNC employees moonlighting as adjunct professors at local universities, expatriates and third-country nationals bringing subsidiaries up to speed, as well as local MNC employees transferred to other countries in the region. International consulting companies, such as PricewaterhouseCoopers, also diffuse innovations.

Firms known as HRM leaders play an important role. Local examples include Kativo, H.B. Fuller's subsidiary in Costa Rica and an industry leader long before it was purchased by H.B. Fuller. In Nicaragua, the Ingenio San Antonio and the local Coca-Cola bottling firm also provided HRM leadership.

The Ingenio San Antonio offered veteran employees the opportunity to purchase homes outside company premises in a nearby residential area. This reduced dependency on the company and gave employees greater control of their personal lives. Management burned the over-100-year-old houses, signaling the end of the paternalistic era. Historically, paternalism served to tie employees to employers; in return for employee loyalty and the acceptance of low wages, employers provided employees with basic needs, small loans during crises, and job stability. It reinforced class distinctions and led to a submissive workforce that would not provide a competitive advantage in the modern era.

Other examples of innovative firms include CSU (Corporación de Supermercados Unidos) in Costa Rica, which implemented radical new management and leadership tools. Incesa, located in Costa Rica and Nicaragua, has always been an innovative firm that has attempted to implement new techniques, such as teamwork.

Intel, Procter & Gamble, PricewaterhouseCoopers, and Chiquita are examples of MNCs that provide leadership in HRM, diffusing performance management tools. They implement such programs as variable compensation systems, stock options and stock purchase, total quality, performance-based compensation, and leadership. Intel benchmarks with other firms, and when it participates in industry or multi-firm forums, other firms take note of its HRM practices and occasionally adopt them, as occurred with their variable compensation plan.

The advancement of women

There are prominent women in executive positions in the public and private sector throughout the region. UNDP statistics (2003) indicate that females comprise 53 percent of the total legislators, senior officials, and managers in Costa Rica, 36 percent in Honduras, and 33 percent in El Salvador and Panama.[8] The percentage of women in INCAE's demanding MBA program has increased dramatically from about 5–7 percent in 1975 to 30–35 percent today. Being well-educated was identified as an important advancement factor for outstanding females in Costa Rica and Nicaragua (Osland et al., 1994).

While these statistics indicate significant progress, not all women enjoy full equality in the workplace. Their status, in general, "varies greatly between and within countries [in Latin America] according to socioeconomic status, regional origin, and skin color" (Htun, 1999: 133). Although labor laws include mandatory maternity leave and job protection, they may not be enforced or companies may try to evade this expense by hiring men or paying women less in the first place. Pregnancy tests to obtain or retain a job are common in Central American maquilas (Htun, 1999). Women tend to be concentrated in lower-status and lower-paying jobs, sometimes earning less than men in similar positions (Htun, 1999).

There are more women executives in the public sector, which is attributed to more openness in hiring and promoting educated women (Yudelman, 1988). Outside Central America, the civil service, based on universal rules, is assumed to be less gender-biased than business (Steinhoff and Tanaka, 1994; Antal and Izraeli, 1993) with shorter work hours (Antal and Izraeli, 1993).

A comparison of personnel practices in a sample of women at the top of private and public organizations in Costa Rica and Nicaragua contradicted the view that the public sector is a more supportive, fair employer for women (Snyder et al., 1995). Many of the private sector subjects worked for MNCs or were CEOs of their own family businesses, which means their experience may vary from low- and mid-level women in local firms. Women in both countries worked for longer than a 40-hour week. Even controlling for marital status (only 50–60 percent of this sample was married) and the presence of children in the home, there were no significant differences in work hours. The majority of women in both types of organizations in both countries generally learned about their jobs through informal channels, such as colleagues, friends, or family in the organization. There were no significant differences in recruitment channels between the two sectors. More than two-thirds of the women in each sector and each country were selected for their positions without any structured competitive process. In summary, the majority of Costa Rican and Nicaraguan women do not owe their positions to universalistic personnel systems in either sector. Nor were there any significant differences in their experience of unfair personnel practices. None of the women in either country perceived discrimination based on color, race, handicapped condition, or religion. However, women in both sectors and countries reported the following forms of discrimination: experiencing pressure due to political affiliation; being passed over for job rewards due to the selection of another person without regard to merit; or experiencing discrimination due to their sex or gender-based assumptions. These senior-level women had little direct experience with sexual harassment of any kind, regardless of sector or country. However, many were aware that other women in their organizations had been harassed. Younger mid-level women in Central America were more likely to experience sexual harassment (Osland et al., 1994) due to their lower status.

Diversity

Discrimination does not receive as much HR attention as in the United States; equal opportunity is sometimes perceived and defined differently. In the early 1990s, a highly competent Costa Rican HR manager advised female industrial engineers to change careers since they would never be hired to supervise men in plants in her multinational or elsewhere; she viewed this not as gender discrimination but as "reality" (Osland et al., 1994). Intel's female country and factory managers are evidence of changing perceptions about women.

Discrimination is usually based on socio-economic status, ethnicity, and gender to some extent; racial discrimination varies by country and is rooted in unique historical conditions. Skin color is less important than socio-economic status. One rarely sees indigenous people in positions of authority. Most Latin Americans are *mestizos*, a mixture of Native American and European ancestry. Education facilitates upward mobility, but "classism" is still a strong cultural value, and individuals with strong connections to dominant families have easier access to opportunities than those of lower socio-economic origins.

A study of the impact of machismo on female careers found few instances of formal workplace discrimination, such as pay inequality or lack of promotion, related to gender (Osland et al., 1994). There were, however, numerous instances of informal discrimination, such as credibility problems, disparaging comments about women, difficulty dealing with an ingrained sense of male superiority, trouble supervising men who did not want to take orders from women, exclusion from the old boys' network, and the perception that assertive women are bitchy and perhaps homosexual. These female executives also reported traces of machismo at home in expectations and pressure from their husbands that were a barrier to their career (Osland *et al.*, 1994). The data for this research were gathered in 1991–1992, and conditions may have improved somewhat for women since that time.

Historically, some MNCs were guilty of discrimination and slow to promote local general managers. It took Chiquita 90 years from its creation in 1899 to name a local general manager. Today, there are fewer expatriates in Central America since the region has developed its own cadre of business executives and professors.

Public sector HRM

The public sector is a large employer in these countries. Jimenez (1994) found that the strength of public sector HR departments was high-quality service delivery due to specialization and technology. He identified the following weaknesses in public sector HRM:

1. it is designed for centralized, static organizations, inconsistent with the need for restructuring public agencies;
2. a general lack of employee ability in the area of organizational transformation;
3. disconnection between mission and employee contributions;
4. poor performance appraisal systems;
5. no link between organizational objectives and HR policies, including compensation; and
6. uncertainty about how changing consumer needs impact the organization.

Downsizing due to budget crises and privatization have altered the social contract between civil servants and their government employers in Central America and elsewhere. As a result, Guillermo Lee Ching, the Director General of the Civil Service Directorate in Costa Rica, states that public-service HRM should be directed at enhancing personal development rather than an organizational career, in recognition of the fact that civil service jobs are no longer permanent. Therefore, Ching (2001: 38) lists the following desirable organizational characteristics that support personal development:

1. a flattened structure organized by processes, not hierarchy;
2. flexible, efficient, results-oriented structures with empowered personnel; and
3. decentralized, multidisciplinary work team orientation, complemented by the use of process advisory groups.

Case study: the Intel–Costa Rica partnership

The traditional companies of the region, such as pharmaceutical, agri-business, consumer products, and clothing manufacturers, have contributed to the development of human resources. They have provided opportunities for residents to climb within the hierarchy, paid for the education of employees and sometimes their children, offered women a chance to be judged on their merits rather than their gender, and diffused modern HRM policies and practices. However, countries understandably want to attract higher value added industries such as electronics. Intel's partnership with Costa Rica is an interesting case study (Spar, 1998) with an emphasis on HRM.

Intel chose Costa Rica for its political and social stability, economic openness and liberalization, and receptive investment environment. Intel was also impressed by Costa Rica's negotiating tactics, unified response, and extensive personal involvement from the top. President Figueres took a personal interest in the project, dining with executives and even taking them on a helicopter tour with himself at the controls. Most importantly, Costa Rica responded favorably to Intel's concerns about its workforce. Specific educational programs were developed to serve Intel, who established a collaborative relationship with Tecnológico de Costa Rica (the Costa Rican Technical Institute). Intel works with local universities to upgrade their engineering programs and sponsors internships; Intel employees teach as adjunct professors in these universities and sponsor internships. Costa Rican employees attend Intel's corporate university. Training programs are translated and adapted when necessary. Intel also works closely with vendors and suppliers to meet their quality standards.

With 2,000 employees, Intel is a leader in HRM. The company tries not to lead the market in terms of total compensation, but may do so when the stock price is up because it gives options to employees, not just senior managers. Intel tracks gender worldwide to avoid discrimination. Women have held the most senior executive positions in their Costa Rican operation.

The impact of culture on HRM

There are several cultural values that influence HRM in Central America. One is personalism, a desire for personalized, individualized attention (Albert, 1996). The formal organizational structure or job descriptions are not enough to guarantee compliance or service; instead people seem to produce work for others primarily because of a personal relationship with them. This loyalty works both ways, and employees also expect loyalty in terms of the treatment they receive from the firm, as manifested in HR policies.

Lack of trust relates to a view of human nature as evil, rather than good (Kluckhohn and Strodtbeck, 1961). It can affect the training and development of employees. A Central American study revealed that general managers of companies engaged in exportation were loath to train their employees for fear they would then go into business as competitors (Quant, 1989). This fear may be warranted, but it also meant these companies were not fully developing and utilizing their human resources. Senior managers of family-owned businesses were less trusting than senior managers of publicly owned companies in a study of outstanding Central American managers (Osland, 1993).

Another value is particularism, making exceptions based on individual circumstances and the obligations of friendship. The struggle between universalism, treating everyone equally according to bureaucratic rules and abstract societal codes, and particularism (Parsons, 1951) is evident in hiring, performance appraisal, and promotion decisions. In a study of mid-level professionals of both sexes and high-level female executives, 70 percent reported that they had obtained their job via personal contacts rather than formal channels (Snyder et al., 1995). Some firms have minimal HR departments and policies, which allow owners or senior managers to make personnel decisions based on relationships; for example, they can reimburse the education costs of some employees with whom they have relationships, but not others who hold the same jobs and qualifications. Occasionally, managers resist codifying personnel regulations because doing so would limit their degree of freedom and force them to submit to the discipline of a bureaucratic, universalistic system (Osland et al., 1999).

Particularism is also evident when laws are not uniformly applied. From the Iberians, the Latin Americans inherited legal pluralism wherein different laws apply to different groups, resulting in special legal privileges for the elites (Rosenn, 1988). Coupled with classism, this may explain widely varying HRM practices for different types of employees. It is not uncommon to find sophisticated policies for the managerial and executive levels and much more basic personnel policies for lower-level employees.

The failure of governments to uniformly enforce labor laws is a major cause of the wide range of HRM practice within these countries. Professional HR organizations foster modern methods, but, as one would expect, the power and influence of HR staff is most limited in firms with the most simplistic approach to HRM. Where HR professionals are given free rein and respect, the result has been innovative and extremely sophisticated practices appropriate for the local context.

Concluding theoretical remarks

In the preceding sections, we provided descriptive information about HRM in Central America and Panama. A theoretical framework is now offered as a lens to see how the various factors interact in creating the HRM system. In most organizations, HRM has an economic function, linked to resource dependency (Pfeffer and Salancik, 1978), where its purpose is to provide the human capital needed by the organization to prosper or fulfill its mission. Still, the company and its HRM system are embedded (Granovetter, 1985) in the socio-cultural milieu of Central American society. Furthermore, the organizational culture is fostered by the founder or owners, or their managerial agents, which creates institutionalism (Zucker, 1987; DiMaggio and Powell, 1983), the process that shapes social behavior based on habitualized, taken-for-granted patterns of interaction. Institutionalism may run counter to economic efficiency and generate non-economic behaviors, such as autocratic leadership in high-power distance countries that impedes competitiveness. Granovetter points out that neither the purely under-socialized economic view of atomized people making rational economic choices nor the over-socialized sociologically determined view of institutionalism is correct. Rather, economic transactions, such as those of HRM, are embedded in a sociological context. The tug of war between resource dependency and institutionalism, ongoing in most organizations, is also crucial to understanding HRM.

The adaptation process of HRM to the socio-cultural context and the tug of war between resource dependency and institutionalism is a dynamic one. Social processes interact with established organizational structure which results in organizational changes to respond to the ongoing evolution of the Central American nations' society and economy. Structurationism (Giddens, 1979), with its focus on the dynamic interaction between participants' actions and the existing structure, provides an overarching perspective of this phenomenon. The objective reality of the structure of HRM is determined by its institutional identity and economic reality. This is linked to the social construction (Berger and Luckmann, 1967) of adaptation to the environment (Thompson, 1967) as perceived by the Central American organization's HR leaders, be they managers, owners, or directors of HR in large organizations. HR leaders' perceptions are filtered by schemas (Solso, cited in Izawa, 1989), cognitive frameworks developed through experience. Figure 7.1 illustrates how HR adaptation occurs.

The dynamic interaction of perceptual schemas of HR leaders, resource dependency, institutionalism, and the socio-cultural context is a social process that creates structures that are "fixed" but malleable over time. Structurationism provides the theoretical theme that grounds the embedded resource dependency in institutionalism with the socio-cultural context and the HR leaders and their perceptual schemas. HRM is not an objective reality affixed to structure but rather is attached to social constructions dependent on the schemas of leaders. HRM is not a living entity whose fate is determined by sociological processes such as institutionalism or economic forces of resource dependency. Instead, HR leaders make decisions within the contexts of economic efficiency, institutional identity, and the socio-cultural context. How does one ground such a theory in practical terms? Here are some of the implications for Central American HR leaders.

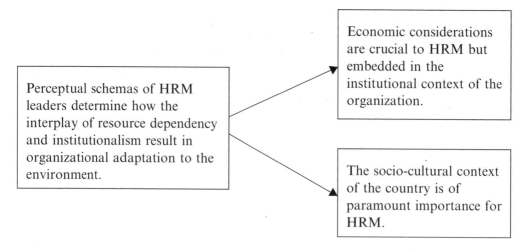

Figure 7.1 Adaptation to environmental influences in the national context

1. Although economic and budgetary concerns are obviously crucial, they must always be viewed in the institutional context.
2. The institutional context is not stagnant or always clear cut; organizations change.
3. When change is envisioned due to globalization, mergers, and so forth, Central American HR leaders need to be aware of their perceptual schemas, how the institutional values are defined, and how both interact with the economic reality of the organization and the socio-cultural context.

Notes

1. Special thanks to Guillermo S. Edelberg, INCAE; Alvaro Gonzales, Chiquita Brands; and Rafael Corrales, Intel, for sharing their knowledge.
2. English-speaking Belize has limited ties with its neighbors and is not considered part of Central America despite its geographic location.
3. The Gini Index "measures the extent to which the distribution of income (or consumption) among individuals or households within a country deviates from a perfectly equal distribution and ranges from 0 (perfect equality) to 100 (perfect inequality)" (www.undp.org).
4. See Table 7.1. For example, Costa Rica and Panama are more affluent (GNI per capita), more developed in terms of HDI, and have more equitable income distributions (Gini Index).
5. GNI = Gross National Income (World Development Indicators Database, World Bank); HDI = the Human Development Index, measures "achievements in terms of life expectancy, educational attainment, and adjusted real income" (www. undp.org).
6. This section is excerpted from Osland (2001).

7. Unless otherwise indicated by a citation, the sections that discuss current practices in Central America are based on written surveys and personal communications with the expert panel. Rafael Corrales is a native Costa Rican who has lived for many years in the United States. He began with Intel in 1997 in finance and chose to transfer into HR over 4 years ago. He won Intel's Internal Achievement Award. Alvaro Gonzales, also a native Costa Rican, has had a long, distinguished career with Chiquita and serves as the senior HRM executive. Dr. Guillermo S. Edelberg, a native of Argentina, received his Doctor of Business Administration from Harvard University in 1963, the first person to do so from a Spanish-speaking country. He worked at INCAE in Nicaragua and Costa Rica from 1974 to 2004. He published a book in 2002 entitled *Current Themes in Human Resources* or *Temas de Actualidad en Recursos Humanos*. Where the Oslands had first-hand knowledge, they too contributed.
8. Data unavailable for Nicaragua and Guatemala.

References

Albert, R.D. (1996) "A framework and model for understanding Latin American and Latino/ Hispanic cultural patterns," in D. Landis and R. Bhagat (eds) *Handbook of intercultural training*, 2nd edn, Thousand Oaks, CA: Sage, pp. 327–358.

Antal, A.B. and Izraeli, D.N. (1993) "A global comparison of women in management: Women managers in their homeland and as expatriates," in E.A. Fagenson (ed.) *Women in management: Trends, issues and challenges in managerial diversity*, Newbury Park, CA: Sage, pp. 52–96.

Berger, P.L. and Luckmann, T. (1967) *The social construction of reality: A treatise in the sociology of knowledge*, Garden City, NY: Doubleday.

Ching, G.L. (2001) "Costa Rica's civil service and its historical responsibility for organizational change," *Public Personnel Management* 30 (1): 37–42.

DiMaggio, P.J. and Powell, W.W. (1983) "The iron cage revisited: Institutional isomorphism and collective rationality in organizational fields," *American Sociological Review* 35: 147–160.

Giddens, A. (1979) *Central problems in social theory*, Berkeley, CA: University of California Press.

Granovetter, M. (1985) "Economic action and social structure: The problem of embeddedness," *American Journal of Sociology* 91: 481–510.

Hofstede, G.H. (1980) *Culture's consequences: International differences in work-related values*, Beverly Hills, CA: Sage.

—— (1983) "The cultural relativity of organizational practices and theories," *Journal of International Business Studies* 14 (2): 75–89.

Htun, M. (1999) "Women in Latin America: Unequal progress toward equality," *Current History* (March): 133–138.

Inter-American Development Bank (2004) "Remittances to Latin America and the Caribbean reach a record $38 billion," press release (27 March), retrieved 4 August 2004 from: http://www.iadb.org/NEWS/Display/ PRView.cfm?PR_Num = 56_04&Language = English

International Labour Organization (ILO) (2003) *Fundamental principles and rights at work: A labour law study (Costa Rica, El Salvador, Guatemala, Honduras, Nicaragua)*, Geneva: International Labour Organization.

Izawa, C. (ed.) (1989) *Current issues in cognitive processes*, Hillsdale, NJ: Erlbaum.

Janssen, M. (2001) "Developing a culturally synergistic approach to international human resource management," *Journal of World Business* 36: 429–450.

Jimenez, M. (1994) *Tecnologías de administración de recursos humanos en Costa Rica [Human resources management technologies in Costa Rica]*, San José, Costa Rica: DGSC.

Kluckhohn, F. and Strodtbeck, F.L. (1961) *Variations in value orientations*, New York: HarperCollins.

Lemoine, M. (1998) "Central American workers in the hands of the maquilas" (March), retrieved 25 May 2004 from: http://mondediplo.com/1998/03/16zonesla

Osland, A. (1994) *Total quality management in Central America: A case study on leadership and data-based dialogue*, doctoral dissertation, Case Western Reserve University.

—— (1996) "The role of leadership and cultural contingencies in total quality management in Central America," *Journal of Business and Management* 3: 64–80.

—— (1997) "Impact of total quality management training and work context on attitudes toward supervisor," *International Journal of Organizational Analysis* 5 (3): 291–301.

Osland, J. (1993) *Outstanding Central American managers*, Alajuela, Costa Rica: INCAE.

—— (2001) "Costa Rica's alternative to labor conflict – Solidarismo," in J. Osland, D. Kolb and I. Rubin, *Organizational behavior: An experiential approach*, Upper Saddle River, NJ: Prentice Hall, pp. 242–243.

Osland, J., De Franco, S., and Osland, A. (1999) "Organizational implications of Latin American culture: Lessons for the expatriate manager," *Journal of Management Inquiry* 8: 253–268.

Osland, J., Snyder, M., and Hunter, L. (1994) "What about machismo? Career and gender issues of Costa Rican and Nicaraguan female executives," International Western Academy of Management Conference, Brisbane, Australia, July.

Parsons, T. (1951) *The social system*, Glencoe, IL: Free Press.

Pfeffer, J. and Salancik, G. (1978) *The external control of organizations*, New York: Harper & Row.

Quant, R. (1989) "Un pez que se muerde por la cola: La capacitación en empresas exportadoras," [A fish that bites its tail: Training in export companies], *Revista INCAE* 3 (2): 21–29.

Rosenn, K.S. (1988) "A comparison of Latin American and North American legal traditions," in L. Tavis (ed.) *Multinational managers and host government interactions*, South Bend, IN: University of Notre Dame Press, pp. 127–152.

Saint-Germain, M. and Morgan, M. (1991) "Equality: Costa Rican women demand 'the real thing'," *Women & Politics* 11 (3): 23–74.

Sheppard, N., Jr. (1993) "AFL-CIO asks U.S. officials to revoke Costa Rica's special trade privileges," *The Journal of Commerce and Commercial* 397 (28035) (10 August): 4A.

Snyder, M., Osland, J., and Hunter, L. (1995) "Personnel practices in careers of women at the top in government and business in Nicaragua and Costa Rica," *Public Administration and Development* 15: 397–416.

Spar, D. (1998) "Attracting high technology investment: Intel's Costa Rican plant," Foreign Investment Advisory Service (a joint facility of the International Finance Corporation and the World Bank), Occasional Paper 11.

Stein, J. (2004) "Lands' End has deal with labor in El Salvador factory," *Wisconsin State Journal* (5 April), retrieved 4 August 2004, from: http://www.madison.com/wisconsinstatejournal/biz/71677.php

Steinhoff, P.G. and Tanaka, K. (1994) "Women managers in Japan," in N.J. Adler and D.N. Izraeli (eds) *Women managers in a global economy*, Cambridge, MA: Basil Blackwell, pp. 79–100.

Thompson, J.D. (1967) *Organizations in action*, New York: McGraw-Hill.

UNDP (2003) "Human Development Indicators 2003," retrieved 25 May 2004, from: http://www.undp.org/hdr2003/indicator/indic_210_1_1.html

US Library of Congress (2003) "Country studies: Panama," retrieved 24 May 2004, from: http://countrystudies.us/panama/53.htm

Von Glinow, M.A., Drost, E.A., and Teagarden, M.B. (2002) "Converging on HRM best practices: Lessons learned from a globally distributed consortium on theory and practice," *Human Resource Management* 41: 123–140.

Workers Rights Consortium (2003) *Assessment re Primo S.A. de C. V.*, 19 March, El Salvador.
—— (2004) *WRC Statement on Agreement with Lands' End*, 5 April, Washington, DC.
World Bank (2002) "World Development Indicators Database," Washington, DC, retrieved 25 May 2004, from: http://www.worldbank.org/data/databytopic/GNIPC.pdf
—— (2004) "World Development Indicators Database," April, Washington, DC, retrieved 24 May 2004, from: http://www.worldbank.org/data/databytopic/GNIPC.pdf
Yudelman, S. (1988) *Access and opportunity for women in Central America: A challenge for peace*, Washington, DC: International Center for Research for Women.
Zucker, L.G. (1987) "Institutional theories of organization," *Annual Review of Sociology* 13: 443–464.

8 Human resource management in Chile

DARIO RODRÍGUEZ, RENE RIOS, EUGENIO DE SOLMINIHAC
AND FRANCISCA ROSENE

Economic and social overview

Between 1985 and 1998, the Chilean economy showed a remarkable performance, growing at an average of 7 percent per year, doubling its national income to over US$5,000 per capita (US$9,000 in PPP). Social mobility increased at a fast rate and consumption patterns changed dramatically. According to the 2002 census figures, more than 98 percent of households have a color TV set and over 30 percent of the population have cellular phones. In the mid-1990s, poverty was reduced from 40 percent to 20 percent.

Growth is apparent in the number of firms that have been created during this period. Currently, there are more than 1,200,000 firms, of which 650,000 are formal enterprises.[1] Of these, 97 percent are small, 2 percent are medium, and 1 percent are large firms. Between 1993 and 1997, the number of firms increased by 22 percent. The economically active population increased by 66 percent from 4.2 million in 1986 to 6.1 million in 2004.

Although labor force in the agricultural sector has decreased from 20 percent in 1986 to 14 percent in 2003, its high participation in the overall labor force market is explained by important export-oriented production activities. The mining sector contributes to 7.1 percent of GNP (2003) and absorbs 1 percent of the labor force, a decline from 2 percent in 1982. Industrial employment is 14 percent and contributes 19.5 percent of GNP. The service sector has also experienced a significant growth. Outsourcing of services previously provided from within the industrial sector explains part of this growth. It grew from 11.3 percent in 1996 to 13.9 percent of GNP in 2003 and accounts for 47% of the work force. The financial sector, in particular, has been among the most dynamic. It accounts for 14.6 percent of GNP and 8 percent of the workforce, up from 6 percent in 1986. This growth is due, in part, to the privatization of both medical insurance and pension funds administration. The latter, the Administradora de Fondo de Pensiones (AFP), manages a total fund of almost US$50 billion, a portion of which is invested in bonds. In turn, the bond market has increased and, due to the country's low risk ranking, many firms are financing their expansion through direct bond issuing.

The export driven economic model relies on a mix of firms with significant differences between them, both in size and economic contribution. Small firms (41 percent) contribute with 1.04 percent, or US$190 million, of total exports. Large and medium-sized corporations (3 percent of all firms) produce 96.1 percent of total exports (US$18.2 billion).

The development strategy established in the 1970s by the military regime and maintained during the *Concertación* governments is a free market economy, export driven, open to international trade and investment. The state has adopted a regulatory role over the markets, having opened many of them to competition via deregulation and privatization. (Rodríguez *et al.*, 1997). Furthermore, financial aids and incentives in several sectors have stimulated market activity. As with many modern states, its steering capacity has been reduced to the maintenance of fiscal and macroeconomic equilibrium, as well as regulating some industries and the labor market.

Historical background: the rupture of the face-to-face bond

From a social standpoint, the deep transformation has not yet completely modified the profound cultural matrix in which the structural and functional differentiation has occurred. The *hacienda*'s cultural womb and social organization consisted of paternalistic relationships between the boss (*patrón*) and the worker (*inquilino*) (Medina, 1971). Authority was exercised arbitrarily but with benevolence (Martinez, 2005). It constituted festive face-to-face interaction in which consumption and sharing were central (Cousiño, 1990; Morandé, 1987). The *inquilino* expected his *patrón* to share the fruits of labor in feasts and celebrations in which this direct face-to-face interaction constituted the most valued characteristic of the relationship.

As the *hacienda* evolved, the boss left for the cities and the relationship was disrupted, leaving the workers with a feeling of abandonment (Cousiño and Valenzuela, 1994). In their migration, they followed their bosses. In this historical and cultural sense, the migrant went to the city to reencounter the departed boss.

Due to these historical roots and the culture of paternalism, the first industries that were established in the main Chilean cities had a structure that resembled the *hacienda* and its labor relations. There are many examples of business firms that built houses, schools, and health services for their employees in order to create an "*urban hacienda*" in the middle of the city.

In the 1940s, the Chilean State played a key role in fostering the industrialization process. Historically, the state has had an important role in implementing solutions for the major societal problems and has been viewed as an effective tool to conduct the various projects of national interest. When the task was defined as the need to overcome underdevelopment through industrialization, it seemed that there were no other actors to face this challenge. Conducting public affairs was the core responsibility of the state, and this took place in a societal system where no significant separation between the various societal subsystems existed. Essentially, the economy was dependent on political decisions (Rodríguez *et al.*, 1997).

The traditional paternalistic relationship began to decay as modernization and reform processes got underway during the 1960s. At that time, the social bond between workers and employers was torn apart. Strikes were frequent and many firms were taken over by their workers. This was viewed by the employers as disloyal behavior, originated mainly from the "infiltration" of political interests exogenous to the firm, with organized actions aimed at a drastic change in property rights. These culminated in an institutional, economic, political, and social breakdown that led to the military regime.

After the military coup of September 1973 there were massive dismissals, both politically and economically motivated. The main outcome has been a long-lasting mistrust between employers and workers. The reinstatement of full property rights, and the subsequent growth of Chilean firms, has not resulted in a full reestablishment of a labor relationship bonded by mutual trust. A modern contractual relationship has become dominant, which lacks the needed trust to become a fully competitive factor. Since trust is a bet for the future that leans on the past (Luhmann, 1979), the shattered personal relationship has not been completely reestablished because mutual trust necessary to lubricate the contractual relationship has not been reconstructed; distrust and suspicion tend to prevail. The challenge is not the reestablishment of traditional labor relationships, but the establishment of a modern working arrangement of rights and duties. This poses complex demands on HRM, particularly in the design of compensation schemes, especially of benefits that need to replace a paternalistic frame with a modern one, with the added tie to productivity at the individual level. Collective insurance and other forms of cooperative distribution of risks have been important developments in recent years, but the measures are not sufficient to indicate that the administration of benefits has become fully modern in conception and operations. Paternalistic decision-making patterns are observable even in many modern, highly professionalized, large companies. As the size and complexity of the firm diminishes, paternalism tends to increase.

The new scenario and current human resource management practices

The functional differentiation (Luhmann, 1997) of the Chilean society has been fast and all-encompassing. It began with the political decision to transform the economy into a free market, lower taxes on international commerce, and foster professionalism in management. The opening of traditionally closed, protected markets to international competition was hard to accept for businesses that had been supported and protected by the state. The most common descriptor used at the time was the word *crisis*. New generations of entrepreneurs took over the firms and, as a means of managing the crisis, made major changes in their organizations (Montero, 1997). This was possible because the country had a better educated labor force and a sufficient number of professionals. There was a deep transformation from firms owned and managed by the state or families to professionally managed companies. In the 1970s, when the Chilean economy dropped its barriers to foreign commerce, engineers[2] and business school graduates were hired to occupy the higher positions in firms; efficient management became a crucial issue that was further professionalized in the years to come. Business entrepreneurs and executives are increasingly aware of the importance of HR and its professional management is seen as a must in order to develop their potential. Nevertheless, this new approach has not prevented them from firing workers as an efficient way to reduce costs in difficult times (Majluf *et al.*, 1999). This is not just, of course, a Chilean trend (Pfeffer, 1997).

Today, the social link that connected worker and firm is not as diffuse and holistic as it used to be; work relationships have turned into very specific contractual links. The relationship is monetary and depersonalized, no longer a familial relationship where loyalty is exchanged for protection, or social benefits are payment instead of money. This new work relationship implies the exchange of work for wage as the predominant form of exchange, excluding other binding forces from the contractual relationship (Rodríguez, 2002).

Unionization remains at a low level, losing ground: it fell 7 percent from 29.3 percent in 1998 to 21.4 percent in 2002. Although the number of unions has increased from 9,858 in 1991 to 15,192 in 2001, the number of affiliated workers has dropped from 701,355 to 599,610. This implies that while the number of unions has grown 54 percent, the number of organized workers has decreased 15 percent, over a total active labor force that grew 22 percent. The unionization rate for the total salaried working force has dropped from 22.4 percent to 15.7 percent (*Dirección del Trabajo*, 2003). Data clearly show a trend towards individualized labor relations and a dramatic change in the role of unions and organized labor.

Labor union leaders provide different reasons for the shift: the apprehension of non-organized workers about the negative consequences on their job stability should they become organized is most popular, with 45 percent citing this motive; perception of no benefits from joining unions is second at 24 percent; and the opinion that more benefits can be obtained directly from employers than by joining the unions is at 13 percent (*Dirección del Trabajo*, 2002).

According to the same source, of a total of 7,192 listed unions in the metropolitan region in 2002, 53 percent or 3,832 unions were inactive. Labor leaders claim that 60 percent of the firms behaved in ways that favored the functioning of unions, while 30 percent perceived them indifferently and 10 percent were against them. In terms of the nature of this relationship, 41 percent of the workers and 48 percent of the employers considered that labor relationships were collaborative and peaceful, while only 27 percent of the labor leaders shared this view. In firms where collective contract negotiations had taken place in recent years, the positive view fell to 32 percent. For the whole metropolitan region, labor conflict measured by the number of strikes dropped from 115 in 1995 to 54 in 2001; the number of workers decreased from 12,363 to 7,059. The duration of strikes fell from 1,522 days to 427. Additionally, the ratio of manpower to days of strike decreased from 151,298 to 79,023. Data show that either the negotiating ability of workers has dropped or that the labor relationships in today's firms are not as conflicting as those of the past.

Social security changed from an underdeveloped welfare state type of labor taxation paid by the employer, with funds retained and distributed by the state, to a system of individual capitalization of workers' savings, administered by the private AFPs. Labor law was reformed in ways that allowed for agreements between employers and employees at the firm level, making it difficult for external organizations, such as union federations, to intervene in the negotiations. Unions were formerly a major source of political influence within the labor movement, especially the leftist parties. New legislation also favored the establishment of individual agreements by giving predominance to the individual labor contract over any collective type of agreement. Unionization became completely voluntary, impeding unions to condition the incorporation of workers to their affiliation status, a legal precept that derives from a constitutional right to freely organize without any type of coercion.

Before these changes, workers built their identity through their membership of a group, union, or business firm. They could not dissent from the group to which they belonged. In the present day, workers are much more self-conscious and proud of their individual identity. Education[3] has played a significant role in this deepening individualism; it remains a determining factor in the differences between people and the differences for which people demand recognition.

It is worth noting that, up to now, we have spoken of workers mostly as males; this is not a distortion. Despite its modernization and open economic system, it seems paradoxical that the female workforce has grown at a slower rate and that female participation in the workforce is lower than in many developing countries. While female participation is 35.6 percent of the labor force in Chile, it is 51.2 percent in Argentina, 61.3 percent in Uruguay, 46.9 percent in Venezuela, 58.4

percent in Ecuador, 60.2 percent in Peru, and 40.9 percent in Mexico. Despite an early historical record of female incorporation in the educational system since the late nineteenth century, the mothering role seems favored even by the most educated, successful professionals.

An individualized workforce that came about due to institutional, situational and socio-cultural factors has resulted in a labor relations system with low overt conflicts. How much of this peaceful labor relationship is due to HRM practices is difficult to establish. Chilean firms experienced a significant growth in very competitive international and local markets,[4] which in turn provided for resources to be distributed to their workforce in the form of wage increases, concomitant with their productivity changes. On average, real wages, (net of inflation rate), grew 19 percent between 1993 and 2001. Thus, the labor system established clear "causal" relationships between labor productivity and compensation increases. The link between productivity and compensation is probably also a result of modern professionalized HRM practices.

In wage and salary administration, a major change has taken place. Today, wage increases are more directly linked to increases in productivity and many workers, especially younger ones, are gradually understanding and accepting this link. During the 1990s, many collective negotiations incorporated objective productivity indicators related to wage increases. At the same time, performance appraisals became more widespread, with many linking their results to compensation, bonuses, or salary increases. However, most Chilean workers and managers are reluctant to consider performance appraisals a valuable evaluation procedure (Koljatic and Rosene, 1993).

In terms of salary composition, variable compensation is low. Even at the managerial level, it does not account for more than 15 percent of total income. Although many firms tie bonuses to group or individual performance, stable flows are widely preferred. Some firms pay bonuses as deposits to their executives' individual pension funds, which are tax exempt.

Benefits administration still responds to a paternalistic relationship and is designed towards the needs of the lower-paid worker, unrelated to his/her productivity. Traditional forms of compensation are present in actions such as holiday bonuses, embedded in the cultural traits of the *hacienda* and alive in the workers' minds.

The traditional job stability offered by companies and demanded by workers until recent times is no longer a characteristic of labor relations (Wormald *et al.*, 2002). Workers no longer want to remain in the same firm. To be promoted within the same organization was, for the older generations, a strong aspiration. Value placed on experience and seniority meant that people were proud of growing old in the same company. Younger workers and professionals, on the contrary, do not want a life-long job; they view it as an unattractive option and prefer to improve their wages by changing employers instead of waiting for a promotion. There are more differences between senior and junior workers than between highly and low-qualified workers in this regard (Rodríguez, 2002). HR managers must deal with both groups, subcultures, and the resulting complexity. This is one of the driving forces for a professional approach in HRM.

Nowadays, another form of complexity characterizes labor relations: workers want employability; they want better wages, not social compensation, fringe benefits, or perks; they do not look for advice in their personal affairs nor economical help. Family and work are neatly set apart. Young workers prefer to be treated more impersonally. They expect that HRM programs, rules, and benefits should be given to anyone in need of them and those that have the right to apply for them, according to general, impersonal, or universal rules. Paternalism and arbitrariness are rejected. They demand that HRM be professional and run by specialists.

Together with the higher organizational relevance of the HR manager and with the increasing importance assigned to his/her role, some firms prefer to outsource part or even all of the HR operations (Koljatic and Rosene, 1993). As such, the first function to be externalized was personnel selection. Large consulting agencies such as Deloitte & Touche and Price Waterhouse were asked to select the person that could best fit the expectations for a certain role. Selection processes began to be much more impersonal and objective, and some of their paternalistic features, such as preference for persons related to other members of the firm, were eliminated.

Recruitment practices cover a wide range of methods: to fill higher executive positions, both public advertisements and networking are used; at the operative level, personal networks seem to be the predominant form of recruitment. The rationale is that the sponsoring worker assumes some responsibility for the performance and/or "loyalty" of the new worker. Most corporations use psychological test screening, although "familism" is not absent from selection processes. In most cases, the sponsored candidate has to go through screening as a requisite. The most important network ties besides family and relatives are those formed by the classmates of their high school years, especially for the middle and upper social classes. In fewer cases, university networks are crucial, particularly for professional and executive levels.

These trends do not represent the whole set of companies. Some of the firms follow modern patterns while others remain within traditional structures. Older enterprises have strong cultures that change very slowly. Newly founded ones may be designed with a more modern managerial blueprint. Significant numbers of recent mergers and acquisitions have added even more complexity to this matter.

The professional class has differentiated itself and the demand for independent professional services has been growing steadily. The provision of labor force via honorary payments has also increased significantly. Consulting firms are available on all management topics.

In general, HRM in Chile has experienced a gradual process of professionalization and has incorporated modern management principles and techniques. In fact, modern Chilean firms exhibit HRM practices that are similar to those observed in developed countries. The vast array of instruments, tools, and practices in use in large and medium-sized firms confirm this trend (Koljatic and Rosene, 1993). However, this cannot be taken as a valid generalization for the bulk of Chilean enterprises, since large and medium-sized corporations amount to 3 percent of firms. This does not imply that the output of the small firms is of low quality, but that their need for professional HRM is a major challenge.

The legal and institutional framework

Six issues from this overall framework are discussed below, namely, risk prevention management, the Chilean social security system, health fostering and protection, labor laws, unemployment insurance, and personnel training and development.

Risk prevention management

The current legislation has its origin in 1968, when Law Number 16,744 on Labor Accidents and Professional Diseases was promulgated. Its fundamental issues have not undergone major modifications until today.

The regulations contained in the system consist of a set of dispositions designed to prevent and cure work accidents and professional diseases, as well as economic benefits from social security coverage associated with these contingencies. This system allows and requires ample worker participation and involvement.

At the firm level, this participative risk prevention system is organized through the mandatory creation of "risk prevention joint committees", also known as "hygiene and safety joint committees". It requires the existence of a specialized department on risk prevention that frequently reports to the HR unit.

Among the most important issues are those related with workers' education on risk prevention with strong technical support on how to introduce safer workplace designs and procedures so as to avoid accidents and professional diseases. This preventive effort is supported by the creation of a special health system and infrastructure for those who suffer a work-related accident. The providers of these health services are mostly entrepreneurial associations that also administrate the insurance premiums that are paid by employers at a variable rate from 0.95 percent of wages, varying according to casualty and accidents. Chile's average premium rate is currently 1.7 percent, significantly lower when compared with European countries such as Belgium (3.3 percent), Germany (2.9 percent), and Italy (3.0 percent). The accident rate has dropped from 35.3 percent yearly in 1969 to approximately 7.7 percent. This rate is similar to those of Spain (8.5 percent) and the United States (7.1 percent) (Undurraga, 2003).

The social security system

The social security system was reformed in 1980 (Raczynski, 1994). The new system is based on individual capitalization of mandatory savings; approximately 10 percent of the wage or salary goes to a personal account managed by the AFPs. The worker can voluntarily save additional tax-exempt amounts in order to increase her/his fund. The amount of the pension will depend directly on the individual savings fund. This system also provides life and disability insurance. The main change from the previous system is that savings are paid for by the worker from her/his income and are not an employer's labor cost. The HR administration is increasingly involved in providing financial orientation and counseling to employees seeking to improve their retirement funds.

Health fostering and protection

The social security system requires a mandatory payment of 7 percent deducted from the worker's salary as a premium for primary health insurance. Health insurance plans are subscribed by employees themselves either in the private (Social Security Health Institutions – ISAPRES) or public health system (National Health Fund – FONASA) (Sp. ISAPRES, 2004; FONASA, 2004). These plans provide sick-leave payments and financial coverage for health expenses for the worker and her/his family.

Increasingly, private firms are providing workers with secondary health insurance that pays for expenses not covered by the mandatory health insurance.

During pregnancy, mothers have the right to paid leaves of absence of six weeks pre-birth and twelve weeks maternity leave. If the child under one year old is severely ill, the working mother has the right to a paid leave that can be used by the child's father instead if the mother so chooses. Payments are made by ISAPRES and funded by the state. Working mothers also have the right to nursery child care services for their children under two years of age, provided or paid for by the employer.

Labor laws

Contractual relations between employers and employees are ruled by a set of legal prescriptions contained in the Labor Code (*Diario Oficial*, 1997, 2003) that provide the relevant legal frame to the HR management. This code establishes two types of contracts based on duration that can be fixed or have an unspecified ending. The former can not exceed one year; if longer, it becomes permanent. The latter involves the right to severance payments in case of termination.

Legal norms contain special prescriptions related to foreign personnel contracts. They cannot exceed 15 percent of the total labor force working for the same employer, except specialized technical personnel, when they can not be replaced by Chileans. Foreigners that work in the country require a resident visa; their work contract cannot exceed a renewable two-year term. The foreign worker's contract requires the employer to pay for home transfer expenses. It is not mandatory for the employer to deduct the social security payments of a foreign employee if s/he is protected in another country. It is only mandatory to pay for work accidents and professional disease premiums. The salaries can be paid in foreign currency.

The labor law allows for four types of unions depending on the nature of the contractual relation that workers have with their employers: firm-level; inter-firm; independent-workers; and temporary-workers. Unions can also associate through higher-level organizations such as federations, confederations, and national central unions. The firm-level union is the most frequent form; it also has the greatest number of members.

Through collective bargaining, direct agreement between employers and workers can be reached in order to establish wage or salary, benefits, and working conditions. Unions are not the sole entities with the right to represent workers for these purposes, since the law also allows the organization of any specific group of workers to collectively negotiate. Evidence shows that this arrangement is used preferably by non-union workers, generally of higher hierarchical level in firms, and that the unions are preferred by workers of lower rank and qualifications.

Unemployment insurance

Starting in October 2002, new unemployment insurance for workers hired since that date is in place. Workers hired prior to October 2002 can voluntarily join in agreement with their employer. The premium is a percentage of the monthly wage or salary, deductible from severance payments, 0.6 percent paid by the worker and 1.6 percent paid by the employer. It pays the unemployed a decreasing monthly allowance up to 5 months, which is calculated from the worker's total savings in a personal account. These are administered by a private consortium of the AFPs. This insurance has been designed to reduce incentives to remain unemployed. Since its inception, over 1.7 million workers have joined this scheme (*Ministerio del Trabajo*, 2004; *El Mercurio*, 2003).

Personnel training and development

Training expenses are tax deductible up to a certain amount. Firms can spend up to 1 percent of their payroll. At the firm level, a joint training committee can be established representing both unionized and non-unionized workers. It approves a yearly training plan that has an additional 20 percent tax break. Training hours are considered work hours.

Evidence shows that training activities are insufficient; on average, a worker is trained once every six years for only 33 hours. During 2002, about 16 percent of the workforce, or 850,000 workers, were trained, and only 28 percent of the firms used the tax exemption (SENCE, 2004).

The costs of change

All these changes in the economic and social outlook of Chile have brought higher standards of living to the population. Chilean workers and firms have had to pay for this improvement. In our view, the workers' main cost is the extensive work schedule, characterized by long working hours and low productivity returns.

Paternalism required loyalty, not efficiency, and modern labor relationships are based on a depersonalized contract demanding efficiency. The transition between these two types of relationships has not been achieved culturally; workers lack a behavioral repertoire to draw conducts from and thus experience permanent uncertainty. New working conditions demand high productivity and competitiveness. Most workers ignore the required behaviors to perform appropriately, so they stay in the workplace for longer hours, unable to achieve the desired increase in productivity. Not fully understanding what is expected from them, the net result is a state of psychological distress. Leadership styles have not adapted concomitantly. From the workers' point of view, leadership is ambiguous. Leaders do not deliver clear straightforward instructions or communicate explicit expectations. This ambiguity acts as a protective mechanism to place responsibility or blame on others of lesser social status. Workers, even the younger generations, still have a high valuation for their bosses' "manners" (*trato*), such as fairness, decency, and caring behavior, in a paternal manner or a more egalitarian mode. The fact that only foreign-owned or operated firms rank in the 15 highest positions of the Great Place to Work Institute (2003) shows that these transitions are hindered by deep cultural and social roots.

Structural unemployment appears as an added cost that has to be dealt with today. Chile's economic history has not been exempt of dramatic moments of widespread unemployment; the nitrate crisis of the early twentieth century is one example. Structural unemployment, in a modern sense, was largely unknown to those who had been able to obtain a job. Today, no firm can guarantee life-long employment, clearly designed career paths within the organization, or salary/wage increases according to seniority. Job instability is a fact, further breaking the allegiance of membership and sense of belonging. The labor relationships lack the bonding capacity that membership and belonging provided for their effort. Loyalty cannot be used today to motivate workers in a credible way. Given this uncertainty, the workers' insurance against unemployment depends on the enhancement of their "employability" skills. Therefore, the expectations placed upon training and the demand for training opportunities are increasing. However, the quality of the regular educational system and many training programs is not sufficient to satisfy these expectations. For many employers, the provision of training opportunities is avoided due to the fear of losing newly trained workers to their competitors.

Challenges for the near future

Chilean society has arrived at a widely accepted consensus about its development strategy: it needs to insert itself in the global economy with the appropriate abilities to maintain its competitive edge. This decision implies that it will likely follow a development path that does not include an industrialization effort to offer complex products in international markets. Even though a substantial part of the entrepreneurial and political elite is looking to find high technology niches, it will most likely remain in back office operations for service industries.

It will continue to develop efficient and competitive food-producing and mining industries, but developments will most likely occur in the service industry due to the competitive advantages that Chile offers in this area. Chile's institutional setting assures property rights and contract enforcement, an educated labor force, ample access to support services, telecommunication development, and a safe urban environment.

According to this development strategy, the country has signed several trade agreements. The unilateral opening of the economy, via tariff reductions, will probably continue in order to correct unwanted trade deviations. At the present time, Chile ranks fifth worldwide in terms of economic openness. Even though trade agreements imply enhanced competition, local firms are already adapted to such an environment, so the new agreements do not pose a serious threat to them. Their challenge consists in changing their scope from a market of 15 million to one of nearly 1.5 billion customers. The change implies a scale of magnitude and quality.

Challenges include performing under higher standards of environmental protection, property rights conditions, and labor matters. Issues exist such as child employment, forced labor, labor satisfaction, work schedule flexibility, and additional training and development.

The challenges to HRM functions are varied. As a whole, HRM has been put under management scrutiny and is considered a strong candidate to have its operations outsourced. Higher labor standards will have to be introduced and enacted, even if management is not fully convinced of their necessity given the local socio-cultural characteristics.

It will have to replace the solid belief foundations of a management style based on permanent life-long labor relationships in a rather stable arrangement that required offers of maintenance services and benefits that adjusted to the life cycle of the workers. Employability, training opportunities, and organizational design appear to be the new focus of justification for management and legitimacy for the workers.

Training activities need to be more focused on productivity and quality so firms' outputs can remain competitive in the global arena. Actions have been taken to establish new accreditation and certification institutions to help pursue this goal.

Another major issue deals with expanding labor flexibility to allow for part-time employment. It involves alleviating severance payments for dismissal, flexible work time, and the corresponding pay and compensation schemes. These need be designed on the basis of a number of hours annually that can be performed during peak demand periods and laid in a latent state during other less labor-consuming months.

Training based on e-learning technologies requires, as a prerequisite, digital alphabetization of workers and the development of capacities by providers so it becomes a meaningful way for workers to develop. Even more so, the use of "blend learning" will require further developments of coordination abilities within the work environment. Internal communications based on intranets and e-mail are modifying leadership and communication styles, demanding the development of higher-level skills. Among these, knowledge management-related skills need to be deployed, including HRM practices related to the attraction and retention of the most critically valued workers. The HR units must enhance their view of the workers as internal clients.

With increased labor market segmentation, economic organizations will be more accountable for the externalities they contribute to create. In particular, we can observe the rapid installation of the issue of social responsibility in many of the leading corporations. Under the current labor law, outsourcing of many routine operations makes corporations accountable for the working conditions of the labor force that is externalized. Although legal liability exists in the form of payment of health insurance and pension funds by the hiring company for the corporations, the effects of outsourcing and the working conditions of the provider's workers will be increasingly at the center of the discussion about corporate accountability. Among these externalities, issues about new health hazards in the work place are significant. Mental health, drug addiction, stress, and AIDS are becoming topics in HRM as more firms need to install programs for both the prevention and the treatment of these items.

An additional challenge for HRM relates to the need to overcome distrust to ensure collaborative and cooperative outcomes from the labor relationships leveraged in the adequate internal layout of firms and organizations. In Chile, workers have been able to adapt to the new organizational and working conditions. Their counterparts, the employers, have not yet been able to overcome some of the relational problems that spring from their views and experience of the history of labor relations. As mentioned earlier, The Great Place to Work Institute (2003) findings consistently reported for the last three years that, in Chile, the top 15 selected companies were foreign firms. These studies focus on the perception of trust between workers and employers. This clearly indicates that Chilean corporations are lagging behind in their efforts to overcome mistrust.

As the trust prerequisite has to be accomplished beforehand, it can easily be understood why HRM in Chile will not only have to deal with new challenges emerging from the openness of its economy, but also with those still stemming from the turmoil of its labor history.

Notes

1. "Formal" meaning that it is registered as active in the internal revenue service.
2. Engineers in Chile enjoy very high social esteem due to their historical role as a corporate group that promoted industrialization in the early twentieth century. Undergraduate business administration programs lead to a "commercial engineer" professional degree. The training of engineers in civil, industrial, and other technical areas puts strong emphasis on management skills.
3. In 1990, the national formal educational level average was 8.6 years; in 2000, it rose to 9.8 years (CASEN, 2000).
4. The Chilean economy is one of the five economies most open to international competition and its internal market is considered one of the most competitive in the world. In the retail industry, large international actors such as Sears, J.C. Penney, Home Depot, and Carrefour were not able to maintain their businesses in Chile due to local competition. Given the small size of the country (15 million inhabitants), large firms efficiently foster concentration, which in turn requires a more active regulatory framework from the state. On this last issue, see Jeter (2004).

References

CASEN (2000) *Encuesta CASEN* [National survey of socioeconomic characteristics], Chile: Ministerio de Planificación

Cousiño, C. (1990) *Razón y ofrenda* [Reason and offering], Santiago, Chile: Cuadernos del Instituto de Sociología de la Pontificia Universidad Católica de Chile.

Cousiño, C. and Valenzuela, E. (1994) *Politización y monetarización en América Latina* [Politization and monetarization in Latin America], Santiago, Chile: Cuadernos del Instituto de Sociología de la Pontificia Universidad Católica de Chile.

Diario Oficial [Official Government Bulletin] (1997), 14 October.

—— (2003), 11 January.

Dirección del Trabajo (2002): http://www.dt.gob.cl

—— (2003) *Estadísticas del entorno socioeconómico y laboral de la región metropolitana* [Statistics about labor and socioeconomic conditions in the metropolitan region] (May), Santiago: Departamento de Estudios.

El Mercurio (2003) "Entrenamiento laboral en Chile" [Work training in Chile] (18 September), from: http://www.elmercurio.com

Fondo Nacional de Salud (FONASA) (2004): http://www.fonasa.cl

Great Place to Work Institute (2003) *Annual Report*, Santiago, Chile.

Jeter, J. (2004) "A smoother road to free markets: Chile's success makes the case for state involvement in economy," *Washington Post Foreign Service* (21 January): E01.

Koljatic, M. and Rosene, F. (1993) *La administración de recursos humanos en Chile: Prácticas y percepciones* [Human resource management in Chile: Practices and perceptions], Chile: Facultad de Ciencias Económicas y Administrativas de la Pontificia Universidad Católica de Chile/Agencia para el Desarrollo Internacional USAID en Administración de Recursos Humanos y Economía Laboral.

Luhmann, N. (1979) *Trust and power*, New York: John Wiley and Sons.

—— (1997) *Die gesellschaft der gesellschaft* [The society of society], Opladen: Westdeutscher Verlag.

Majluf, N., Abarca, N., and Rodríguez, D. (1999) "Country learning: The changes in Chilean management," in H. Siegwart and J.W. Mahari (eds) *Corporate development*, Köln: Wirtschaftsverlag Bachem, pp. 217–236.

Martínez, P.G. (2005) "Paternalism as a positive form of leadership in the Latin American context: Leader benevolence, decision-making control and human resource management practices," in M.M. Elvira and A. Davila (eds) *Managing human resources in Latin America*, London: Routledge, pp. 75–93.

Medina, J. (1971) "De la hacienda a la empresa" [From the hacienda to the firm], in H. Godoy (ed.) *Estructura social de Chile* [Chilean social structure], Santiago, Chile: Editorial Universitaria, pp. 102–10.

Ministerio del Trabajo (2004): http://www.mintrab.gob.cl

Montero, C. (1997) *La revolución empresarial chilena* [The Chilean entrepreneurial revolution], Santiago, Chile: Dolmen.

Morandé, P. (1987) *Cultura y modernización en América Latina* [Culture and modernization in Latin America], Madrid: Ediciones Encuentro.

Pfeffer, J. (1997) *New directions for organization theory*, Oxford: Oxford University Press.

Raczynski, D. (1994) *Social policies in Chile: Origin, transformations and perspectives*, Michigan: Kellogg Institute.

Rodríguez, D. (2002) *Gestión organizacional* [Organizational management], Chile: Ediciones Universidad Católica de Chile.

Rodríguez, D., Cereceda, L.E., and Wormald, G. (1997) "Del estado modernizador a la modernización del estado" [From the modernizing state to the modernization of the state], *Estudios Sociales* 94 (4): 55–73.

Servicio Nacional de Capacitación y Empleo (SENCE) (2004): http://www.sence.cl

Superintendencia de ISAPRES (Sp. ISAPRES) (2004): http://www.sisp.cl

Undurraga, E. (2003) "Es mejor prevenir que curar" [It is better to prevent than to cure], *Revista Capital* 112 (July): 110–111.

Wormald, G., Cereceda, L.E., and Ugarte, P. (2002) "Estructura de oportunidades y vulnerabilidad social: Los grupos pobres de la región metropolitana de Santiago de Chile en los años noventa" [Opportunity structure and social vulnerability: Poverty groups in the metropolitan region in Santiago, Chile in the nineties], in R. Kaztman and G. Wormald (eds) *Trabajo y ciudadanía* [Work and citizenship], Montevideo: Cebra, pp. 133–238.

Archives

Asociación Chilena de Seguridad (ACHS): http://www.achs.cl

Índice Gubernamental: http://www.gov.cl

Instituto Nacional de Estadísticas (INE): http://ine.cl http://www.ine.cl/03-empleo/rama/TPrama.htm

Instituto Nacional de Estadísticas (INE) (2003) *Censo nacional de población y vivienda 2002* [National Population and Housing Census], Chile.

Ministerio de Educación: http://www.mineduc.gob.cl

Ministerio de salud: http://www.minsal.cl

Mutual de Seguridad del la Cámara Chilena de la Construcción: http://www.mutualseg.cl

Servicio de Cooperación Técnica (SERCOTEC) (2003): http://www.sercotec.cl

Superintendencia de Administradoras de Fondos de Pensiones (Sp. AFPs) (2004): http://www.safp.cl

9 Human resource management in Colombia

ENRIQUE OGLIASTRI, JAIME RUIZ AND IVAN MARTÍNEZ

Human resource management (HRM) as practiced in Colombian businesses is quite diverse. This diversity is the result of the marked differences which coexist between different types of companies at this unique juncture, represented by the beginning of the twenty-first century and the dramatic changes originating from international business centers. This review provides a focus on context as well as a historical perspective. It refers to companies which operate in Colombia, nationally owned or not, and the differences in HRM between various companies. First, a review of the Colombian environment and the evolution of HRM will be presented. Then the presence of a strategic perspective will be analyzed. Finally, the current state of selection, contracting, the labor market, compensation, training, development, negotiation, and company labor relations trends will be evaluated.

The environment of human resource management in Colombia

In 2004, Colombia was the third largest country in Latin America after Brazil and Mexico. The country's population stood at 45 million with a growth of 1.3 percent from the year before, and 33 percent of the population were below the age of 14. Life expectancy was 71.8 years and the literacy rate was 92 percent. The GDP per capita stood at US$1,915, which represented 5 percent of that of the United States. According to the United Nations, Colombia is considered a "medium human development" country with a 0.779 value on the UN's Human Development Index (HDI) (UNDP, 2003).[1]

In 2002, the economically active population in Colombia consisted of 20,100,000 people, of whom approximately 17,108,000 were employed. Employment was distributed according to branches of economic activity: 57 percent in the service sector; 22 percent in agriculture; and 18 percent in industry. Divided by gender, 59 percent of jobs were held by men and 41 percent by women (DANE, 2003).

The union movement was legalized in 1935 with the creation of the Confederación Sindical de Trabajadores (Union Workers Association). By 2004, unionism had suffered notably, representing just 5 percent of the working population. In its most recent census, the Labor Ministry identified 970 company unions, 1,091 trade unions, and 177 industry unions, making up 98 percent of unionized workers (Molina, 2004).[2]

Although Colombia has had a continuous democratic political system, it is a country with great social inequalities and an exclusively centralized power structure (Ogliastri and Dávila, 1983, 2004 [1987]). In terms of values, the GLOBE study found high degrees of collectivism oriented to family and small primary groups, low uncertainty avoidance, and rejection of prevalent elitism (Ogliastri et al., 1999; Ogliastri, 2004).

In order to develop a coordinated global picture of the system in Colombia (Peres, 1998), it is necessary to first explain management differences according to company size. In 2001, 9 percent of all firms represented large companies with 57 percent of employment; 22 percent represented medium companies with 27 percent of employment; 47 percent represented small with 14 percent of employment; and 22 percent represented micro-companies with 2 percent of employment (Arbeláez et al., 2003).[3]

Unemployment decreased from 20.3 percent at the end of 1999 to nearly 13 percent in 2003 (DANE, 2004). Observing the evolution of employment between 1992 and 2001 suggests that the medium, small, and micro-companies maintained a constant volume of employment while the large companies experienced job losses (Arbeláez et al., 2003).

Approximately 65 percent of production processes in large companies were semi-automated and about 10 percent were manual (Arbeláez et al., 2003). Barely a fourth of these companies used automated or computerized production processes. The automation level was even lower in small and medium-sized businesses, showing little of the innovation that would allow these companies to participate in processes of market liberalization and competition.

The evolution of human resource management in Colombia

Colombia has not been untouched by international business theories, movements, and trends. During the first half of the twentieth century, the function called personnel administration was performed by people with backgrounds in industry, a military career, or former practice as a labor lawyer. Between 1950 and 1960, when the theories of Taylor and Fayol were established and implemented in the most advanced companies, the field started to call itself industrial relations. IR began to receive important contributions from the field of psychology. Organizational development was widely accepted between 1965 and 1975 in private companies and official entities (Infante *et al.*, 1977; Ogliastri, 1980). During this period, internal processes such as factor-based performance evaluation, application of psychological tests for employee selection, job evaluation, and internal process consulting became popular. The field became known as human resources and was consolidated with the combination of psychology and industrial engineering. Beginning in 1980, quality orientation, expressed by the formation of primary groups, quality or participation circles, and the formation of internal quality auditors, took priority (Ogliastri, 1987).

In the 1990s, the management of human talent became related to business objectives and organizational strategies. At the beginning of the new century, there was a focus on competencies, balanced scorecard application, downsizing, outsourcing, coaching, organizational learning, emotional intelligence, leadership, and outdoor training, to name but a few. These topics reflect companies' internal evolution as well as the international context of new administrative technologies and trends.

López (1998) notes: "Proposed American theories have been accepted and implemented in Colombia during those periods in which they were in full force in America. ... The proposals that we can now call 'contemporary management' are disseminated simultaneously in both countries." Despite this flow of information, key topics related to human resource management such as anti-discriminatory actions, "organizational justice," and "corporate citizenship" had not made it to Colombia.

One study of 394 Colombian companies showed the most common nomenclature in the field in the year 2000: "human resource management", 36 percent; "human behavior management", 13 percent; "personnel", 12 percent; "human talent", 6 percent; "industrial relations", 6 percent; and "human development", 4 percent (SENA, 2000a).

Relationship between the human resources function and strategy

How strategic was the role of human resources in Colombian companies? Despite frequent talk about strategy, results were not quite evident. True integration might be achieved if human resource policies were explicitly drawn up, written, and documented, and specifically associated with business results and organizational practices, instead of responding to some "best practices" coming from generic overseas trends.

The point of departure for all of a company's functional areas could ideally be an organizational strategy founded on a vision, mission, and values upon which policies would originate. Due to the high level of environmental uncertainty, Colombian companies could hardly function under strategic parameters to guide their actions and results.

Small, medium-sized, and family-owned companies, due to greater uncertainty and volatility in the face of socioeconomic ups and downs, were more oriented toward a non-explicit vision of their businesses. The area of human resource management, even in the multinationals, operated in a state of emergency with changes in direction and unpredictable alterations that caused the performance of their functions not to be very "strategic".

AON Consulting (2002) found that the most sought-after skills of those individuals responsible for HRM were: organizational leadership (29 percent); strategic planning (23 percent); and knowledge of the business (17 percent). Of the companies analyzed, 57 percent had their HR function totally centralized, and only 3 percent had the function totally decentralized. It was also reported that in 42 percent of the companies, HRM was at the second-highest level of the organization and in 46 percent it was at the third-highest level. AON found trends toward the outsourcing of HRM, including the use of headhunting and temporary employment agencies. At the same time, the practice of maintaining strategic aspects inside the organization and contracting the rest grew.

One study conducted by SENA (2000a) indicated that "54 percent of HR personnel's time is dedicated to operational tasks, 24 percent to strategic direction, and 22 percent to consulting tasks."[4] The cited AON study also reported that 23 percent of those interviewed were involved in strategic business planning, 43 percent indicated that they worked on human resources strategic planning, and 23 percent "considered doing it". AON concluded that current business leaders' perspective of HRM was significantly more favorable than before.

Nevertheless, fewer HR managers are positioned at the second hierarchical level and HRM policies increasingly involve other executives. One study undertaken by Human Capital (*Dinero*, 2003) reported that 75 percent of the companies contacted considered HRM to be strategic while the other 25 percent considered it to be "a service function". The data may have suffered from ambiguities in language and validity, but they indicate that the topic of strategy and its implications was on the minds of business executives.

There is a tendency to question whether the salary and training budget assigned to HRM adds value to the production process; HRM should demonstrate to the presidency that it represents an investment, not a cost. The scarcity of indicators and control systems to appropriately evaluate results and allow strategic decision making is a hindrance.

Despite the lack of adequate instruments for evaluating management impact, large companies did rely on clear policies that oriented the HRM decision-making process. In the small and medium-sized businesses, there was a greater degree of informality, a greater capacity to respond to emergencies, and fewer strategic criteria in the management of human resources (Cámara de Comercio de Bogotá, 1999).

In synthesis, there were many differences in human resource management between the small or medium-sized businesses and the large companies. The HRM specialist, more than a member of the strategic team, was considered a facilitator of change processes, recruiting, hiring, contracting, firing, labor negotiation, compensation, training, and performance evaluation.

Labor market, recruiting, and hiring processes

Between 1997 and 2003, the Colombian economy managed to maintain single-digit inflation figures while the official unemployment figures ranged between 21 percent and 11 percent, reaching approximately 14 percent in 2003. Various elements contributed to these figures, such as the fall in demand for goods and services, the decrease in GDP growth, a drop in exports, and an increase in imports. The five years leading up to 2004 constituted a crisis. Some multinational companies had removed their plants from the country and many manufacturers had either closed down plants or decreased plant personnel.

Government administrations streamlined government entities with the goal of eliminating 30,000 jobs and diminishing the fiscal deficit. This process began in 2002; in the first year, 10,000 government workers left their jobs. In 1999, SENA (2000b) predicted that there would be a reduction of approximately 15,000 jobs in banking and financial institutions during the next decade. This prediction was proven correct five years later.

The armed conflict in Colombia generated forced migration from the countryside, straining the economic and social systems of the larger cities and pushing unemployment from 11 percent to 21 percent. The large number of job seekers did not necessarily meet employer requirements. For example, hotel managers declared that their greatest problem was finding trained personnel with a customer service orientation for the tourist sector.

This situation produced various responses. In regions surrounding industrial cities, such as the towns outside of Cali and Bogotá, work-training programs were established in conjunction with elementary and secondary schools. These programs aimed to improve students' training levels to respond to industry and business requirements and ease the challenges of recruiting and hiring.

The highest levels of turnover were found in the sales area of consumer goods companies. In general, these companies preferred candidates who were referred by their own employees to those identified through other recruiting sources such as universities or headhunting firms. As in all of the cases that have been mentioned, the topic of career planning was an important part of the strategic discourse, even though it was not concretely reflected in practice on the job.

In one study by PricewaterhouseCoopers (2001) conducted in South America, the 19 participating Colombian companies responded that the most attractive factors for potential employees were the company's image, career growth opportunities, and compensation.

The Colombian economy was going through one of its worst crises. The job market situation did not make the selection processes any easier, as they were neither systematized nor oriented by clear policies, except in large companies and multinationals. The high level of unemployment did not ease the process of selecting qualified candidates for suitable positions, which aggravated the socioeconomic situation for the displaced population.

Contracts and flexibility in labor relations

The 1992 labor reform in Colombia was oriented toward greater flexibility and transparency in labor relations, and expected to increase overall levels of employment. The most important changes were: (a) more flexible payments to workers; (b) severance payments of one month's salary per year worked, paid annually to a special fund in each worker's name and no longer retroactive; and (c) private administrative funds for pension and severance payments were created.

In 2003, some aspects of the 1992 labor reform were regulated and changed, which increased the flexibility in contracted working hours and decreased the length of the workday, which had been considered a generator of overtime hours. Temporary employment, apprenticeship contracts as regulated by SENA, and the function of family compensation institutions, entities that channel company contributions in order to provide income stability for their employees, were more clearly defined. The motivation for the 2003 reform was to stimulate job creation according to the administration and Congress.

The contractual structure of the large companies in the country was significantly modified. In 1992, 80 percent of the personnel were permanent and 20 percent were temporary; by the end of 2001, around 60 percent of the jobs were permanent and approximately 40 percent were temporary (Arbeláez et al., 2003). This trend could be observed in small and medium businesses as well.

Flexibility was oriented toward reducing costs in a competitive and global economy. Turnover, measured by the variations in average seniority, indicated a much higher mobility in the private sector than in the public; differences in average seniority ranged between 5 and 12 years (Rey, 2003). In the private sector and multinationals, there was greater flexibility; in the public sector, one could practically be ensured lifetime employment (Jiménez, 2003).

A growing phenomenon related to work flexibility is the associated work organizations (OTAs), cooperative groups organized by laid-off employees with the support of their previous employers. In this structure, companies subcontract workers' services, and in doing so change the nature of the relationship with the workers such that it is regulated by commercial code instead of labor laws. These cooperatives contribute to a decrease in businesses' labor costs without diminishing workers' income, but at the cost of taxes and other regulations.

In summary, tendencies toward more outsourcing and employment flexibility, processes which are controversial for workers and HRM, were found. Businesses emerged from groups of employees who had left other companies and became providers of services to their previous employers in less costly relationships than those established by the labor law. Although some companies had established strategic criteria in order to maintain or subcontract some workers or functions, the majority of companies did not have explicit, consistent guidelines to make such decisions. The HRM function accompanied these processes, but did not provide leadership in planning the changes in the size of these companies' workforces.

Compensation or remuneration

Regarding compensation, diversity in the business structure was also evident. In small and medium-sized businesses, remuneration was found to be personalized to a great degree, especially in the medium and high organizational levels of the companies. At the worker level, remuneration is set according to the legal minimum salary, which is subject to annual negotiation between the government and the labor unions. Additionally, salary increases are negotiated in each company as corresponds to the Colombian labor and union system, and normally begin based on the legal and extralegal benefits agreed upon in the past.

After the Colombian economic crisis that started in 1997, businesses began to modify their compensation structures. They went from fixed compensation plans to payment structures based on results and performance, not simply seniority. The performance evaluation process had had many problems and was found to be discredited by the field of HRM; they believed that it "was only used to determine salary increases and was a formal and tedious process that had no impact on work productivity".

Variable compensation, compensation according to sales volume, had been applied for a long time in sales areas and at executive levels according to results and achievement of corporate goals. According to Human Capital, the consulting firm, fixed compensation was offered in 40 percent of cases, flexible compensation in 35 percent, and variable compensation in 25 percent (*Dinero*, 2003). The practice of flexible payments by utilizing benefits in kind, such as meal tickets, education, recreation, and generic drug subsidies, expanded, causing salaries, associated taxes, and supplementary payments to seem lower.

Compensation in Colombian companies presents a fairly complex panorama with notorious inequities and disparities (Ruiz, 2002). It is common to find differences of 50 to 100 times between the maximum and minimum salaries in the same organization.

There is also clear gender discrimination in terms of salary and hierarchical levels. More men participate in higher positions in organizations; women are positioned in support roles. These imbalances have increased, more frequently entrenched in the private sector than in the public. These indicators reveal paternalistic cultural behavior with an absence of rational strategies for managing human talent compensation.

In summary, employee compensation was tied to the national system that fixed the minimum salary each year and to the internal negotiation processes of each individual company. The crisis inspired variable forms of payment, including payment in kind, which had no tax implications and went directly to addressing families' basic economic needs. Significant salary differences and inequities related to gender were detected according to hierarchical levels and company size.

Employee training and development

By 2004, the role of employee training and development did not seem to have achieved a level of strategic development in Colombian companies. Even though employee training was part of the survival strategy and corporate competition during moments of crisis, it still had not been oriented toward intellectual capital or explicit knowledge management in the majority of companies. A diversity of approaches and an inconsistency between words and actions predominated.

Training and development concentrated on two approaches: quality and competency management. In nearly all economic sectors, the quality approach came from the implementation of the ISO 9000 certification as one of the requirements for contracting services or providing goods; it was one of the most important forms of company recognition. Competency management had received wide acceptance as a process for organizing HRM in the medium term.

Preparation for change, formal succession planning, individual development, and training in basic skills were the main objectives of training programs. There was a tendency toward active training methods instead of formal seminars.

Approximately 72 percent of training was conducted at the workplace. Options for specialized institutes with new technologies and methodologies were scarce (Arbeláez et al., 2003). Although on-the-job training is not necessarily a bad thing, as in the case of competency management, this easy response also covered those companies which did not have specific training programs.

One study conducted by the Corporación Industrial Las Granjas covered a sample of 90 companies of different sizes from various industrial sectors out of 237 operating in the industrial area of Bogotá. The study concluded that only 39 percent of those surveyed had any formal training policy. This was more frequent in the service sector than the manufacturing sector and in companies with over 100 employees (Lucero and Spinel, 2002).

It was also found that service companies and medium-sized companies defined training without consulting either line supervisors or their employees. Reactive training, spontaneously organized without elaborating a budget or a plan, was more common in manufacturing than in service companies. Overall, only 30 percent of the companies had a previous budget and some sort of structure for training; the majority were in the service sector with businesses in existence for at least 20 years with over 100 employees (Lucero and Spinel, 2002).

In large companies, the employees or their managers were often the ones to request training from HRM. They openly proposed courses via internal e-mail. In some companies, the training was conducted by the employees themselves. Training needs were determined mainly by surveys, performance evaluations, 360-degree evaluations, the results of strategic projects, and employee competency development plans. As time went on, the event and the presenter were evaluated less than the impact of the training on organizational processes, business objectives, growth, and projects.

Trends in labor relations and negotiations

In 2004, the labor relations focus in Colombia was less present in annual negotiations. Labor relations involved strategic problems and implied drastic organizational decisions more frequently. Traditional unionism dwindled and the fundamental interests of the workers required longer-term thinking for the stability of the company. In addition, labor negotiations changed radically during the 1990s.

In the past, labor negotiations were a well-understood and simple process. One side asked for the moon and the stars and the other offered breadcrumbs. They showed no interest, offered direct or veiled threats, presented exclusively unilateral advantages, tirelessly negotiated points one by one, exaggerated or distorted arguments, and worked until the early hours of the following day. It was a field for tough negotiators who knew how to manage emotions, mutual aggressions, and extreme bargaining tactics. Some companies, such as Ecopetrol, the largest in the country, continue to use these methods.

Even though these procedures still existed in 2004, the majority of the labor negotiators had taken to the new theory of negotiation, at least in theory if not in practice. From a competitive perspective of the world in which everyone fought to survive against others and assumed that for some to win, others must lose, there had emerged hope that collaboration could become a means to obtain mutual benefits. A completely distributive labor relations perspective, which asks "How much do you take and how much do I receive of the net sum?" has evolved to mean processes for the creation of mutual value, benefits for all parties, and collaboration instead of war. Labor relations are no longer controlled by intimidation tactics, but rather from a base of mutual respect for colleagues who do different jobs. Modern leaders no longer believe that labor relations are defined annually or during intense negotiations, but rather understand that managing relationships must take place during the day-to-day work within the organization. The organizational environment, in and of itself, has become more important than either the legal or political arena, both of which are often external to the business itself.

In the past, negotiation points were resolved one by one. Within the last decade, negotiators have grown accustomed to working on a block of issues, interchanging concessions in order to achieve greater benefits at lower costs, seeking "value". From a process of pure haggling, labor negotiations have evolved into the application of standards or objective criteria to resolve increases, such as the consumer price index, inflation, productivity gains, inflation outlook, and a national social agreement between unions, business, and the government. Participation in the warlike exercises of labor relations is no longer equal to a punishment or military service for business executives; labor relations are understood to be an opportunity to exercise the sophisticated art of strategy during the course of the entire business year (Ogliastri, 2001).

Salary and benefits negotiations have changed in character and in their degree of importance. Other types of negotiations have been emphasized and could be fundamental in the future, such as negotiations about managing bankruptcies, closures, mergers, accelerated technological change, outsourcing, and company reorganizations.

Conclusions

The main characteristic of HRM in Colombia is the difference between large, multinational, or governmental organizations and the small, medium-sized, or family businesses. The former have rational and "bureaucratic" rules and regulations that keep pace with cutting-edge managerial innovations and technologies. In small, medium-sized, and family businesses, paternalism prevails and from the process of selection to training, there is very little long-term vision.

A marked contradiction exists between the HRM discourse and the reality of its implementation. In theory, specific terms, projects, and descriptions are announced, permeated with all sorts of up-to-date administrative technologies promoted by private consultants. In practice, there are significant limitations originating from various kinds of organizational, technological, budget, and cultural restrictions that result in partial implementations, truncated change processes, misunderstood innovations, immobility, and shifts in priorities.

There is very little research activity on HRM found in the universities, which results in teaching based occasionally on translated texts and concepts which are not pertinent to the national realities, while the executives of multinationals and consultants actually access and apply vanguard technology.

HRM maintains its position as a support area, based on a psychological perspective that sees managed human resources as a variable to be adjusted to management's strategies. In this sense, to respond to the central question posed by this work, we can say that the discourse of HRM is a strategic variable for Colombian organizations, but in reality it is found to be anchored in combined paternalistic, bureaucratic, and systemic practices.

The situation of internal conflict brought about forced displacement of rural citizens to the subhuman, precarious social conditions of cities. These workers were not absorbed into companies besieged by international competition in the process of employee reductions or into the public sector, oriented toward decreasing their scope of activity.

A clear tendency is observed in both the laws and in practice to make employment and compensation more flexible and to rationalize and organize HRM processes around the strategies of the business.

The Colombian economy is in a period of stagnation and political, economic, and social crisis that has formed a generation of executives, professionals, and workers who have confronted the most difficult emergencies and challenges with tireless ingenuity and resolve. Colombia has tremendous natural resources and a culture of work and innovation proven throughout the years, which will undoubtedly allow its people to come out ahead of the obstacles and challenges of the twenty-first century.

Notes

1. This index has a maximum value of 0.994 for Norway and a minimum of 0.275 for Sierra Leone.
2. There were notable differences in the calculations of union membership ranging between 850,000 and 1 million members.
3. Companies are classified as follows: micro – up to 19 employees; small – 20–99 employees; medium-sized – 100–200 employees; large – more than 200 employees.
4. SENA, the National Educational Service, is a governmental entity financed by company contributions and dedicated to bringing technological training to workers.

References

AON Consulting Colombia, SA (2002) *Estudio de tendencias de recursos humanos en Colombia año de 2002* [Human resource trends in Colombia, 2002], unpublished manuscript.

Arbeláez, M.A., Zuleta, L.A., and Velasco, A. (2003) *Las micro, pequeñas y medianas empresas en Colombia: Diagnóstico general y acceso a servicios financieros* [Micro, small, and medium businesses in Colombia: General diagnosis and access to financial services], Colombia: Fedesarrollo, p. 13.

Cámara de Comercio de Bogotá (1999) *Testimonios de gestión humana* [Testimonies of human management], Bogotá: Foro de Presidentes.

DANE (National Department of Statistics) (2003) *Documentos técnicos sobre mercado laboral* [Labor market technical documents], Bogotá.

—— (2004) "Balance de le evolución del mercado laboral colombiano, en el cuarto trimestre del 2003" [Balance of the evolution of the Colombian labor market in the fourth quarter of 2003], from: http://www.dane.gov.co/inf_est/empleo.htm

Dinero (2003) Gestión del talento. Las seis claves del éxito [Talent management. The six keys to success], 188 (August): 34.

Infante, A., Dávila, C., Sudarsky, J., and Ogliastri, E. (1977) *Desarrollo organizacional* [Organizational development], Bogotá: Editorial Universitaria de América.

Jiménez, B.F. (2003) *Análisis descriptivo sobre rotación de personal en una empresa mayorista de software a la luz de la demografía organizacional* [Descriptive analysis of turnover in a software wholesaler in the light of organizational demographics], unpublished master's thesis in Business Administration, Universidad de los Andes, Bogotá.

López, F. (1998) "Educación en administración y modas administrativas en Colombia" [Education in administration and administrative trends in Colombia], *Revista Universidad Eafit* (January–February): 29–59.

Lucero, P. M. and Spinel, F. (2002) *Estudio sobre la estructura y necesidades de capacitación en la corporación industrial "Las granjas" de Bogotá* [Study of the structure and necessities in the industrial corporation "Las granjas" in Bogotá], unpublished thesis in Business Administration, Universidad de los Andes, Bogotá.

Molina, O. (2004) "Alianzas y estrategias del sindicalismo colombiano: Ventajas y conveniencias" [Colombian union alliances and strategies: Advantages and agreements], *Documentos Movimientos Sociales*, from: http://www.fescol.org.co/documentos-politica.html

Ogliastri, E. (1980) "Auge y caída de los grupos vivenciales en Colombia" [The rise and fall of sensitivity training in Colombia], *Lecturas en Organizaciones*, 5 (May), Ingeniería Industrial Universidad de los Andes, Bogotá.

—— (1987) *Gerencia japonesa y círculos de participación. La experiencia de América Latina* [Japanese management and participation circles. The Latin American experience], Bogotá: Norma.

—— (2001) *¿Cómo negocian los colombianos?* [How do Colombians negotiate?], Bogotá: Cambio y Alfaomega.

—— (2004) "Colombia: The human relations side of enterprise," in R. House, F. Brodbeck, and J. Chokkar (eds) *Studies of managerial cultures in 20 countries*, London: Sage.

Ogliastri, E. and Dávila, C. (1983) "Estructura de poder y desarrollo en once ciudades intermedias de Colombia" [Power structure and development in eleven medium-sized Colombian cities], *Desarrollo y Sociedad*, 12, CEDE, Bogotá.

—— (2004 [1987]) "The articulation of power and business structures: A study of Colombia," in M. Mizruchi and M. Schwartz (eds) *Intercorporate relations. The structural analysis of business*, Cambridge: Cambridge University Press.

Ogliastri, E., McMillen, C., Altschul, C., Arias, M.E., Bustamante, C., Dávila, C., Dorfman, P., Coletta, M.F., Fimmen, C., Ickis, J., and Martínez, S. (1999) "Cultura y liderazgo organizacional en 10 países de América Latina. El estudio Globe" [Culture and organizational leadership in 10 Latin American countries. The Globe study], *Academia, Revista Latinoamericana de Administración* 22: 29–57.

Peres, W. (1998) *Grandes empresas y grupos industriales latinoamericanos* [Large companies and Latin American industrial groups], Mexico: Siglo Veintiuno Editores y CEPAL.

PricewaterhouseCoopers (2001) *Primer estudio de mejores prácticas y tendencias en la gestión de personas* [First study of best practices and trends in human resource management], unpublished manuscript, Bogotá.

Rey, C.J. (2003) *Análisis descriptivo desde la perspectiva de las variables edad, sexo y antigüedad: Estudio de tres casos* [Descriptive analysis from the perspective of age, sex and seniority variables. Study of three cases], unpublished master's thesis in Business Administration, Universidad de los Andes, Bogotá.

Ruiz, G.J. (2002) *Nóminas de personal y demografía organizacional: Tres ejemplos de análisis* [Payroll of personnel and organizational demographics: Three examples of analysis], unpublished manuscript, School of Business Administration, Universidad de los Andes, Bogotá.

SENA (National Educational Service) (2000a) *Estudio de caracterización de recursos humanos* [Study of the characterization of human resources], Bogotá.

—— (2000b) *Estudio de caracterización ocupacional del sector de servicios financieros en Colombia* [Study of the occupational characterization of the financial services sector in Colombia], Bogotá: Communications Division.

UNDP (2003) *United Nations human development report*, Madrid.

Human resource management in Mexico

L. FERNANDO ARIAS-GALICIA

I have been in touch with human resources practices for the last 50 years in Mexico, from the academic viewpoint and as a white-collar worker executive and consultant. From 1996 to 1997, I served as president of the *Asociación Mexicana de Capacitación de Personal*, equivalent to the American Society for Training and Development. Through the years, I have regretted the lack of a systematic research effort to better understand, influence, and evaluate organizational interventions in the human resource field. As a result, decisions concerning employees are usually made based on managers' personal beliefs and attitudes.

In this chapter, I have adopted an executive briefing style instead of writing a scholarly paper; references have been kept to a minimum. When writing, I kept in mind the foreign executives going to work in Mexico. Additionally, I took into consideration the need for international management students to have a general view of human resource management in Mexico. From the second section onwards, you will find an account of personal impressions and experiences rather than a collection of assertions based on research papers published in peer-reviewed journals, which are so scarce in this field. Many papers are published in management journals; however, they tend to be essays instead of research articles. Often, these papers are written in a "how to" style, paraphrasing books or papers published in the United States.

Santayana, the American philosopher, once wrote, "If people do not know history, they are doomed to repeat it." I think it will be fruitful to briefly review Mexican history, emphasizing issues about work, law, and economics. This will aid understanding of cultural traits as well as aspects of today's legislation.

History at a glance

Mexico has a long and interesting history, which dates back 15,000 years. The first recorded strike in North America took place in Mexico City. In 1582, the municipal council decided to cut the wages of the cathedral's musicians and singers; the performers decided to stop appearing for religious services. After a few days, they received their old salary and were paid for the days that they were out of work.

It seems that recent events are more important in understanding culture. This review will therefore depart from the mid-nineteenth century. In 1847, the United States declared war on Mexico; Mexico lost about 50 percent of its territory (including modern-day California, Texas, Arizona, New Mexico, and Nevada).

Mexico was invaded again by France in 1862. Maximilian of Hapsburg and his wife, Carlota, were designated Emperors of Mexico by Napoleon III and a minority of Mexican people. On 5 May 1862, the Mexican army defeated the French in Puebla, but eventually most of the country was dominated by the French. Benito Juárez, the legitimate President of Mexico, continued fighting and ultimately forced the foreign army out of the country. Maximilian and his close generals were executed.

Throughout this period, the economy suffered. Industry was rudimentary; agriculture, forestry, and cattle-raising could not develop.

Porfirio Diaz was elected and remained in power for 33 years. He brought an era of peace to Mexico. Telegraphs and railroads were introduced; industry began to flourish. However, about 90 per cent of the population was illiterate. Diaz adopted an extremely liberal policy. As was internationally customary in those days, unions were forbidden and wages were fixed by employers. Social security did not exist, children worked in mines and factories, and long working hours were the rule rather than the exception.

In the *haciendas* (large areas of land dedicated to farming) a corrupt system was customarily in place to exploit people, called *la tienda de raya*. Workers received low wages but were forced to buy food, clothing, and candles from the hacienda's store at very high prices. This same system was also used at factories throughout the country, making peasants and workers almost permanently in debt and practically slaves to their employers. When the haciendas were sold, peasants were included in the deal. If anyone attempted to escape, he was harshly punished.

Porfirio Diaz ruled the country with a strong arm. All expressions of discontent were fiercely quashed. Dissatisfaction with the regime grew; Diaz finally resigned in 1910.

Revolting took place for several years following Diaz's resignation. In 1917, Congress passed a new constitution. This was the first time laws regarding work were included in a ruling document. Article 123 included many old aspirations of laborers; the laws are still in force today and will be described later.

Many employers see these laws as paternalistic and excessively protective. The language reinforces this opinion: the term "employer" is not used; instead "*patrón*" (from the Latin "father") is utilized. For another example, a worker who is inefficient or often late cannot be dismissed. To be fired for being absent, a worker must accumulate four incidences within 30 working days. When discharging a worker for one of the motives permitted by the law, the *patrón* must deliver an explanatory letter to the employee listing the reasons for termination. If the *patrón* fails to deliver said letter, he is automatically guilty for an unjustified firing in the eyes of authorities; the *patrón* then has to pay the former employee three months of wages in addition to 20 days' worth of salary for each year the worker was employed. Without any doubt this paternalistic approach of the law has its roots in the history previously outlined and in the fact that a great number of modern workers are semi-illiterate.

In 1938, after a strike by oil workers, President Lazaro Cardenas nationalized foreign oil companies. This caused an upsurge of national pride and is still viewed as a great achievement, since foreign engineers and managers left claiming, "In a few months you will beg us to come back." This did not happen, and today PEMEX (*Petroleos Mexicanos*) is the largest company in the country.

The Partido Revolucionario Institucional (PRI) ruled the country for 70 years. Many people think this was a perfect monarchy; it was disguised as democracy and every six years there was a new president supposedly elected by the people. In practice, there was no free speech and no free election of representatives by workers. Opposition was tolerated to a limited degree in order to give the impression of democracy. As a result, people expected that the president in office or the government solved all problems, instead of taking an active role in this endeavor.

Corruption was part of the system. Union leaders were bribed with seats in the Congress or governorships of states. The PRI had absolute control over unions that were large bodies of politicians. In order not to "rock the boat" fringe benefits were introduced in the labor law, thus increasing costs for companies.

In the 1950s and 1960s, there was a strong economic upsurge. Gross national product grew at 7 percent or more for several years. This brought a renewed sense of optimism and confidence. Unfortunately, from 1970 onwards, the economy slowed down. In the last few years, there have been very complex crises in the economy.

Today

It is not difficult to grasp the impact of history on national culture. First, an overview: Mexico comprises approximately 2 million square kilometers. A wide variety of climates exist throughout the country; generally speaking, the southern part is tropical and the northern states tend to have a desert-like terrain. The central area is mild in temperature and suitable for agriculture. Oil and tourism are the main sources of foreign currency, as well as money sent by relatives working in the United States.

Mexico has signed free trade agreements with many countries. There is controversy about the benefits coming from these treaties. One thing is certain: a lack of planning and entrepreneurship has hindered the profits from these endeavors.

As of April 2004, there is a fierce controversy about foreign investment in oil and electricity. Many politicians are opposed to it on the grounds of losing national self-regulation. Many critics claim that without such investment, problems of scarcity will eventually arise and cause trouble in the future.

Now, about 97 per cent of businesses in Mexico are small, with 15 or fewer employees. Large Mexican corporations comprise a small percentage of firms. Some of them are transnational. Bimbo, a bread company, has plants in several countries in South America, Spain, and the United States. Cemex, a cement firm, is considered the third largest producer of cement material in the world, with plants in Europe, Latin America, Asia, the United States, and Canada. Corona beer is sold in many countries all over the world. These examples are exceptions rather than the rule.

Large transnational firms are present in Mexico, mainly from the United States, Japan, France, Germany, and so on. As a matter of fact, in April 2004, only one bank was still completely owned by Mexicans. In large corporations, organizational culture is a mixture of the traits described below with values, policies, and procedures from the parent company.

Large organizations in the private and public sectors are prone to adopting international practices, very often without sound reasoning and evaluation. Therefore, as many companies attempt to become certified in the ISO 9000–2002 system, "quality", "just in time", "downsizing", "quality circles", "autonomous work groups", "continuous improvement", and "outsourcing" are commonly used terms. This does not mean that all executives and employees have necessarily adopted the spirit of these practices. These fads attempt to change the prevailing culture, even without declaring this goal explicitly.

Culture

There is not a single type of Mexican culture. In general terms, people from the south tend to be very friendly and polite. Before going into business, they talk about family and current events such as politics and sports; they take some indirect ways of expressing concerns. Saving face is very important. Family topics are paramount.

By contrast, people in the north are more direct and concise in their relationships. They tend to be frank and open, avoid verbosity, and get down to business more quickly. They are reputedly industrious and hard workers; this is particularly true for people in Monterrey, the second most industrialized city in Mexico.

People in the central part share many softened characteristics of both areas.

Hofstede (1980) found four very important dimensions:

1. *Individualism–collectivism.* Mexicans prefer to work in an environment characterized by close social relationships in which group members care for and support each other. Loyalty to the group is a prevailing value. Family ties are strong.
2. *Power distance.* Mexicans follow the superior's orders because s/he is entitled to be obeyed. These views are reinforced by the existing labor law: when mentioning workers' obligations, it says, "Perform work under the Patrón's orders (or his/her representative), to whose authority the worker is subordinate in all matters referring to work." Besides, one of the reasons employers may dismiss workers without any responsibility is for disobeying orders regarding work from the employer or the employer's representatives. Mexicans view talking about one's own superior's orders to a higher executive as an act of insubordination. Titles and hierarchies are very important. In many firms, however, empowerment programs have been very successful. Self-managed work teams are becoming more and more popular in many industries, profiting from the collectivistic inclination of Mexican workers.
3. *Uncertainty avoidance.* Mexicans prefer clear rules and formalism. Therefore, bureaucracy is a very heavy burden in organizations, particularly in the public sector.
4. *Femininity–masculinity.* Masculine societies put emphasis on self-assertion and the acquisition of money and material goods. Feminine cultures value warm interpersonal relationships, quality of life, and interest in others' matters. Mexicans scored higher in the latter approach.

Of course, values are changing, particularly among young people. The above sketches should be viewed with care; they simply reflect general trends. Eva Kras (1988) described the main differences between management ideas in the United States and Mexico. Important Mexican cultural features are: family is the first priority, which means that many firms are family companies; fear of losing face is paramount; confrontation is avoided; dress and grooming are status symbols; title and position are more important than money; truth is tempered by diplomacy; leisure is considered essential for a full life; autocracy is often exercised in firms; there is basically a theoretical mindset instead of a practical one; promotions are based on loyalty to superiors; deadlines are flexible; planning is aimed at the short-term vision instead of the long-term; and competition is avoided since harmony is most valued.

Of course, culture is not a fixed entity; it is evolving constantly. Diaz-Guerrero (1995) has shown how values changed in Mexican youngsters over one decade. Also, Inglehart (1997) found a general trend towards postmodernism, deemphasizing traditional authority and allowing a wider range for individual autonomy. His research included Mexico. Perhaps all societies are moving towards a kind of global culture while maintaining some local aspects. Undoubtedly, all the cultural traits described above impact human resources practices.

Human resource planning

Most human resources executives do not have a seat at the board of directors. In fact, many of these departments are located at the second or third level in organizations. Human resource planning does not usually have a strategic role. Most of the time, employees and executives work in a hectic environment. Long-range planning is difficult in rapidly changing times.

Recruiting

Newspaper advertisements, posters on the front doors of organizations, radio clips, and television spots are all means to let potential workers know that there are openings in an organization. Referrals from other employees are not uncommon. Particularly in small firms, relatives are also good sources for recruiting.

The *Secretaría del Trabajo y Previsión Social* (Labor Ministry) has an office whose intention is to put unemployed people in contact with employers. This service, called Chambatel, can be accessed by phone. Many universities and associations, as well as some government offices, organize periodical "*Ferias del Empleo*", employment fairs where employers set up booths to offer jobs.

Selection

Although there are laws forbidding any kind of discrimination, women of certain occupations, age, disabilities graduating from public colleges and universities are frequently sources of such bias. This violation of human rights is not typically recognized, as people are not aware of such malpractices and do not sue organizations. Notwithstanding, it is not strange to see women in executive positions these days. As a matter of fact, in the last few years more and more women have entered the labor force.

Interviews are the universal way to screen candidates. Most of the time, they are unstructured and undertaken by people untrained in this technique. Only specialized HR personnel in large organizations are apt to profit from well-conducted interviews.

In many organizations, tests are customarily administered to applicants. However, these instruments are very seldom subject to a check for reliability and validity; many do not even have Mexican norms. Tests are usually copied and passed from hand to hand. In many organizations, secretaries or white-collar workers – employees without technical training – administer, score, and interpret results.

There are firms that sell computerized tests, which seems to be a technological advance. However, old tests are merely put into the machine without proper reliability, validity, or standardization.

Although trained psychologists are often in charge of the selection process in large firms, the theoretical approach in their training leads these professionals to accept any test offered in the market without rigorous questioning.

Many organizations also use assessment centers. Again, there is no published research regarding the reliability and validity of this technique in Mexico. In recent years, emphasis in competencies has been enforced. With this approach, in which observable behaviors as the end result of training are paramount, many organizations and academics are attempting to refocus the HR processes in order to use competencies as the major axis around which procedures are built.

Many competence norms have been published by the *Secretaría de Economía* (Economy Ministry). They are applied to a great many tasks, such as cleaning rooms in hotels, driving motor vehicles, and other training.

Training

There are many problematic issues in the Mexican educational system. Large percentages of the GNP have been directed towards education. According to the census in 2000, 10 percent of the population aged six and older had never been to school; only about 12 percent of the population aged 24 and older had received at least one year of higher education. Illiteracy is greater among women.

In the last few years, the government has opened technical universities in which students get can their degrees in computing, administration, and other trades after two years. The schools require an equivalent or greater number of attendance hours than traditional colleges.

Many critics say that the educational quality does not reach international standards. In international comparisons of reading comprehension, mathematics, and science, Brazilian children have scored the lowest, followed by Mexicans. This is a dramatic hindrance to technical and economic development.

According to the labor law (*Ley Federal del Trabajo*), training is mandatory for organizations and all personnel must be trained. Training is a right; according to the law, its aim is to increase quality of life and productivity. In practice, many organizations tend to deliver courses in "human relations" or similar subjects just to give the appearance of complying with legal regulations. Many companies have a pre-employment training school. They offer applicants a "scholarship" to attend and then select the best people. This is particularly true for technical personnel.

As previously stated, Mexican culture is not prone to the objective evaluation of results. It is granted that courses are beneficial and few people care about results. So, cost/benefit analysis of training is not very frequent in organizations. This is true for nearly all HR functions.

In the last few years, unemployment has increased in Mexico, as it has in many countries around the world. The government has launched a program to train unemployed people in crafts such as plumbing and carpentry; they receive a certain amount of money each month. Poor women are eligible to receive a loan to start a small business. The long-term results of these programs remain to be seen.

Safety

Workers and companies should pay fees to the social security system (*Instituto Mexicano del Seguro Social*). These fees are increased according to the degree of industry danger; a commercial firm pays much less than a foundry. Fees are also increased if a company reports large numbers of accidents.

Large companies are very careful about safety. However, many managers complain about workers' carelessness regarding safety because of "machismo"; it is not a macho thing to wear protection against accidents. It does seem that this attitude is disappearing slowly.

In small shops, keeping safe work conditions is not the rule. One can see numerous small firms that do not practice cleanliness or protection against accidents. There are special standards when producing dangerous materials, machinery, and many other products. These are published by the *Secretaría de Economía*.

Wage and salary

In Mexico, it is not customary to delineate between wages and salaries as in the United States. All types of remunerations are covered under the heading "*Salarios*" or "*Sueldos*". Therefore, in this chapter "wage" and "salary" are used interchangeably.

According to the law, all income delivered by the employer to the worker in the form of a regular wage, overtime, piece rate, or fringe benefits, should be included in the calculation of salaries. All of this is taken into account when paying fees to the social security system (*Instituto Mexicano del Seguro Social*). It is important to note that blue-collar workers, by law, receive their wages weekly.

Overtime should be paid at 100 per cent more than the regular wage, up to nine hours a week. After that, the rate is 200 per cent. If employees are asked to go to work on a Sunday, they should receive an extra 25 per cent salary at least.

By law, unions may ask for an increase in wages each year and for new work conditions every two years. Collective bargaining is customary in large organizations. Corruption is not rare; there are many "white" unions or "*sindicatos blancos*" that are created to offer companies mild bargaining conditions and are not really representative of employees. They profit from the ignorance and functional illiteracy of workers.

Fringe benefits

According to the law, workers have the right to the following:

1. Forty-eight work hours per week, which may be distributed to allow workers to rest on Saturday afternoons. In practice, many employees work 40 hours a week. It is becoming more frequent for white-collar employees to work at home since computers allow access to information or programs. By law, workers should have at least one paid day off a week.
2. A six-day paid vacation after the first year of work. Afterwards, vacations are increased by two days up to twelve for each additional year of seniority. After four years, the increase in paid vacations is two days every five years.
3. A vacation bonus: 25 per cent of wages that would be earned if working regularly.
4. Mandatory days off are: 1 January, 5 February (Constitution Day), 21 March (Juarez's anniversary), 1 May (Labor Day), 16 September (Independence War Day), 20 November (Revolution War Day), 25 December. Collective contracts in many factories include 12 December (Virgin of Guadalupe Day). There are also other days off according to local festivities. For instance, in Puebla, 5 May is the celebration of the 1862 victory of the Mexican army over the French invasion. In many companies, when there is a mandatory day off on a Tuesday or Thursday, it is customary to take another day off (called "puente" or "bridge") so workers may have a long weekend. In these cases, employees work longer hours for a week in order to compensate for the extra day off.
5. Workers are allowed to participate in the firm's earnings apportion. A percentage is fixed by a commission. Workers then receive a proportion of

earnings according to two criteria: number of days worked in the fiscal year and salary amount.

6. Women are entitled to a paid leave six weeks before childbirth and six weeks after. These may be extended up to 60 days if there is the danger of miscarriage or any dangerous situation arises. After the birth, two extra breaks of half an hour each are allowed for nursing the baby. Social security offers the benefit of public day-care centers after maternity leave ends. Currently, it is illegal to ask for a certificate of non-pregnancy when hiring women.

7. Employers should pay 5 percent of salaries including all fringe benefits and overtime to an institute (INFONAVIT) in order to provide workers with loans to buy housing or renew houses.

8. The legal age for working is 16. Youngsters between 14 and 16 may be hired provided that they have their parents' permission and work fewer hours in jobs that are not dangerous, among other provisions. In practice, however, it is not uncommon to see children working in small shops or agriculture jobs.

9. Workers should receive an annual bonus of at least 15 days of wages before 20 December. People working for less than a year are entitled to be paid a proportional bonus.

10. The social security system provides retirement wages, which depend on salary earned, age of retirement, and years worked.

Many companies offer their employees additional fringe benefits. In particular, bank employees are reputed to have a very good package of fringe benefits. The law provides special work conditions for several categories of employees: aviation pilots, sailors, musicians, actors, university professors, and sports stars, who do not usually work under a fixed scheme.

Attitudes and motivation

In general terms, people tend to be satisfied with their jobs, supervisors, and peers. A general trend is that the higher echelons are more satisfied than the rank-and-file workers.

Research in a variety of Mexico City firms found that male workers valued working in a clean and safe place the most, followed by not being dismissed if performance complied with standards. In third place, they wanted to have a considerate and fair boss. At the bottom of their preferences was having more paid days off. Female workers preferred in the first place not to be dismissed if performance complied with standards; second in their preferences was to work in a clean and safe place. Third was to have a job that allows them to be salient in the community. Working with nice and friendly peers was the last. Male white-collar workers selected in the first place to have the opportunity to put their own ideas to work; second place was having a job that allows them to be salient in the community. Third was to have a considerate and fair boss. Last was to have more paid days off. The order of preferences for female white-collar workers was first to have a considerate and fair boss, and second to have a job that allows them to be salient in the community. Third, they wanted to work in a clean and safe place. Fourth was to have more paid days off. For salespersons, the order was: to have a job that allows for salience in the community; a tie between not being dismissed if performance complies with standards and having the opportunity to put their own ideas to work; and, finally, to have more paid days off.

Recent investigations have shown that affective commitment is the result of organizational climate and organizational support. Affective commitment, in turn, leads to the intention to stay within the organization. Job satisfaction contributed greatly to affective commitment. This line of research involved employees from diverse organizations as well as medical doctors and nurses in several cities of the country.

Another set of investigations led to this generalization: stress is related negatively to job satisfaction and the relationship with happiness is also negative. The main source of stress and happiness is not the job but the family.

The importance of family led to the launch of another set of studies. Results showed that good planning had a positive impact on happiness and a negative one on family conflicts. Heavy workloads showed, as expected, positive associations with these conflicts as well as with taking work home, and a negative relationship with happiness.

In another line of research, middle managers' wives showed significant negative relationships between marital satisfaction and stress, as well as conflicts with their husbands because of little family time. On the other hand, associations were positive between marital satisfaction and family closeness, having meals together, romantic love, and the husband's educational level.

Continuing with the female theme, development seems to be an important factor that contributes to happiness, particularly in the case of women. Male and female workers were surveyed in a factory. Women showed higher levels of stress and were more dissatisfied with the job and supervisor; however, they were happier. Interviews conducted determined that the source of happiness for women was independence: they could make their own decisions about buying things.

In another set of analyses, it was not strange to find negative associations between stress and clarity of goals, clarity of standards to evaluate work, open communication with bosses, formal communication coming from the organization, planning, and integration within units in the organization. On the other hand, positive relationships were found between stress and frequent organizational changes and workloads.

Other HR issues

1. *Absenteeism.* In many firms, absenteeism increases on Mondays. In the nineteenth century, it was a well-established habit. My hypothesis is that it is related to hangovers: on Sundays a great many workers drink heavily.
2. *Turnover.* My experience suggests that workers, particularly blue-collar, leave their jobs suddenly because of affective reasons rather than cognitive ones. On the other hand, it is customary for white-collar workers to give notice of at least two weeks. This period increases to at least one month in the case of executives.

Conclusion

This broad picture of current practices coming from history and culture has many exceptions, of course, except in the legal aspect. There are a number of similarities apparent with other countries because it seems plausible that organizations are managed in similar ways around the world. Differences do arise from specific cultural traits.

It is expected that managerial practices from industrialized countries as well as the media and books used at universities and colleges have an influence in cultural change. One can guess that human resources practices will resemble those in advanced countries more closely in the future. Both human resources managers and accountants confront a paramount challenge: to show how these practices impact profits. Until then, the human factor in organizations will not receive all of the attention it deserves.

References

Diaz-Guerrero, R. (1995) *Psicología del Mexicano* [Psychology of the Mexican], Mexico: Trillas.
Hofstede, G. (1980) *Culture's consequences: International differences in work related values*, Beverly Hills, CA: Sage.
Inglehart, R. (1997) *Modernization and postmodernization. Cultural, economic, and political change in 43 societies*, Princeton, NJ: Princeton University Press.
Kras, E.S. (1988) *Management in two cultures. Bridging the gap between US and Mexican managers*, Yarmouth, ME, USA: Intercultural Press.

11 Human resource management in Peru

MARY F. SULLY DE LUQUE AND LYDIA A. ARBAIZA

Peru, known for its ancient relics and industrious culture, offers great opportunities in many aspects of the modern world. Over the centuries, Peruvian business practices have included human resource management in various forms. The formal development of human resources in business practices, however, has only become apparent within the last generation, often as multinational companies have interacted more dynamically with domestic businesses in Peru. The diversity of practices in human resources varies significantly depending on several factors, such as company, industry, and economy type (i.e. formal or informal).

In this chapter, we provide a brief overview of the pertinent background of Peru, to assist in understanding the historical, social, and economic milieux. We will discuss the concept of human resource management as it has been understood and implemented in organizations, covering such themes as labor market workforce and economy type, as well as selection, compensation, and retention. In the conclusion, we discuss implications of human resource management and suggest implications for Peru. The intent of this discussion is to underscore the evolution of, and challenges in, managing human resources in this diverse and multifaceted society.

Historical background

The initial populace of the Andes arrived in the region around 8000 BC and, through the following millennia, experienced the rise and fall of numerous complex civilizations (CountryWatch Review, 2004). In the fifteenth century, the Incan tribe of the southern Andes began an unprecedented expansion after several centuries of relatively stationary existence, eventually conquering a 380,000-square-mile area in and around what is now Peru. As various tribes and cultures were overpowered, the Incans assimilated and applied constructive customs and knowledge into their own culture to satisfy the collective needs of the expanded state. The emergence of the Incan Empire had a direct effect on the unique set of work values demonstrated by native Peruvians today. Their trade systems, routes, assimilation of other cultures' values, delivery of technology, and development of great feats of engineering and art influenced the whole continent, transmitted from generation to generation via oral and artifact history. The creation of a calculation device (*Quipus*)[1] allowed for communication and the development of complex accounting systems, large-scale planning, and irrigation systems.

Spaniard Francisco Pizarro began exploring the Incan Empire early in the sixteenth century and later overtook *Cuzco*, the Incan political capital, solidifying Spanish control of the Empire. For the next two centuries, Spanish control was largely unchallenged. The land tenure system put into practice by Spain gave the colonizers command of indigenous land and labor. This led to tremendous cultural and economic divisions between the minority elite and the indigenous people. On 28 July 1824, Peru declared independence from Spain. Toward the end of the nineteenth century, the country embarked on industrial and commercial development based on natural resources. The Lima-based oligarchy maintained control of the economic and political structure of the country during most of the nineteenth and twentieth centuries, and blocked the advancement of the entrepreneurial middle class for decades (CountryWatch Review, 2004). Throughout the twentieth century, Peru saw periodic shifts from civilian rule to military coups, the rise of social democratic movements focused on social and land reform, and often democratically elected yet authoritarian-styled presidents (Booth and Sorj, 1983; Chaplin, 1976).

Social and political influences

Linked to human resource management are the factors of social and political influence. The third largest South American country, Peru, had approximately 26.7 million people in 2002, with an estimated 37 percent under the age of 15. From 1998 to 2002, life expectancy increased from 66.1 to 67.2 years for males and from 71 to 72.3 years for females. Approximately 73 percent of the population live in urban areas. A large portion of the nation's workers are young and willing to work for relatively low wages in order to make a living and help their families. Population growth in 1997–2002 averaged 1.6 percent yearly and is expected to remain steady for the next few years.

Approximately 45 percent of the Peruvian population is indigenous; part of the population are Incan descendants. Many Peruvians, approximately 37 percent, are *mestizo*, which refers to a mix of indigenous and European descent, mainly Spanish. Peruvians of European descent comprise about 15 percent of the population; there is also a small, approximately 3 percent, population of descendants from Africa, Japan, and China. Distinct geographical regions of Peru parallel the socioeconomic rift between the *mestizo*–Hispanic culture of the more prosperous coast and the more traditional Andean cultures of the highlands and mountains. This has led to Peru's dual economies (EIU, 2003).

Primary education is free and compulsory, based on provisions in the revised constitution of 1993; 83 percent of school-aged students in Peru, at all levels, attend public school. Due to a concerted government effort, school enrollment has risen to 7.5 million in elementary and secondary schools. The literacy rate is estimated at 90.4 percent for men and 86.8 percent for women. The 74 universities in Peru, 58 percent private and 42 percent public, have a total enrollment of 415,000 students.[2]

Within South America, however, the standards for public education in Peru are amid the lowest. Within Peru, there is a huge disparity between public and private education, as well as urban and rural systems, especially for girls.

In 2001, after the corruption and authoritarianism of the previous decade, the new government of President Alejandro Toledo has revived confidence in the democratic system (*Background Notes*, 2003). Under Toledo's tutelage, the executive branch has become more accountable and transparent, and Congress has greatly improved investigative and oversight powers. Despite these advancements, the president has received low approval ratings – 10 percent for the first quarter of 2004 – although various political parties have provided some consensus for the sake of democracy (Amiel, 2004).

Economic influences

Economic influences are also important in the assessment of human resource management (HRM). In 1990, the Peruvian economy began a dramatic change from the strong protectionist policies, excessive import duties, and government control of vital economic sectors of the previous 20 years. Under the auspices of former president Fujimori, the country saw reduced inflation and the eradication of two significant guerrilla organizations (Degregori, 1990; Palmer, 1992). Since 1990, the infrastructure has significantly improved through private investment in telecommunications, power equipment, and airport facilities (EIU, 2003). Transformation was achieved through market-oriented economic reforms and privatization, which has met many requirements of long-term growth.

Following several years of economic stagnation from 1998 to 2001, the Toledo administration embarked on successful economic recovery by implementing conventional economic policies and enacting measures to attract investment (*Background Notes*, 2003). Peru has 4 percent of the population of the world, yet produces only 2 percent and exports only 1 percent of the world-wide total. The real gross domestic product (GDP) grew by 4.9 percent in 2002, 4 percent in 2003, and is estimated to grow at 4 percent in 2004 to US$2,126 per head. Although this is a moderate growth rate for an emerging economy, it is relatively robust compared to other Latin American economies (Amiel, 2004). Banking, retail services, agriculture, mining, and manufacturing are key area sectors. In 2002, Peruvian exports produced the country's first trade surplus in 11 years: US$7.65 billion in exports versus US$7.44 billion in imports. Major trading partners of Peru include the United States, the European Union, Japan, Colombia, Brazil, China, and Venezuela. Table 11.1 shows a comparison of Peru's GDP to that of other South American countries.

Since the mid-1990s, the Peruvian apparel industry has had astonishing growth in the international market compared to other Latin American countries (Cortazar, 1997). In 2003, Peru saw a marked increase in exports of non-traditional products, such as textiles, notably through a program that gives Peruvian exports duty-free entry into the US market in exchange for aggressive work to eradicate drug crops by the Peruvian government. Tourism is another area of growth. A top travel destination in South America, Peru's travel industry reported a significant increase in traffic for 2003 with strong growth anticipated for 2004 (Hunt, 2003). In 2001, the World Travel and Tourism Council projected that travel and tourism added 3.9 percent to the GDP, accounting for 747,181 jobs, or 8.6 percent of total employment (EIU, 2003). Other areas of growth were agriculture and fisheries.

Committed to monetary discipline, the Peruvian central government has continued fiscal restraint, which is imperative for controlling inflation. This sound monetary policy has resulted in stable prices. In 2003, inflation met the predicted estimates at 2.6 percent, with the core inflation index at 0.8 percent (Amiel, 2004). Consumer prices are expected to rise moderately over 2004 and 2005, at 2.4 percent and 2.1 percent respectively. The fiscal deficit has shown constraint, meeting the IMF target of 1.9 percent in 2002. Primary products, such as mining and fisheries production, provide the majority of export earnings; however, such

Table 11.1 Comparative economic indicators, 2002

	Peru	*Ecuador*	*Chile*	*Colombia*	*Brazil*
GDP (US$ billion)	56.9	20.8	63.3	81.8	440.1
GDP per capita (US$ billion)	2,127.2	1,679.4	4,208.1	1,866.4	2,500.1
GDP per capita (US$ at PPP)	5,044.3	4,109.2	10,334.1	6,431.5	7,643.6
Consumer price inflation (av; %)	0.2	12.5	2.5	6.3	8.5
Current-account balance (US$ billion)	−1.1	−1.5	−0.6	−2.0	−7.3
Current-account balance (% of GDP)	−2.0	−7.2	−0.9	−2.5	−1.7
Exports of goods fob (US$ billion)	7.7	4.9	18.3	12.0	60.9
Imports of goods fob (US$ billion)	−7.4	−6.0	−15.8	−12.1	−47.9
External debt (US$ billion)	29.1	14.4	40.0	36.0	201.3
Debt-service ratio, paid (%)	48.9	20.1	22.1	42.0	78.2

Source: Economist Intelligence Unit, Country Data.

dependence subjects the economy to the volatility of weather conditions and commodity prices (EIU, 2003).

Labor market and workforce

The state of the labor market and workforce is intricately interwoven with the state of human resource management. The economy has been modestly expanding, but economic growth is not creating jobs. From December 2001 to December 2003, employment fell from 3.59 to 3.57 million, and the unemployment rate increased from 7.9 percent to 9.7 percent (Amiel, 2004). Surveys conducted in metro-Lima in 2002 reported that unemployment averaged above 10 percent (CountryWatch Review, 2004), maintaining the labor market as the economy's main weak spot. Some estimates suggest that only one-third of the labor force are appropriately employed (Amiel, 2004).[3] In an ongoing trend, income distributions are unequal, with the poorest 20 percent of the population receiving less than 5 percent of the national income (EIU, 2003).

Since March 2000, the legal minimum wage for workers has been 410 *nuevos soles* per month. In the formal sector, most workers receive more than minimum wage, and wages for professional staff are high (CountryWatch Review, 2004). In 1993, an 8-hour maximum workday and a 48-hour maximum work week, or a 45-hour work week for women, were established. The labor code additionally stipulated 24 hours of rest per week for all workers, and 30 days paid annual vacation. However, workers willingly relinquish any such benefits to secure regular employment. From 1990 to 2002 in metro-Lima, the actual average number of hours worked increased from 48 to 52 hours per week; 52 hours to 55 for men and 42 hours to 48 for women (MTPE, 2003).

A recent survey of HR managers, 40 percent from national and 60 percent from multinational companies (DBM Peru, 2004), reported that company wages of managers would increase (47 percent) or remain stable (44 percent). Half, or 52 percent, of the multinational companies predicted wage increases, with 39 percent of national companies reporting smaller increases. The greatest wages increases will be seen in mining and energy (67 percent), finance (60 percent), and consumption (54 percent). The hiring levels show variable tendencies. Although 49 percent of the managers predict an increase in the hiring of personnel in 2004, only 38 percent – mainly in multinational companies – predict that they will not hire this year.

Historically, Peru has had a strong history of labor union movements (Collier and Collier, 1991; Parodi, 2000). Numerous major work strikes took place in the late 1980s. In the early 1990s, however, the severe economic environment made it increasingly difficult for workers to respond to demands for work stoppages (Political Risk Services, 2003). During the economic restructuring implemented by the Fujimori administration, trade unions were dealt an unyielding blow (Parodi, 2000). With increased economic austerity and political gravity, a reluctance to participate in unions grew. Labor strikes came to be considered as opportunities for others to gain work. As a result, the union movement was weakened and reduced to a very low percentage of the total workforce. Dissatisfaction with the current state of employment found May Day 2004 marked by strikes.

The growth of human resource management

The concept of managing human resources has existed throughout Peruvian history. In the Incan culture, there is evidence that societal members were given specific duties to ensure the productivity of the communities and survival of the societies; their roles changed as they matured. Management of human resources is conceptualized quite differently today. The focus has shifted from utilizing the individual to developing the individual; from employing human resources to service core competencies to framing human resources as a core competency. For Peru, the progression toward realizing the full potential of the individual as a core competency is not yet a reality, though many inroads have been made.

The first recorded labor laws in Peru were introduced in the twentieth century. These were the earliest attempts to address injustices toward workers in the society. During the mid-twentieth century, harsh treatment of employees was not uncommon, especially in industrial jobs (Parodi, 2000). In many companies, employees worked without breaks, even for meals, and were required to buy their own supplies, the price of which was often deducted from wages. The relations between the workers and the company were non-standardized and inconsistent, based on each person's individually signed contract, which was subject to renewal every few months.

Laws enacted in 1970 brought to an end many contemptible employment practices. These laws addressed the inequities in power relations and created an arena for the growth of labor unions. As unions emerged, a new relationship developed based on the premise that worker benefits were determined by collective bargaining (Parodi, 2000). The unions brought standardized job evaluation procedures as well as work and wage schedules. Workers could express dissatisfaction or take time off without the risk of losing their jobs. This basic seed of appreciation for human resource issues was crucial for the advancement of the human capital component of organizations. Labor unions negotiated with companies for worker benefits, from wages and work hours to pensions and perks (Haworth, 1989; Collier and Collier, 1991). When present, the role of HRM was to protect the employee; employee growth and development may have been consequences, but they were not intentional goals.

Turbulent economic and political circumstances in the 1980s overwhelmed the country and disrupted the management of human resources (Crabtree, 1992; Graham, 1992). During periods of extreme societal distress, many common-place practices and procedures are suspended, with organizational and societal survival becoming paramount to individual needs. Indeed, this was the case for Peru. In the late 1980s, with soaring inflation and indiscriminate terrorism, defense-mode behaviors emerged in organizations. All actions turned inward. The function of human resources took a definitive turn away from preserving the employee to protecting the organization.

The 1990s inaugurated a movement of pragmatism. With the election of Fujimori as president, Peru began to embrace the forces of a market economy (Cameron and Mauceri, 1997). Neo-liberal reform of labor laws replaced older, less labor-efficient regulations, affecting both public and private sectors. To accomplish many of his reforms, Fujimori enacted an authoritarian style of government, implementing a new constitution in 1993 that bolstered centralism and enhanced the power of the chief executive, thus reducing the power of the legislature. The business environment flourished during this period as greater interest in HRM emerged.

From the middle of 1997, the HRM model of competencies began to adapt in some organizations to address globalization, continuous change, technological development, and high competitiveness. This helped to balance organizational results and human resources potential within the organizations. Nevertheless, this concept has traditionally been associated solely with labor issues.

Influences on human resource management

Many larger companies are embracing progressive company-driven HRM practices, although small to medium-sized companies lag behind. There are aspects of HRM that are strategically important to most companies, but the placement of human resources as a core competency is atypical and underappreciated. Although labor is abundant and trainable, organizational managers frequently complain of the shortage of highly skilled workers. This statement underscores the importance of treating HRM as a strategic competence.

Diversity in the organization is modestly influencing the managing of human resources in Peru. From 1970 to 2002 in metro-Lima, the number of working women increased dramatically from 34.2 percent to 51.8 percent. The number of working-age men remained relatively constant during the same time period, shifting only from 72.4 percent to 75.3 percent (MTPE, 2003). Diversification of the workforce brings with it many human resource concerns, from three-month maternity leave and harassment issues to pay inequity and promotion bias toward males.

If the onus for representing individual interests shifted from labor unions back to the organizations, HRM concerns would seem more salient. However, many businesses have been using contract work to avoid implementing HRM systems. In some manufacturing companies, the use of contract workers has existed for over 15 years. Some organizations avoiding *"grupos sindicales"* or unions prefer to employ companies that offer them the service of managing the workers. Contract employment exists in every business sector in Peru. Companies hire service providers who take care of salaries, compensation, holidays, and training. Rather than management positions, contract employment is mainly related to labor positions, such as seasonal, labor, or administrative positions where service providers offer qualified personnel on an "as needed" basis.

Organization size

Peru does not have many large organizations compared to other countries in the world. In 2002, metro-Lima listed 13 percent of its companies as medium to large with over 50 employees. Another 13 percent were listed as small or *pequeña* companies with 10 to 49 employees. An additional 19 percent were micro-businesses with 2 to 9 employees, 35 percent were independent employees, and 10 percent were considered "other" businesses (MTPE, 2003). The increasing importance of *"pequeña y micro empresas"* (PYMEs) in the economic development of Peru has been the focus of much attention. These types of organizations are more flexible, highly entrepreneurial, and have great potential for strategic growth in HRM.

PROFUTURO, a medium-sized pension system enterprise in Peru, has successfully integrated human resource management as a core competency (Arbaiza, 2002). Their model of human resource management has been a major contributor to the successful evolution of the organization in the past five years, resulting in a significant impact on their business performance. This was accomplished through traditional implementation of HRM practices, the commitment and involvement of the CEO, as well as the active participation of everyone in the firm. To ensure HRM as a core competency, collaboration between areas was essential; each area acted as a client or a provider of other areas depending on the issue to be resolved. To nurture a culture of participation, communication was fundamental.

When employers and employees shared the firm's culture, results followed. By 2001, PROFUTURO AFP had recruited 23 percent of the subscribers from the overall Peruvian Pension Fund System. It manages a portfolio worth US$510 million out of a system total reaching US$3,400 million. Financial resources were dramatically improved by human resources. The company proved that for HRM to become a major player it needed to radically change its mindset; the results were remarkable (Arbaiza, 2002).

In larger organizations, especially multinationals, a greater use of contemporary management theories is exhibited; many of these companies assert HRM as a strategic competency. This process is reflected in the organizational culture, knowledge acquisition, creation, and innovation of the organizational members (Chávez, 2002). It is not uncommon for these companies to practice six sigma, capabilities maturity models (CMM), TQM, or MSF, usually driven by elite executive members, and compulsory for lower levels. Some Peruvian organizations have undertaken this strategic process. Investing approximately two years in the initial phase of creating the design and assimilation of the determined competencies, companies complement this later by developing and applying selection, training, development, evaluation, and compensation processes.

Formal economy organizations

The Peruvian economy is based on the informal and the formal economy, including traditional international and local organizations. The landscape of organizations in the formal economy sector is usually broken down into industrial, financial services, natural resource development, and service organizations. Traditionally, industrial, financial services, and natural resource development sectors have been led by international organizations and the Peruvian government, bringing HRM practices influenced by these organizational cultures. In contrast, the service industry has mostly been developed by Peruvians and investment from other South American countries.

General responsibilities of HRM departments include selecting employees by conducting interviews and background checks, as well as training employees by developing and implementing programs. In large organizations, human resource managers coordinate HR activities with regional and corporate offices. The development of incentive programs has gained importance within HRM departments in formal organizations to address the ongoing problem of retention. Recruitment is predominantly, or 70 percent, based on the requisite qualifications for the relevant position, whereas the remaining 30 percent is based upon background information including schooling, university experience, family, and friends. Social contacts through family and academic connections are important. Companies advertise in newspapers, use headhunters, or utilize their HR department.

The characteristics of HRM in organizations vary, but there are some general tendencies. Remuneration has been primarily based on seniority and job title, especially in public organizations. Incentive programs and "pay for performance" are becoming more familiar, notably in sales positions. Management by objectives is a widespread practice. Upward movement in the organization hierarchy is based on connections, social structures, performance and customer focus. Deep hierarchies exist in many organizations, built on multiple checks and balances to avoid corruption. Hierarchies also provide clear definition of the chain of command and job descriptions. These dispositions are in line with the high power-distance cultural dimension characteristic of Peru (Hofstede, 1980).

Training was identified as another of the most important responsibilities for human resource managers in Peruvian companies. From multinational pharmaceutical companies to family-owned retail petroleum companies, from textile plants to private pension organizations, training surfaced as imperative. This is particularly important given that there is a shortage of skilled workers in the country. A textile manufacturing company took proactive steps to address the shortage by creating training schools, typically registering up to 140 workers in the program at a time (Cortazar, 1997). Larger and multinational companies typically pay for training. Former Peruvian minister Alfonso de los Heros (1999) recommended several measures for managing human resources in business growth over the next decade, especially the need to increase labor quality of employees through training and development. This would be accomplished with careful attention paid to the protection of weak labor sectors, women, young people, and unemployed men over 45 years of age.

Motivational issues are salient in HRM in formal organizations. Evaluation and incentives can be developed based on the employee's ability to communicate with all levels of the organization, understand the challenges of subordinates, include family and social considerations in the workplace, and be political enough to represent subordinates and protect them from other directors or departments within the same business. Due to the competitive labor market, employees often show an eagerness to do more in order to prove their value and increase their stay in the organization.

Relationship-based negotiations, particularly the relationships involving long-standing customers, can create highly developed networks and political systems inside and outside of the organization. To attract new customers and encourage customer satisfaction and loyalty, some companies promote the unique and creative thinking of employees, who come up with ideas such as the creation of a customer response system. In team meetings, humor is often used to promote clear objectives. This may include making fun of situations or other groups in order to generate results through peer pressure. This group-based activity is characteristic of the high in-group orientation reported in Peruvian culture (Hofstede, 1980). As such, individual and group-oriented recognition, in the form of department or company events, are important employee incentives. These types of activities assist in addressing the reoccurring challenge identified for the human resource manager: the issue of retention.

Informal economy organizations

The development of business, based on the need to work for survival and scarcity of credit, through innovative, informal enterprise encourages individuals to develop their capacity and effort (de Soto, 1989). Many scholars believe that there is great entrepreneurial wealth in Peru that, in a few decades, with improved financial credit lines and education, could serve as a model for third world countries to become part of the first world. From 1990 to 2002, employment in the formal economy in metro-Lima decreased from 43 percent to 38 percent, while employment in the informal economy grew from 57 percent to 62 percent (MTPE, 2003). Outside metro-Lima, in greater Peru, there are more workers in the informal economy (MTPE, 2003). As a result, the greatest change in the market of the past decade has been the increase in the informal economy.[4] Villarán, a researcher in the field of human resources, argues that it is common to equate informality with poverty and that often there is confusion between micro- and even small firms and the informal sector. This obscures the distinctiveness of the informal sector and underestimates its role in the economy (Späth, 1993).

Informal employment is considered an activity such as employment in commercial, service, or manufacturing enterprises with a typical workforce of ten or fewer people. The informal economy is comprised of a large network of small shops, stalls, and street-sellers. Merchandise for the informal economy is often acquired on the black market from backstreet sweatshops or organized smugglers. With minimal overheads and taxes, the informal network provides stiff competition for formal outlets and has held back the development of a modern retail sector (EIU, 2003).

Informal organizations may be smaller organizations in which family provides the labor, working long hours at the expense of education. In some cases, family members work for no pay, live in the same household, and share the profit in terms of food, clothing, and the like. Because the organizations are small, promotions will be based on trust or family ties. Training or education is sometimes paid by the bosses or owners if they are certain that the experience or knowledge will be used in the business; loyalty is more precious here than in the formal economy.

From 1970 to 1990, street vending in Lima increased dramatically, from 2.5 percent of the economically active population to 13.1 percent (EIU, 2003). Street vendors, as well as small shops, require little or no formal advertising. Word-of-mouth advertisement for smaller companies is similar to the development of a brand for medium-sized organizations. Pay-per-performance strategies are often utilized; each informal employee is supervised by an informal manager of a specific area, and is literally paid on a daily basis. Employees in this system must buy their life necessities on a daily basis. If they do not perform, they are no longer employed. Necessity drives innovation on customer acquisition and product development. Incentive systems include development of referral systems by employees to move customers to specific stores. Strong competition among referral systems and learn-as-you-go behaviors have led to the development of sophisticated tracking systems.

Typically, development of social networks at work, use of barter systems, and relationships are used to aid other informal organizations in the development of profits. Employees of these small businesses have often developed relationships with the owners of informal businesses; they know each other and trust each other with their merchandise. This leads to the development of social networks that find and refer customers to informal organizations. Interestingly, it has been discovered that, within the informal economy, there is also the notion of informal credit. In an investigation conducted recently, it was found that informal credit, or credit on a daily or even hourly basis, can be negotiated at high interest rates. Some businesses in the informal economic sectors have marshaled their efforts to form informal clusters of trade districts. These cluster locations may include hundreds of shops of the same trade in the same area. An example of the small firms' efficiency is the *Complejo Gamarra*, which manufactures and markets clothing and fashion wear (Späth, 1993). Gamarra is a commercial area encompassing 25 blocks in Lima. With hundreds of storefront shops strategically located in a highly commercial area, Gamarra provides tens of thousands of jobs (Cortazar, 1997). The area is distinct due to the combination of economic activities present: production, trading, and services, as well as a combination of different business sizes. The group has its own magazine and radio station. With this growth, HRM concerns become more prominent. An economic organization, PROMPEX, began providing guidance by contacting "apparel and quality experts to provide advice to companies and to offer conference and assistance on quality control, personnel management, marketing, and export trade to manufacturers in the area" (Cortazar, 1997: 110).

Emerging HR influences

Recurring themes surface in the best practices espoused by human resource managers in many Peruvian companies. In recent interviews with HR executives in Lima, succession management was ranked as a top priority. Another theme considered important was evaluation. Assessment was noted as a crucial component to aligning the needs of the employees with those of the organization, and vice versa. Accountability translates into measurement. Communication was a multifaceted theme occurring throughout the organization, considered essential to the best practices of the organization. This includes interpersonal communication, networking communication within and across organizations for better work performance, 360-degree feedback, and customer relations.

Succession management is a top concern for companies where talent is scarce. A survey of HR managers from 60 percent multinational and 40 percent national companies reported that focus on leadership succession was of great concern for the future (DBM Peru, 2004). Fifty-one percent of companies reported that they would increase investment in succession management, 61 percent of national companies and 52 percent of multinationals. The consumer goods sector committed to the largest investment at 77 percent. With this increase, processes for developing the human capital will acquire greater importance.

Over the past decade, Peruvian organizations have undergone substantial change in many areas. Beginning in 1992, privatization in Peru has come to the forefront of development. Sales of state-owned energy generators and distributors, mining and refining interests, the telephone monopoly, and banks have led the privatization process. In some instances, Peruvian citizens and company employees were allowed to participate in the process. Bowen (1998) notes that in some of the larger and more politically sensitive companies, Peruvian company workers acquired up to 10 percent of the equity and packages of retained shares in selected companies which were then offered to the public at discounted prices. The privatization of the pension system in Peru is another example of reform. Arce (2001) suggests that privatization involves two elements: participation and transparency. Careful consideration of these elements will determine the success of the process.

Another organizational change that has been occurring in Peru is decentralization. Decentralization of governmental systems in Peru helps meet local concerns, creating policies in line with the human resources of regions. The process of decentralization also assists in balancing the dual economy that exists in Peru. Countering the marginalization of the rural economy, decentralized structures can address this problem (Buchenrieder and Heuft, 2003). This is especially true in agricultural promotion, where HRM issues have largely been ignored, but where enhancing human resources is vital for development. Fundamentally, decentralization can only be achieved if there is greater accountability within the system, and this can happen only if constant, transparent flow of information is guaranteed (Buchenrieder and Heuft, 2003). Realizing the strategic advantages of HRM as a core competency would facilitate this change process and instill the trust that is currently absent.

Conclusions

The business landscape in Peru is undergoing transformations. There have been structural transformations in the public and private sectors, formal and informal transformations in the economy, and dynamic transformations in the labor arena. For HRM, these transformations are opportunities for strategic growth; however, this growth requires enlightenment for both labor and industry. Crucial items include participating in strategic planning as well as aligning the employees' view with the corporate view. Acknowledging employees' needs and encouraging them to share responsibility as active participants in the process are important.

Hopefully, trust can be recovered in the transformation process. Through years of corruption, manipulation, mismanagement, oppression, and under appreciation, the Peruvian employee has lost trust in the system. The redevelopment of this trust is essential for the success of human resource development generally, and HRM specifically. In a speech at an APEC CEO summit in October 2003, President Toledo ended the discussion by stating that a company's vision must also focus on the social climate. If it does not, local communities will ultimately turn against it. He closed by reiterating that for all to prosper, government and business must be committed to partnership and good practices. Human resource management has the potential to play an important role in this process.

Notes

1. A *Quipu* is a device made of a main cord with smaller varicolored cords attached and knotted.
2. With several excellent universities and professional graduate business programs countrywide, many have, or are in the process of seeking, accreditation in the United States and Europe.
3. Urban underemployment is classified according to hours worked and wages received.
4. Several categories comprise the informal economy: independent workers that are not professional or technically skilled, employees in families who do not receive pay for their services, people working in their home and/or micro-companies.

References

Amiel, R. (2004) "Quarterly review and outlook," Global Insight Inc., Waltham, MA, retrieved from: http://www.globalinsight.com

Arbaiza, L. (2002) *PROFUTURO AFP: Organizational change driven by a human resource management model*, presented at the conference "The Missing Middle", organized by the University of Durham and EFMD, England.

Arce, M. (2001) "The politics of pension reform in Peru," *Studies in Comparative International Development* 36 (3): 90–115.

Background Notes (2003) "Background notes: Peru" (December), US Department of State, Bureau of Western Hemisphere Affairs, Washington, DC, retrieved from: http://www.state.gov/www/background_notes/peru_0300_bgn.html

Booth, D. and Sorj, B. (1983) *Military reformism and social classes: The Peruvian experience*, London: Macmillian.

Bowen, S. (1998) "Peru storms – and shines," *Latin Trade* 6 (5): 30–36.

Buchenrieder, G. and Heuft, A. (2003) "Decentralization in Peru's agriculture policy: A critical review from 1993–1998," *Oxford Development Studies* 31 (3): 341–363.

Cameron, M. and Mauceri, P. (1997) *The Peruvian labyrinth: Polity, society, economy*, University Park: Pennsylvania State University Press.

Chaplin, D. (1976) *Peruvian nationalism: A corporatist revolution*, New Brunswick, NJ: Transaction Books.

Chávez, G.E. (2002) "Las Competencias en la Gestión de Recursos Humanos," [Competencies in Human Resource Management] *Gestión empresarial Management* 59 (January–February).

Collier, R. and Collier, D. (1991) *Shaping the political arena: Critical junctures, the labor movement, and regime dynamics in Latin America*, Princeton, NJ: Princeton University Press.

Cortazar, M. (1997) "Peru: 3000 years of textiles and apparel," *Apparel Industry* 58 (9): 102–10.
CountryWatch Review (2004) *Peru*, Houston, TX: CountryWatch.
Crabtree, J. (1992) *Peru under Garcia: An opportunity lost*, London: Macmillian.
DBM Peru (2004) "DBM Peru," Lima, Peru, retrieved from: http://www.dbmperu.com
Degregori, C.I. (1990) *El surgimiento de Sendero Luminoso [The rising of Sendero Luminoso]*, Lima: Instituto de Estudios Peruanos.
De los Heros, A. (1999) "Rol de los recursos humanos en el desarrollo económico" [The role of human resources in economic development], *Análisis Laboral* 269 (November).
De Soto, H. (1989) *The other path: The invisible revolution in the third world*, New York: Harper & Row.
Economist Intelligence Unit (EIU) (2003) *Country profiles, 2003*, London: Economist Intelligence Unit Ltd.
Graham, C. (1992) *APRA: Parties, politics and elusive quest for democracy*, Boulder: Lynne Rienner.
Haworth, N. (1989) "Political transition and the Peruvian labor movement, 1968–75," in E.C. Epstein (ed.) *Labor autonomy and the state in Latin America*, Boston: Unwin Hyman, pp. 195–218.
Hofstede, G. (1980) *Culture's consequences: International differences in work-related values*, Thousand Oaks, CA: Sage.
Hunt, C. (2003) "Tour ops: Chile, Ecuador, Peru among hot spots," *Travel Weekly* (17 November): 34–36.
Ministerio de Trabajo y Promoción del Empleo (MTPE) (2003) *El empleo en el Perú: 2002–III [Employment in Peru: 2002-III]*, Peru: Dirección Nacional del Empleo y Formación Profesional.
Palmer, D.S. (1992) *The shining path of Peru*, New York: St. Martin's Press.
Parodi, J. (2000) *To be a worker: Identity and politics in Peru*, Chapel Hill, NC: University of North Carolina Press.
Political Risk Services (2003) *Peru country forecast: Political framework*, East Syracuse, NY: Political Risk Services Group.
Späth, B. (1993) *Small firms and development in Latin America: The role of the institutional environment, human resources and industrial relations*, Geneva: International Institute for Labour Studies.

12 Human resource management in Uruguay

GASTON J. LABADIE

Uruguay is one of the countries that compose Mercosur, the Southern Cone Common Market, along with Argentina, Brazil, and Paraguay. Due to its comparatively small economy, Uruguay has traditionally been subject to external shocks coming from its main neighboring trade partners. Since the mid-1970s, Uruguay has implemented significant economic and social changes, such as liberalizing trade, lowering tariffs, and introducing reforms within the labor relations system. These transformations have brought changes in the distribution of production and employment by economic sector, increased competition for Uruguayan businesses, and induced changes in the role of human resource management (HRM). There has also been an increasing professionalization of the management role led by specific university programs that started to train specialized professionals in the early 1990s, which are better suited to the demands of the "new" environment.

There has been hardly any systematic empirical research on HRM in Uruguay, except for some students' theses, and only one study that deals with the matter directly (Rodriguez *et al.*, 2001, 2003). There has been a Personnel Managers' Association in Uruguay (*Asociacion de Dirigentes de Personal del Uruguay* – ADPU) since 1972. Its activities have been largely devoted to disseminating legal and regulatory changes or specific "position papers" of managers or business leaders, at either the national or international level.[1]

The present chapter will discuss some of the changes that have taken place in the last 20 years in the Uruguayan labor market, institutions, and labor force and have impacted the role played by human resource managers. Followed by a summary of the research evidence on the changing role of unions, it will depict some of the results of recent systematic research on human resources practices and the role played by human resource departments (HRD) within Uruguayan private firms. The conclusion will offer an empirically based profile of human resource managers as well as some speculations regarding the current and future challenges within the country.

Changes in the Uruguayan labor force and labor relations system and their impact on human resource management

With a population of 3.4 million and a labor force of 1.4 million, Uruguayan society had a very early social and welfare state development. With a very low population growth rate since the mid-1950s and early "ageing" of its population in comparison to other Latin American countries, Uruguay is considered among those that have a high Human Development Index according to the United Nations, ranking 37th in the world in 2001 and 40th in 2002.

Labor force trends in the past 15 years indicate that only 5 percent of people within the labor force in 2001 had not completed primary education. Those with secondary education increased slightly to include 40 percent of the labor force and those with technical education remained in the same proportion. Those with university education increased significantly from 8.4 percent to 20.7 percent in 2001. Women have increased their education and participation rates in the open labor market from 45.2 percent up to 54.8 percent. Concurrently, there has been a further increase of service employment, which accounts for over three-quarters of the labor force, together with a decrease in the secondary sector that took place as a result of the de-industrialization that followed the opening of the economy. At the same time, public sector employment went down from almost one-fourth of the labor force to 16.6 percent in 2001.[2] The proportion of professionals and technicians has increased by over 5 percent, up to a total of 17.9 percent; managers have almost doubled to 6.5 percent; workers in personal services, including independent and informal workers, have increased 4 percent to constitute 21.5 percent of the labor force; and blue-collar workers have decreased the most, down from 28 percent in 1986 to 18 percent in 2001.

During this period, there have been significant changes in the institutional context in which human resource managers perform their activities. Uruguay had a unique system of wage councils from 1946 until the advent of the military coup in 1973. Collective bargaining was banned during the military regime, but with the return of democracy in 1985, labor unions regained the right to bargain and the system was re-instituted. Wage councils implied a trilateral representation of employers, workers, and the state. These councils set minimum wages by industry and labor category. If the government delegates gave their consent to the wage agreement, it applied by decree to the entire sector, and not just the firms and unions involved in the original bargaining.

This mechanism instituted a centralized bargaining system, with wage changes that were synchronized in the whole economy and allowed little room for firm-level negotiation, although it was allowed for wages above and beyond those that were collectively agreed.

Union membership, which had been proscribed by the military, quickly recovered high levels in 1985, reaching 26 percent of the total employed population; 19

percent in the private sector and 48 percent in the public.[3] Since then, in all industries where private employment is predominant, union membership and density have decreased significantly, down to 15 percent in 1997; 7 percent in the private sector and 47 percent in the public.

The changes that took place during the nineties account for this fact. The system that was instituted in 1985 became a source of labor market rigidities and had an impact on HRM practices. Research has shown the significance of unionization relative to other institutional constraints to understanding the relevant sources of rigidities in employment, mobility, and performance within Uruguay (Cassoni et al., 1995) and has also modeled its impact on firm performance (Cassoni et al., 2002). The response of wages to macroeconomic conditions has been examined at the macro level, concluding that wage compression and lower response are the consequences of collective bargaining (Cassoni et al., 1996). Unions were able to successfully negotiate higher wages for blue-collar workers with higher union density between 1985 and 1991. While employment fell in that period, unions were able to protect against job loss by reducing the rate of change of employment in relation to wages and decreasing the rate of change of employment relative to changes in output. This rate fell by more than 50 percent with respect to the period when there was no collective bargaining (Cassoni et al., 2000; Cassoni and Allen, 2004). All of these results were tested with a "right to manage" model, which fitted the data quite appropriately and implied that there was no bargaining over employment, only over wages. Therefore, the "objective function" that unions had from 1985 to 1991 was centered on maximizing wages. The results of this bargaining strategy did not apply only to their members, since the labor relations system enforced these gains for non-union workers within the industry and job category.

Starting around 1991, the government abandoned the tripartite negotiation and relaxed the enforcement of collective agreements at the industry level. Lower import tariffs became binding constraints around 1993, increasing the exposure of firms to international and regional competition. As a result, some collective agreements started to explicitly consider employment as part of their negotiations, suggesting that there was a change in the union's objective function. Cassoni and Labadie (2001) have shown that these new practices can be modeled by a recursive contracts model. This implies a more decentralized bargaining practice in general, with job stability clauses, lack of synchronization in wage changes, and a new role for firm-level unions that negotiate specific work conditions, as opposed to industry-level unions, without the ability to negotiate HRM policies.

As a result, in the 1980s, strong unions bargained at the industry level almost exclusively over wages, and managed to get a higher proportion of rents in relatively more economically protected sectors. In the 1990s, when protection was no longer possible, without the enforcement of collective agreements from the state, and with declining membership in the context of increased unemployment, unions started bargaining at the firm level. The new labor relations system was able to guarantee some job stability, depending on the industry. In some cases, unions moderated their wage demands or even allowed wages to fall. In others, the negative impact of increased openness of the economy was buffered by changes in the composition of employment (blue-collar versus white-collar), but in all cases, unions tried to smooth the effect of demand fluctuations. Empirical evidence shows that unions in exporting industries were more concerned about employment than the rest, willing to accept lower relative wage increases; the industry that is practically monopolized by a large public enterprise got both wage and employment increases due to union action (Cassoni and Labadie, 2001). Consistently, union membership has remained very high at the industry level in the public utilities sector. In all other sectors, union membership at the industry level has decreased significantly, while union action has remained active at the firm and plant level.

Impact on human resource management

This new environment generated new demands, requiring a different approach to HRM than the previous one.

The wage council system that was re-instituted in 1985 had traditionally been the Uruguayan labor relations establishment. In practice, and particularly for the vast majority of smaller firms, it meant that the level and timing of the whole wage-setting process was located outside their sphere of managerial decision making. It was via the delegates of the larger firms which were represented in the employers' associations that wage levels and their timing were agreed upon, and once the state had approved them, they were enforced at the industry level. Therefore, with wage setting outside of their control, and with a work relationship heavily regulated by law and ILO conventions, the human resource function, particularly in smaller firms, became marginal.

Further, since the Uruguayan labor force works in a market with very few organizations that have a large number of employees, there is a limited role for the human resources practices that are usually applied in large corporations. In fact, human resource management took place within the broader business practices in the country that lacked adequate managerial strategies (Stratta, 1991). In this economic and institutional context, the main managerial activity was more oriented towards "rent-seeking", trying to get more special protections from the state (Sapelli, 1989, 1992; Rama, 1991; Aguiar, 1992), with a relative absence of efficiency-improving practices.

The HR department was only strategically relevant in larger firms, in concentrated sectors that had larger unions, to develop the collective agreements that were required in economically protected sectors, with rents to be distributed, and unions that were concerned almost exclusively with their real wage level in an economy with high inflation. HR professionals tended to be experienced practitioners that had worked within the firm, eventually working with lawyers, but not trained managers. Avoiding strikes through negotiation, and developing appropriate collective agreements with the right wage levels and rules of adjustment, was the main concern of "human resource managers". This was especially the case in the manufacturing industries, which employed close to one-third of the labor force until the early 1970s, with a significant presence of blue-collar workers – a social landscape that has completely changed in recent times.

Among smaller firms, HR management practices were almost exclusively limited to payroll control and payment as an auxiliary role to the general administration. Even today, in these firms, which are mostly family businesses, decision making is highly concentrated, with board meetings devoting high percentages of their time to operations that should be left in the hands of lower managerial levels or even the shop floor (Vilaseca, 1999).

Since the early 1990s, the changes previously highlighted have called for a managerial role more oriented towards a "profit-seeking" behavior, with more innovation-prone activities, careful development of strategies, and managerial practices seeking to attain competitiveness in a more open economy.

In 1991, a manager of one of the largest manufacturing firms in the country stated:

> It is necessary to make plans from the perspective of human resources. Let's make a "*Human Resources Master Plan*" for the firm, taking into account the challenges (threats and opportunities) that it means to get into demanding and competitive markets. … Let's assume that efficient and competitive human resources guarantee efficient and competitive firms, and this is our responsibility, since we promote this change, this is our role.
>
> (Damonte, 1991: 9)

It is in this context that the more current HRM policies and practices can be studied.

Human resources practices in Uruguay[4]

To characterize the more recent human resources policies and practices in Uruguay, we report data from a study performed in 116 firms in Uruguay towards the end of the 1990s. Data was collected using a questionnaire on best human resources practices developed as part of a comparative study on the subject (Von Glinow *et al.*, 1995).[5] The sample of private firms studied focused on the largest firms in Uruguay, with only 22 percent having fewer than 100 employees, 68 percent having between 101 and 999 employees, and 10 percent having over 1,000 employees, covering most of the firms in the country within that category. The resulting sample had an industry composition biased towards manufacturing, with 41 percent of the firms in this sector, an identical percentage of service industries, and only 13 percent from other industries. Most of the firms (45 percent) reported having more than half of their workforce unionized, 20 percent reported having a lower proportion, and 35 percent reported not having unions. The vast majority (85 percent) reported having a specialized HRD.

Given these characteristics, the results summarized are representative of the largest and relatively "more advanced" firms within Uruguay.

Table 12.1 presents the frequency with which firms use different selection procedures, training and development practices, alternative compensation mechanisms, and performance evaluation methods.

Personnel selection

Most Uruguayan large firms (80 percent) almost always use the interview as a way of selecting their human resources; 73 percent evaluate the skills for the job; and 57 percent consider proven work experience. The majority do not use tests of technical skills, and 23 percent never use them. Only about 40 percent consider interpersonal skills or the value alignment of candidates in their selection process, and 30 percent never consider them. However, the higher the knowledge of international practices that HR managers have, the lower the relative importance of the interview and the higher the reliance on technical tests and value identification with the organizational culture.

Training and development

In accordance with previous studies on the matter (Silveira, 1991), training and development is used 70 percent of the time to improve the technical skills of employees and to a lesser extent (50 percent of the time) to train for future activities. Only about a third of the firms use training to socialize workers in the values of the organization or to train new employees, but significantly, a higher proportion of the firms never use it. Only 27 percent of the firms use training and development as an incentive for their personnel, and half of them never do. The vast majority of the firms never use training as a way of improving human relations among employees. Those firms that have a higher orientation towards employees provide the most training as an incentive; 81 percent do it most of the time. They also train employees as part of their induction process; 78 percent of them do it almost always. Providing training to make employees into

Table 12.1 Best human resources practices

Practice	Almost always (%)	Frequently (%)	Never (%)
Personnel selection			
Personal interview	80	13	7
Skills for the job	73	23	4
Proven work experience	57	29	14
Prospects for future high performance	53	33	14
Odds of remaining in the firm	50	28	21
Tests of technical skills	49	28	23
Ability to develop personal relationships	44	28	28
Value identification with firm	43	27	30
Training and development			
Improve technical capacity	70	16	14
Train for future activities	50	31	19
Train for multi-tasking	44	23	32
Correct previous deficiencies	39	33	28
Socialize employees in values of the firm	36	27	37
Train new employees	34	29	37
As incentive to employees	27	24	49
To improve human relations	13	20	67
Performance evaluation			
To acknowledge employee good work	50	25	25
To use in promotion	43	35	22
Develop a career development program	40	26	34
To assess goals achieved	37	33	30
To keep record of employee's performance	36	31	33
To listen to those evaluated	35	30	35
To determine appropriate pay	25	35	40
To collect data for payroll administration	23	44	33
Compensation			
Benefits are an important part of compensation	35	21	44
The benefit package is generous	29	24	47
Compensation is planned in the long run	27	27	46
Material incentives are a priority	26	17	57
Pay system is oriented towards the future	22	24	54
Seniority is specially compensated	15	30	55
There is incentive pay	15	25	60
Compensation depends on goal-attainment	14	25	61

Source: Survey on Best Practices on Human Resources Management, Universidad ORT, Uruguay.

multi-tasking or multi-skilled workers appears to be associated with the perception of an increased competitive environment.

Performance evaluation

One-fourth of these large firms never use performance evaluation and those 50 percent that do it systematically do it as a means of acknowledging the employee's good work. About 40 percent use it as an input for promotion evaluation (33 percent do it frequently), or for a career development plan, but 34 percent never use it at all. One-fourth use it to determine the appropriate pay, while 40 percent never do. Those that have a higher orientation towards employees tend to use more performance evaluation as the basis for promotion; 85 percent of those that do it almost always and 55 percent of those that do it frequently.

Compensation

Monetary pay is the dominant compensation practice in Uruguay. Only 35 percent of the firms report providing benefits as an important part of their compensation scheme; 44 percent report never doing it. Only 27 percent report having a planned compensation policy and only 15 percent systematically provide incentive pay or variable compensation depending on the accomplishment of objectives. It is those firms that have a higher orientation towards employees that provide more benefits as an important component of the total compensation.

While there is variance among organizations, the general depiction of HR practices in larger firms in Uruguay suggests that the policies adopted do not follow the "best practices" recognized in the literature. One mediating cause could be related to the relative influence that the HRDs and managers have in their respective organizations.

Role of the human resource department and profile of HR managers in Uruguay

Organizational importance of HRD

A 71 percent majority of HR managers consider that their department is important or very important, against 6 percent stating that it is not. However, 23 percent of them consider that their department is neutral. It is in smaller firms with fewer than 50 employees that the HRDs tend to be considered unimportant; 50 percent of the total respondents are in that category. In most of these cases, the

HR department does not work with the upper echelons of management. Further, by their own admission, 55 percent of them do not have a medium knowledge of the best human resources practices.

In the largest firms, those with 1,000 employees or more, the HR departments tend to work with the top management team to a large extent (84 percent). Also, 58 percent report having higher levels of knowledge of best human resources practices.

In terms of decision making, one-fourth of the HR managers state that they should decide about some matters more frequently than they actually do, and 39 percent are neutral in that respect. Almost half, 45 percent, consider that they do not receive information from the top frequently enough, while 75 percent of them frequently or very frequently provide ideas to higher levels in the organization.

It seems that in the largest firms, HRDs play a strategic role in decision making. In most of the other large organizations in Uruguay, HRDs and managers seem to be more information providers than members of the top decision-making teams. They apparently do not have jurisdiction over all the decisions they claim for themselves, not having the prestige and salience that would be required in a framework of "best practices".

Best practices and managerial profiles[6]

The literature on best practices, or, more broadly, practices with a quality focus, emphasizes that they constitute strategic vehicles for firms. Since they imply that policies are complementary or alternative to one another, the different practices should be examined together. Scholars have pointed out three managerial profiles depending on the intensity of use of best practices: simple, professional, and strategic. An analysis of this kind was performed by Rodriguez et al. (2001, 2003), and the dimensions measured and scaled were: "orientation towards employees", "organizational careers", and "standing of HRDs". Once combined, these dimensions led to the characterization of the profiles, which are "styles of working towards employees and personnel rules, including attitudes, actual behaviors, and beliefs" (Rodriguez et al., 2001).

Orientations towards employees refer to the importance assigned to employees in the performance and competitiveness of the firm, from the importance of having employees embedded in the ideology of the firm to boosting productivity through personnel involvement and participation. Practices concerning the organizational careers of employees denote all practices in the cycle from the recruitment to the retirement of an individual, including material and symbolic rewards such as benefits, training, and development. Organizational standing of the HRD refers to the relative position of the department in terms of status, prestige, and participation in the strategic decisions of the firm (Rodriguez et al., 2001: 3).

Firms with simple managerial profiles are those wherein the management of human resources has a short-term and reactive orientation. Careers result from informal relations or unstructured events. Evaluation and training are largely informal and implemented when problems arise. They are unrelated to the broader objectives of the firm such as performance. Well-structured HRDs are rare and human resources functions are marginal for the firm.

Firms with professional managerial profiles have medium-term orientations towards their employees, try to implement a good working climate, have formal and systematic personnel rules, and are concerned with employee satisfaction. Human resources practices are designed systematically for each step of the work career and the department has well-defined functions and structures. While procedures tend to be formal and practices systematic, these efforts remain unrelated to the larger objectives of the firm.

Firms with strategic managerial profiles have a long-term orientation towards employees and human resource management focuses on the continuous improvement of the quality of employees. Firms with strategic profiles have a clear design of the organizational career of their employees and consider them as a direct input to enhance the broader organizational performance. For this reason, decisions made by the HR department are considered central to the functioning of the firm and included as part of the strategic plan of the organization, sharing executive status. On the basis of these ideal types, scales were developed for the three dimensions, and a cluster analysis was performed. The three configurations empirically identified are not "pure" but hybrids (Rodriguez *et al.*, 2001, 2003).

Most large firms (43 percent) in Uruguay present a quasi-simple profile; 28 percent have a professional profile; and 29 percent have an incomplete-strategic profile. This summarizes the state of best practices in human resource management in the country. Most of the firms probably remain skeptical as to the actual value of these best practices and therefore do not develop them. If this is the case in this sample, it is probably more so within the broader population of organizations. In those firms that have a quasi-simple profile, the HRD has an unexpected organizational standing in terms of prestige and importance, quite consistent with our earlier interpretation of its role within large firms that have a highly unionized work force. A similar inconsistency appears in the case of the professional profile, in which payment practices have lower values than expected and are more traditional than expected, but the HRD has a higher status than expected in the ideal type.

There is also a small group of large firms that are "incompletely strategic" because their payment practices tend to be below the expected values, with more professional or traditional payment schedules; bonuses, incentives, and variable pay remain rare within the Uruguayan compensation landscape. The distinctive characteristic of those firms that have adopted the relatively more modern practices is that 67 percent are concentrated in the services and financial sector; 56 percent tend to be multinational subsidiaries; while 13 percent have foreign capital combined with national. However, 61 percent of those that have a professional profile are also multinational, while in 63 percent of those that present a quasi-simple profile, the capital is national in origin.

Conclusions and challenges for the future

The current state of human resource management in Uruguay, empirically characterized, indicates that there is a great deal of opportunity for improvement within the area. Even among large firms, too many are still practicing a simple or "craft" style of HR management. In all policies, and particularly in those related to compensation, performance evaluation, and training, the actual practices performed have ample space to introduce the most accepted practices and more current innovations.

Since it is in the compensation and pay practices that firms seem to be particularly unaligned, even when they have other strategically oriented best practices, the relevance of the institutional environment should be seriously taken into account. Labor union behavior in the past and present in some industries, as well as meticulous or costly regulations that limit the actual possibilities of implementing bonuses, incentives, and variable pay, have clearly impeded the appropriate developments in accordance with international best practices. It is this institutional environment that has provided the strategic importance of HRDs, linked to the role they played in the relationship to union behavior, but were not allowed to develop to their full potential.

Given the changes in the institutional and economic environment, and the fact that the actual composition and educational background of human resource managers is changing, it remains to be seen if there is going to be an adoption of better human resource management practices. New generations of professionally trained managers are entering the labor market with greater awareness and knowledge of best practices that would eventually allow them to innovate if the appropriate institutional environment allows for these changes. Eventually, these new managers will replace the older practitioners or collective negotiators that have occupied the role in the past. It is likely that these better management practices are lagging behind what is actually required by the relatively "new" international competition that Uruguayan firms are facing, with their challenges in terms of quality, productivity, and flexibility to adapt to new markets.

The role of the human resource manager should adapt to other changes that are taking place. The human resource manager has to do more than be a change leader and develop best practices within the firm. Outsourcing decisions and more flexible modalities of work contracts are also challenges to the HR manager, who has to contribute appropriately in the "make or buy" decision, in administering many of those activities that are contracted out and are part of a "networked" organization, and eventually managing the human resources of the "supply chain", as limited as it may be. This is particularly true when organizations are small and there is no significant scale or differentiation to have specialized personnel to manage these situations.

In all probability, it is especially in small economies like Uruguay that HR managers face the greatest challenges, in terms of the breadth of the training they require and in terms of their innovation capacity to deal with institutional constraints from the environment and the internal structures, practices, and values of many family businesses.

Notes

1. See the chapter on Uruguay, with three papers from different positions by HR managers, in Aldao-Zapiola and Hermida (1995).
2. Given its significance in terms of employment and the fact that the largest organizations in Uruguay are all state-owned, and since public utilities have largely remained as public enterprises, a full characterization of HRM should include this sector. However, due to the diversity of institutional settings and practices within the public sector, such a task is beyond the scope of this chapter.
3. This clearly contrasts with what happened in Chile after the military regime. See Allen *et al.* (1994).
4. We wish to thank Mary Ann Von Glinow for sharing the questionnaire that was used as the basis for data collection.
5. Methodological details and other procedures can be found in Rodriguez *et al.* (2001).
6. This section is largely based on previous joint work with Ana Laura Rodriguez, whose leading role as main author I wish to acknowledge specially.

References

Aguiar, C. (1992) "Organizaciones empresariales y producción de reglas. Algunas reflexiones sobre el caso uruguayo" [Enterprise organizations and rule generation. Some speculations in the Uruguayan case], in K. Bodemer (ed.) *Organizaciones empresariales y políticas públicas* [Entrepreneurial organizations and public policies], Montevideo: CIESU-FESUR-ICP, pp. 135–158.

Aldao-Zapiola, C.M. and Hermida, D. (1995) *Relaciones industriales y recursos humanos en América Latina* [Industrial relations and human resources in Latin America], Buenos Aires: FIDAP, ADPA, WFPMA.

Allen, S., Cassoni, A., and Labadie, G. J. (1994) "Labor market flexibility and unemployment in Chile and Uruguay," *Estudios de Economía* 21: 129–146.

Cassoni, A. and Allen, S. (2004) "Unions and employment in Uruguay," in J. Heckman and C. Pagés (eds) *Law and employment: Lessons from Latin American deregulation*, Chicago: NBER and University of Chicago Press, pp. 435–96.

Cassoni, A. and Labadie, G.J. (2001) "The outcome of different bargaining models: The effects on wages, employment and the employment mix," *Documento N° 14/01*, Montevideo: Departamento de Economía, Facultad de Ciencias Sociales, Universidad de la República.

Cassoni, A., Allen, S., and Labadie, G.J. (2000) "The effects of unions on employment: Evidence from an unnatural experiment in Uruguay," *Working Paper 7501*, Cambridge: National Bureau of Economic Research.

—— (1996) "Wages and employment after reunionization in Uruguay," *Cuadernos de Economía* 99: 239–277.

Cassoni, A., Labadie, G.J., and Allen, S. (1995) "Uruguay," in G. Marquez (ed.) *Reforming the labor market in a liberalized economy*, Washington, DC: Center for Research in Applied Economics, Inter-American Development Bank, pp. 137–191.

Cassoni, A., Labadie, G.J., and Fachola, G. (2002) "The economic effects of unions in Latin America: Their impact on wages and the economic performance of firms in Uruguay," *Research Network Working Papers R-466*, Washington: Research Department, Inter-American Development Bank.

Damonte, R. (1991) *El papel del dirigente de personal en el desafío de la integración* [The role of the human resource manager in the face of the regional integration challenge], Montevideo: Apuntes ADPU, pp. 7–11.

Rama, M. (1991) "El país de los vivos: Un enfoque económico" [The country of "street wise" people: an economic approach], *Revista Suma* 11: 7–36.

Rodriguez, A.L., Labadie, G.J., Font, L., Prego, R., and Cedrola, G. (2001) "Best practices and managerial profiles among firms in Uruguay: A quantitative description," *Documento de Trabajo N° 10*, Montevideo: Facultad de Administración y Ciencias Sociales, Universidad ORT Uruguay.

—— (2003) "Prácticas de gestión de recursos humanos en Uruguay: Un análisis cuantitativo" [Human resource management practices in Uruguay: A quantitative analysis], *Relaciones Laborales* 1: 13–34.

Sapelli, C. (1989) *Tamaño del estado y crecimiento económico* [Government size and economic growth], *Serie Foros* 1, Montevideo: CERES.

—— (1992) *Tamaño del estado. Instituciones y crecimiento económico* [Government size. Institutions and economic growth], Santiago, Chile: CINDE.

Silveira, S. (1991) "Innovación tecnológica y estrategias de formación del capital humano en las industrias dinámicas uruguayas" [Technological innovation and strategies of human capital development in the dynamic Uruguayan industries], in G. Labarca (ed.) *Formación y empresa: El entrenamiento y la capacitación en el proceso de reestructuración productiva* [Training and business: Training and development in the process of productive restructuring], Montevideo: Cinterfor, pp. 385–416.

Stratta, N. (1991) "La innovación industrial: El perfil del cambio modernizador en Uruguay" [Industrial innovation: The profile of modernization and change in Uruguay], in G. Argenti (ed.) *Uruguay: El debate sobre la modernización posible* [Uruguay: The debate over the modernization that is possible], Montevideo: CIESU, pp. 225–269.

Vilaseca, A. (1999) "¿Cómo son gobernadas las empresas uruguayas?" [How are Uruguayan firms governed?], *Revista de Antiguos Alumnos del IEEM* 2 (3): 96–104.

Von Glinow, M.A., Teagarden, M., Bowen, D., Frayne, C., Nason, S., Huo, Y., Milliman, J., Arias, M., Butler, M., Geringer, M., Scullion, H., and Drost, E. (1995) "Toward a theory of comparative management research: an idiographic case study of the best international human resources management project," *Academy of Management Journal* 38 (5): 1261–1287.

13 Human resource management in Venezuela[1]

HENRY GÓMEZ-SAMPER AND PATRICIA MONTEFERRANTE

Management development in Venezuela was introduced by the oil industry in the 1920s, when most of the population formed a closely knit, rural society. Oil camps were worlds apart, setting standards for housing, lifestyles, and personnel practices for decades to come. This chapter describes abrupt changes in the management of human resources over a comparatively short span of time in a country where state oil revenue plays a central role in the distribution of wealth. Venezuela is today a largely urban society, split between those who are culturally linked to the world, *vis-à-vis* an underclass residing in *barrio* settlements, who earn their livelihood mainly in the informal economy.

Venezuela's changing fortunes

Following the Second World War, Venezuela's urban population grew rapidly. Oil income, together with immigration from Europe, triggered the establishment of local assembly and packaging plants for imported goods. Protectionist policies in the 1950s encouraged the growth of local manufacturing, and social legislation patterned on the French model spun an array of worker benefits. State enterprises flourished. Trade unions, allied with political parties, brought industry-wide collective bargaining. These developments led Venezuelan companies to establish personnel administration departments and, in due course, local universities to offer degree programs in both human resource management and industrial relations (Bitar and Mejias, 1984; Garbi and Piñango, 1989).

Nonetheless, prevailing management practices removed the personnel manager from the top management layer. The role of personnel managers was police-like, concerned with verifying worker absenteeism, running time clocks, keeping track of payroll taxes, and reprimanding employees. To be sure, the expansion of local manufacturing in the 1970s introduced, in larger firms, newer practices for recruitment, selection, and training. Personnel managers soon gave way to human resource development managers. Despite the human capital promotional rhetoric, however, to this day such managers rarely share fully in forging company strategy.

Two decades of economic recession, followed by social and political turmoil at the turn of the century, together with competitive realities in a globalizing economy, have impacted Venezuelan management practices perhaps more than they have elsewhere. Few of the local conglomerates that sprouted with oil prosperity in the 1970s have survived. Multinationals based in the industrialized world (or in more stable neighbor countries) acquired retail chains, power stations, banks, and insurance companies; while those taking over chemicals and processed foods opted to close undersized plants. State enterprises in steel-making, airlines, and telephone communications were privatized, also by foreign firms. Human resource departments, like companies, downsized; and functions formerly performed by employees were outsourced. Venezuela's informal economy mushroomed, and in 2004 accounted for almost three-fifths of the labor force.

In sum, Venezuela no longer stands out as Latin America's rich country. Companies, state enterprises, and public agencies that were once big spenders have scaled down. Decades of economic mismanagement, coupled with high population growth, wasted untold public resources. Today, most Venezuelans have little access to the kind of health, education, housing, infrastructure, and other services that once made this country the envy of its neighbors.

Employment in a downsizing economy

Local management consultants, business executives, academics, and human resource management practitioners interviewed for this study reveal that local perceptions of current organizational realities differ little from those that prevail elsewhere in a changing world; except that the impact of change on local business practices may have been sharper and swifter than in the region at large. Locally owned business is also coming to grips with social and political threats in a country where democratic institutions, fragile to begin with, have withered.

Venezuela's economy shrank following 2002. Repercussions stemming from measures taken by an increasingly authoritarian government to punish the private sector for its widespread support of a short-lived coup in that year came to a head soon after. Even the state-owned oil company was punished for joining private firms in a civic strike; some 18,000 managers along with research and development and information technology specialists were sacked. In a slowing, downsizing economy, as many as 2.2 million Venezuelans of working age in 2004 were unable to obtain conventional employment.

In a turbulent employment context, clear-cut decisions have been expected from human resource managers of private firms: staff reduction, shorter hours, pay-cuts, and especially the outsourcing of such non-basic functions as plant and office maintenance, security, customer attention, and information technology. Small and medium-sized firms reportedly fared worse than larger companies, and many closed (Americaeconómica, 2003). To forestall job losses, even trade unions agreed to support whatever pay-scale decisions companies chose to implement (*Dinero*, 2002). What Ulrich (1997) observed elsewhere was now taking place in Venezuela: the average individual's employment security based on government policy and business practice was being replaced by self-reliance and opportunity.

Labor market projections infuse Venezuela's already sad experience with greater complexity (Daza, 2003). Given demographic transition, the population entering work age (15 or older) exceed the number of those leaving employment at 65. Over the past decade, the labor force is estimated to have increased by 4 million, whereas the number of formal jobs rose by only 470,000; in other words, seven out of eight people seeking work must do so in the informal economy. The situation is exacerbated by years of economic decline. As a result, greater numbers of women enter the labor market, children drop out of school at an earlier age, and the proportion of family members who become breadwinners has increased.[2]

The shrinking labor market fuels Venezuela's informal economy and foretells a bleak social outlook. Additionally, it fosters brain drain (see Box 13.1). Of ten working-age persons, it is estimated that three are employed in either the public or private sector, two are unemployed, and five work in the informal economy. According to Daza (2003), three out of five formal economy job offers currently require at least 14 years of schooling. Yet in 2002, only 7 per cent of salary-earners had completed higher education (Ortega, 2003).

Managing under a legal straitjacket

Venezuela's human resource management has been strongly conditioned by excessive regulation of the labor market. Management practices relating to human development have seldom been a product of improved organizational strategy; instead, they have largely been shaped by reactive responses to the legal framework.

As in much of Latin America, attempts at labor regulation reform reveal two underlying tensions: first, an excessively protective view of the workforce, shared by a politicized trade union movement and a good many legislators; and second, largely unheard demands by productive sector organizations that seek flexible employment provisions to help make business become competitive (Bronstein, 1998).

Box 13.1. Venezuela's Brain Drain: A Cause for Concern

I had long planned to leave because the economic, political, and social outlook was worsening. The last straw was when my husband was kidnapped when visiting his father's rural hostel in Yaracuy, in May 2001. Thanks to our European Community passport and the help we received, doors were opened for us.

(Orthodontist, age 38, migrated to Spain in September 2001)

Opportunities in Venezuela were few, the crime rate was high, and whenever I dealt with the government I had to fight the bureaucracy. Australia is a politically stable country; health and personal security are excellent, and schools are modern and well equipped.

(Sales manager, age 37, migrated to Australia in 1996)

For years I felt the country offered me little, except for my family who remained here. Basic needs can no longer be met: personal security, employment, a better quality of life. Getting ahead is more difficult here.

(Engineer, age 25, migrated to Canada in July 2004)

Human resources specialists are concerned over the impact that the brain drain will have on recruiting qualified professional staff in the coming years. It is estimated that as many as 200,000 Venezuelans now live in the United States. An untold number of first-generation Venezuelans of Spanish, Italian, or Portuguese origin have returned to their parents' country; often they have access to a European Union passport and speak a second language. Many others have migrated to Colombia and neighboring countries.

Source: http://www.mequieroir.com

Reforms during the past decade have failed to reduce significantly the overall cost of labor (Márquez, 2002). The base law, enacted in 1990, was amended in 1997 following arduous negotiations between government, trade union leaders, and the private business federation. Retroactive severance benefits that rendered labor costs excessive were modified. Worker layoff penalties imposed on organizations were partially reduced. Also, salary (for purposes of severance and layoff indemnity) was redefined to include perks, commissions, bonuses, and other specified benefits. But workers can only be let go for disciplinary reasons; technology, losses, or inadequate skills are not a valid cause for discharge except when closing operations. Accordingly, companies generally discharge employees for "unjustified" reasons and pay double indemnity.

A noteworthy reform made in 1999 was to permit the setting up of companies that operate with a temporary workforce. Many organizations use this option in order to cut labor costs by outsourcing non-basic functions, but observers suspect that this feature might not last long, in light of the uncertain political and institutional climate. In fact, some feel that companies would be well advised to create contingency reserves to protect themselves from future severance pay demands by laid-off temporary workers contracted through another company.

Still another legal handicap that fuels labor costs and distorts hiring patterns is a mandatory ban on laying off workers who earn less than a sum equivalent to about twice the minimum wage. The ban was decreed for "emergency" reasons in April 2002 and renewed several times. Observers consider the measure self-defeating, as it discourages firms from hiring low-wage workers.

Stifling labor regulations impact Venezuelan organizations by curbing employment flexibility and limiting their ability to compete locally and internationally. Provision must be made for mandatory benefits that cost more than 70 percent over base pay (Daza, 2002). This makes Venezuela's labor costs the highest in Latin America, with charges that are 10 percent above Peru and 30 percent higher than Chile.

Relations between employers and trade unions represent another contentious issue. Trade unions appeared in Venezuela following the end of the Gómez dictatorship in 1936, and were of Marxist orientation, closely allied with political parties. When oil revenue was ample enough in relation to the population – and Venezuelan industry was protected from foreign competition – labor peace prevailed. But political strife has led trade unions allied with the government to make undue demands on business. Some companies about to close a plant have been pressured to hand over management and facilities to the workers.

Managing people

In today's global economy, organizations expect management to fulfill strategic human capital needs, anticipating and dealing with change, aligning policy and practice to competitive demands. Venezuelan organizations do not always fit this picture. We now review changing staff recruitment, selection, evaluation, compensation, and human development practices in Venezuela and what appear to be prevailing trends.

Depending on the organization, and depending on the knowledge and skills of managers charged with running its human resources unit, local practice varies. Certain Venezuelan organizations qualify as world class; but many local human resource managers spend their time administering payroll and attending to the demanding legal responsibilities entailed in employment. (See Box 13.2.)

Box 13.2. Changing Management Practices at Cadena Capriles

Desirée Bujanda, in 1999, became the human resource manager at the Capriles media group. Only one year earlier, Miguel Angel Capriles López, son of the group's founder and now the company president, had ushered sweeping editorial, cultural, and technological changes in the design, promotion, and sale of the firm's newspapers, magazines, and other publications in both print and other media.

On her first visit to the office, she immediately grasped how this organization had been managing its people. Her office, located on the 13th floor of the headquarters building, was dismal. Furniture and equipment were delapidated, water leaked through a window, and few employees had reason to go there. Her support staff appeared to be deeply unmotivated; she categorized them as belonging to a work culture that could be described as "doing is better than thinking".

Before 1999, the position had been known as "personnel superintendent". Records were on file for each employee. There were no prescribed recruitment, selection, or compensation practices. The payroll was not coded, payroll management was assigned to the finance department, and lower-rank employees were paid in cash.

Desirée noted that changes were already taking place. Newspapers were being redesigned, and print processes converted to automated and electronic means. These changes required fast assessment of staff capabilities and the hiring of technologically qualified talent. The task she had before her was not easy for someone without media experience.

Today, five years later, Desirée's office is pleasant to work in; she reports directly to the president, is part of the executive committee, is involved in all aspects of organizational change, and has learned both the business and its jargon. Recruitment, selection, and compensation policy have been spelled out. Her highly skilled staff includes some holdovers.

Key factors in the changeover at Cadena Capriles are a chief executive who believes in tapping human energy to fulfill organizational goals, and a proactive human resource manager who built a management unit that is deemed capable of responding to the company's strategic needs.

Source: Interview with Desirée Bujanda, and the firm's corporate website: http://www.la-cadena.com

Many who speak for top management attribute business success to human capital; but whether they mean it requires examining their organization. Few old-school business people consider human resource management to be a critical function. Area managers are often viewed as less talented and qualified than those charged with production, finance, or marketing. Evidence to this effect is compelling, for human resource managers tend to earn less than their colleagues. Of course, some organizations may only require routine practices in personnel management.

Leading executive recruitment agencies report that a good many Venezuelan firms are searching for human resource managers with qualifications that go beyond traditional needs. Candidates are sought who are knowledgeable in recruiting and developing human capital to implement organizational strategy, able to deal with financial issues, and capable of serving as change agents. Be that as it may, comparatively few managers heading the human resources unit of their respective organizations possess such capabilities, and the undergraduate study programs of local universities that offer this field of study do not generally prepare students for such demands (Granell, 1999).

Some companies have sought to fill their need for better qualified managers of human resources by drawing on other professions, such as engineering, administration, and psychology. Other companies have designated managers from departments that are better attuned to business and organizational strategy as heads of human resources. Yet an emerging legal straitjacket may soon put an end to such moves. A law soon to become effective requires public and private organizations to designate only graduates in human resources and industrial relations as heads of corresponding management units. Pointedly, managers lacking the degree, or managers with other degrees but less than 10 years' experience in human resources, would not qualify to sign collective bargaining contracts or represent the firm in labor disputes aired in the courts.

In sum, Venezuela's legislators appear to be woefully ignorant of market demands in terms of both the qualifications for managers of human resources as well as the workforce benefits that deter competitiveness. Companies that seek human resources strategists and change agents tend to make do with whomever they have on hand, or draw from the available pool of talented individuals who appear to possess the knowledge, attitudes, and skills that best suit their needs.

Human resource management practices

Table 13.1 compares human resource management practices in two time periods, the mid-1990s and the present. The earlier practices are drawn from a contemporary study, whereas current practices are based on in-depth interviews held with specialists consulted in preparing this study.

Table 13.1 Human resources practices in Venezuela, in the mid-1990s and early 2004

Practices	Mid-1990s	Early 2004
Recruitment	Emphasis on strengthening talent and strategic recruitment. Campus recruiting, student fellowships, and internships. Promoting staff.	Reduced campus recruitment and external efforts. Use of the internet by some organizations.
Selection	Profile sought: flexible, talented, broad education, competences suited to the strategic needs of the organization. Some firms specify leadership, ability to learn, and other novel criteria. Personal interviews are most frequent method. Some companies employ multiple interviews and newer methods.	Profile sought: technical skills consistent with knowledge and personal attributes. Strong emphasis on competences, especially in large firms. Personal interviews are most frequent method. Some firms also employ role-playing, group dynamics, and business games.
Evaluation	Trend towards change in evaluation methods: defining competences, multiple reviews, sharing results with person assessed, disconnect evaluation from salary. Individual review. More emphasis on factors than objectives. Results shown to but not discussed with those assessed.	Most firms employ performance measurement instruments. Individual evaluation most frequent. Some large firms employ multiple assessments, e.g. 360-degree. Link with compensation still common. Reluctance to provide feedback to those assessed. More rigorous application of selection procedures.
Compensation and incentives	Variable compensation only for top management and, occasionally, middle managers. Criteria most often used include merit, market, and cost of living. New benefits: automobile loans, broader insurance, contribution to savings plan, housing loans.	Variable compensation not limited to top management. Performance incentive bonuses. Cost of living pay adjustments. Fewer benefits, maintaining insurance and savings plans. Employment increasingly depends on the individual's self-development.
Staff development	Performance evaluation seldom used in career planning and development, but interest in doing so is expressed. Few firms formally assess potential growth. Trend towards design of management succession and career plans. Ambiguity in defining company commitment	In transition. Change in traditional development pattern. Rethinking of management succession and promotion.
Development and training	Outlays for training rise, but represent declining share of revenue. Formal plans based not on strategy but on needs detected, mainly in functional areas. Difficulty assessing effective results of training.	Reduced outlays by medium- and small-scale firms. Large firms maintain support for activity. Greater formal approval of staff development outlays. Training appears better geared to organizational needs. Coaching begins to be employed. Little training on-line.

Source: For the mid-1990s, IESA–Hay Group (1994); for 2004, interviews with a panel of academics, consultants, executives, and management practitioners.

Recruitment

Practices to recruit professional talent have made an about-face. In the mid-1990s, leading firms would actively promote employment openings. Company recruiters participated in fairs or visited university campuses to interview graduating students. Today, promotion is largely led by career services units based at the universities, or by students who organize events or search out prospective employers, in some instances by placing their *curriculum vitae* on the internet.

Non-professionals are generally recruited by means of notices published in the press or, for unskilled workers, posted outside the plant gate. Such notices tend to generate immediate response and long lines of applicants.

Selection

Venezuelan organizations increasingly specify the criteria employed for screening job applicants. Initiative, self-reliance, creativity, and ability to work in a team are often mentioned by firms that are cognizant of their organizational culture. White-collar workers without some post-secondary education or other training are rarely selected. Personal interviews are the general rule for all applicants, but some companies employ personality and other testing methods.

Comparatively sophisticated selection competences such as those listed above, let alone the latest testing methods, would make it appear that organizations applying them employ best business practices. Unhappily, all too often staff evaluation, development, promotion, and compensation practices leave much to be desired. Incongruence between selection criteria and other human resource management practices reveals a lack of strategic vision in managing people, akin to the country's traditional management shortcomings.

Nonetheless, even in firms where human resource management practice can be faulted, the general trend is towards improvement.

Evaluation

Most local firms employ some means for measuring staff performance. Individual assessments are the rule, although some companies now employ multiple methods, such as 360-degree feedback. Frequent use of this tool is found in service organizations, especially in areas such as customer relations, marketing, and sales.

Little change from prevailing practices in the mid-1990s is reported with respect to over-reliance on performance evaluation for purposes of determining compensation. Informed observers consider that performance evaluation is often perceived as a means for either rewarding or penalizing the staff member assessed, overlooking the opportunity to detect problem areas or attend to the individual's development needs.

Compensation and incentives

Variable compensation is increasingly being applied to both higher- and mid-level management posts. Incentive bonuses are common practice, linked chiefly with the firm's success or that of a particular management unit. Yet adequate organizational performance assessment, a requisite for applying variable compensation practices, is rarely in place.

Merit, market conditions, and cost of living continue to be the main criteria applied for assigning salary increases. Nonetheless, a slowing economy has led most organizations to approve only minor raises. These aim to offset the rate of inflation, but generally fail to do so.

Most firms have cut benefits from the mid-1990s level, with only savings and health insurance plans remaining in place. On the other hand, companies report giving greater attention to programs aimed at improving employee morale, motivation, and commitment to the organization, including such activities as holding social events, get-togethers with ranking executives, and outings for employee children (Hay Group–Venamcham, 2003).

Staff development and training

Life-long learning programs in companies that once employed career development plans have generally been discontinued. Economic, social, and political turbulence have taken their toll when it comes to long-term company commitment to staff.

Employee responsibility for self-development appears to be emerging as a common theme among leading firms, in keeping with current employment conditions in Venezuela and elsewhere. This mode presumably requires companies to assess individual self-improvement needs, organize or inform the employee about appropriate opportunities for developing particular skills, and facilitate participation. Few companies in Venezuela are equipped to undertake so ambitious a set of tasks, but progress in this direction appears to be underway.

Immediate training needs continue to be sponsored by larger firms, among other reasons in order to compensate for poor educational skills among non-professional staff. Medium-sized and small firms hard hit by economic decline appear to have cut back generally on all training.

A salutary by-product of economic decline has been closer alignment between organizational needs and the level of support allocated to management training. In the past, staff would often vie to enrol in short courses focusing on the latest management fad. How salutary it becomes, however, depends on the extent to which training approvals address the organization's strategic needs. Approvals may often reflect notions held by superiors, overlooking what is best for a staff member's development. Few firms have made a serious effort to align human resource management practices, including staff training, to strategic organizational goals.

Coaching has become a staff development tool in some Venezuelan companies. However, few local managers have the leeway required to dutifully attend to this task. Firms that favor coaching generally assign the task to specialized consultancy services.

A small number of Venezuelan companies offer their staff the opportunity for skills training and development online. In all likelihood, the reason the approach is so little used is that human resource managers of the traditional bent are unaware of its benefits.

The challenge at hand

Human resource management in Venezuela faces a number of challenges that must be addressed in the coming years. Some of these challenges pertain to human resources professionals, together with the associations or guilds to which they belong, while others relate to the management units that are charged with fulfilling organizational needs.

Specialists in human resources must assume a more proactive role than they have in the past in shaping the future of their profession. Burning local issues pertaining to the field that await urgent attention include labor regulation reform, social inequities that influence human behavior in organizations, international competitiveness, and gearing study programs to market demands. Additionally, by establishing closer links with academic centers and consultancy firms, these specialists must press for research to broaden the country's sparse stock of knowledge in human resources.

Management units concerned with human resources in business firms, public agencies, and not-for-profit organizations must understand and participate fully in making decisions that focus on strategic organizational goals. To begin doing so, human resources specialists employed by such units must learn new knowledge, reshape long-standing attitudes, and acquire relevant business skills. Only then will they stand on the same ground as managers from other units, and acquire the capability for spearheading change in Venezuelan organizations.

A moot question is how human resource managers in the future, once Venezuela's economy attains a degree of stability, regain legitimacy in the eyes of their charges. Workers attached to many companies who were summarily outsourced to temporary employment services, and subsequently dismissed, resent how the hand-over process was implemented; this in a country where attitudes towards business have traditionally ranged from skepticism to outright hostility.

The road that lies ahead for human resource managers in Venezuela is tortuous. Without a doubt, economic, social, and political pressures will cause distractions along the way, making today's issues seem more important than tomorrow's. There is no management recipe to assist them in the task at hand. They must cope with the challenge day in and day out, without losing sight of what comes next.

Notes

1. The authors gratefully acknowledge valuable comments made by a panel of distinguished academics, human resource management consultants, and management practitioners enlisted for the study: Héctor Riquezes, Juan Carlos Larrañaga, Cristian Burgazzi, Piotr Szabunia, Carolina Castillo, José Gregorio Silverio, Carmen Cecilia Torres, and José Ramón Padilla.
2. The number of women in the labor market rose from an average of 30 percent from 1975 to 1987, to a striking 55 per cent in 2002, becoming almost two-fifths of the labor force (Ortega, 2003)!

References

Americaeconómica (2003) "Un 15% de las empresas venezolanas cerraron en el primer trimestre del año" [Fifteen percent of Venezuelan firms shut down in year's first quarter] (April), retrieved February 2004, from: http://www.americaeconomica.com/numeros3/206/noticias/chempresasvenemi.htm

Bitar, S. and Mejias, T. (1984) "Más industrialización: ¿Alternativa para Venezuela?" [Is more industrialization an option for Venezuela?], in M. Naím and R. Piñango (eds) *El caso Venezuela: Una ilusión de Armonía* [The Venezuelan case: An illusion of harmony], Caracas: Ediciones IESA, pp. 102–121.

Bronstein, A.S. (1998) "Pasado y presente de la legislación laboral en América Latina" [Latin American labor legislation – past and present], San José, Costa Rica: International Labor Office, retrieved January, 2004, from: http://www.oit.or.cr/oit/papers/pasado.shtml

Daza, A. (2002) "El costo de la regulación laboral en Venezuela" [The cost of labor regulation in Venezuela], *El costo de la regulación laboral y de las decisiones judiciales en Venezuela* [The cost of judicial decisions and labor regulation in Venezuela], Caracas: National Investment Promotion Council, pp. 13–56.

—— (2003) "El mercado laboral en Venezuela: Hechos estilizados" [Stylized facts about the Venezuelan labor market], Mimeo, Caracas, retrieved January 2004, from: http://www.anri.org.ve/canales/seguridad/foro_seg_soc/mercadolaboral.pdf

Dinero (2002) *Se desvanece la industria* [Industry vanishes], 168.

Garbi, E. and Piñango, R. (1989) "La gerencia de recursos humanos" [Human resource management], in M. Naím (ed.) *Las empresas venezolanas: su gerencia* [The management of Venezuelan firms], Caracas: Ediciones IESA, pp. 247–268.

Granell, E. (1999) "La gestión de los recursos humanos en Venezuela" [The management of human resources in Venezuela], in S. Dolan, R.S. Schuler, and R. Valle (eds) *La gestión de los Recursos Humanos* [The management of human resources], Madrid: McGraw-Hill/ Interamericana, pp. 364–370.

Hay Group–Venamcham (2003) *Aprendizajes de la crisis* [Learning from the crisis], Flash 2003-2, 15 (34) (undated bulletin with comprehensive information concerning human resources management practices following a two-month national work stoppage, gathered from a survey of top managers drawn from 102 chiefly multinational firms in manufacturing, trade, and services).

IESA–Hay Group (1994) *Recursos humanos y competitividad en organizaciones venezolanas* [Competitiveness and human resources in Venezuelan organizations], Caracas: Ediciones IESA.

Márquez, V. (2002) "Opciones de política para hacer manejable el costo laboral" [Policy options to render labor cost manageable], *El costo de la regulación laboral y de las decisiones judiciales en Venezuela* [The cost of judicial decisions and labor regulation in Venezuela], Caracas: National Investment Promotion Council, pp. 111–157.

Ortega, D.E. (2003) *Descripción y perfiles de desigualdad de ingresos en Venezuela, 1975–2002* [Income inequality in Venezuela – description and profiles, 1975–2002], Caracas: United Nations Development Program.

Ulrich, D. (1997) *Human resource champions*, Boston: Harvard Business School Press.

14 Emergent directions for human resource management: research in Latin America

MARTA M. ELVIRA AND ANABELLA DAVILA

Sound human resource management (HRM) is paramount to the future success of business organizations in Latin America. This book's chapters consistently stress that effective personal and social relationships are key to effectively managing human resources in this economically growing region. The chapters also highlight tensions between the strategic HRM approach demanded by global competition and *local* approaches to HRM, rooted in Latin American cultural values. Work plays a central role in Latin American life, providing much more than a means of sustenance, which creates an intricate implicit social contract between workers and their employers. Thus to succeed HR managers must be sensitive to the worker expectations that are embedded in this contract as they look to making changes in their human resources systems.

Latin America's view of human resources is typically person-centered, meaning that the HR professional is seen as an advocate at the service of employees rather than strictly an agent of the organization. This person-centered view of HR management faces increasing pressure from the performance-centered view predominant in global companies. The tension of balancing employee interests and performance outcomes through HR practices parallels another tension faced by Latin American organizations. As described in our first chapter, they must do their business in a hybrid cultural environment, where regional and national values, and global and local practices, coexist. Resolving these seeming paradoxes could become HR researchers' and professionals' contribution to society and business in Latin American today. Thus, we present a research framework and agenda that considers the need to modernize HR practices while maintaining the profound humanism underlying social contracts (and, by extension, employee relationships) in the region. Modernizing HR in Latin America is not inevitably at odds with a profound humanism and in fact cannot be accomplished without deliberate attention to the social contracts.

The case of Mexico's Grupo Bimbo illustrates the potential benefits of understanding Latin American work values in order to implement HR practices that are both culturally acceptable and effective. Bimbo is a large multinational organization with operations in the United States and 14 countries in Europe and Latin America. It is considered to be one of the world's most important baking companies in brand and trademark positioning, sales, and production volume. It is a serious competitor but achieves this while adhering to policies that are entirely consistent with the Latin American social contract. The company has been labeled as an organization "entirely human" (Flores-Vega, 1995). One of the person-centered policies Bimbo adheres to is avoiding employee layoffs even during downturns. Though costly, this commitment to employees has stood the test of time. In return, Bimbo benefits from increased employee loyalty and sustained financial success, which executives attribute to this and other similarly humanistic policies. This very public commitment to its people also enhances the firm's reputation for corporate ethics, social responsibility, and altruism. From our perspective, Bimbo understands the importance of values such as the social contract and commitment to long-term employment in Latin America and has been able to make this social contract beneficial.

Bimbo has accomplished its successes in a region where political and economic instability and strong globalization forces make merely surviving a major accomplishment. The challenges for full business development in Latin America range from outsourcing to inequality to the integration of women in the workplace. To meet these challenges, the research in this book suggests that it is not enough for HR to fulfill a generic profit-seeking and performance-enhancing strategy. It must also pursue a strategy that is culturally adaptive and considers the historical and cultural context in which HR practices are embedded. This notion is entirely consistent with recent work in international HRM that highlights the need to understand the field in the context of various cultural and country situations (Brewster, 1999; Budhwar, 2004; Schuler *et al.*, 2002; Von Glinow *et al.*, 2002). As Gaugler (1988: 26) states: "An international comparison of HR practices clearly indicates that the basic functions of HR management are given different weights in different countries and that they are carried out differently."

Given this context, understanding and solving HR challenges requires using a broad strategic HRM framework that encompasses the various institutions involved in employment relations. The evidence in this book suggests that in the context of Latin America's collectivistic culture, the central institutions include the family and community, as well as governments and firms. Thus, the development of HRM theories that consider the big picture is needed to account for the Latin American context.

The research in this book has laid the groundwork for developing such theories, providing an analysis of Latin American HRM overall and for selected countries, and highlighting the historical, economic, cultural, and institutional environment in which HR management develops. The chapters in Part I of the book delve into the work values, the macroeconomic and political environment, and leadership and social capital aspects that can be considered regional contextual characteristics shared across Latin America. Part II examines how these contextual factors vary within countries and reviews some of the issues that influence HRM policies within each country. For example, a large informal sector exists across Latin American economies but appears most pervasive in Peru, with its elaborate system of informal entrepreneurial networks. Similarly, paternalistic labor laws reach across the region, but the spread of market liberalization that is reducing the reach of these paternalistic laws varies widely among countries.

In the remainder of this chapter, we provide an overview of the most critical HRM challenges discussed throughout the book and reframe those challenges as opportunities for a research agenda on Latin American HRM. We then propose a strategic human resources framework to pursue such an agenda.

HRM challenges in Latin America

Despite differences across Latin American countries, they share several challenges. Underlying these challenges is the integration of HR practices into the hybrid cultural and economic system which balances regional and national values, and global and local practices. Firms need to find ways to effectively combine traditional, local practices with global HRM practices that frequently clash with their core cultural values.

Before further analyzing the challenges, we need to recognize the essential values guiding HR decisions across the region. The research presented here converges on several themes about the values surrounding work relationships, including a concern for the welfare of individuals and their families, maintaining a harmonious organizational climate, creating an organizational sense of community, and respect for legitimate authority. Consistent with these observations, a study by Ogliastri *et al.* (1999) finds that Latin Americans rank these values highest in the world. Underlying these fundamental values appears to be what we call a humanistic, i.e., person-centered, approach to HRM strategies and practices, fitting for an environment that places the person at the center of social, economic, and political activity. As Albert (1996: 333) notes, interpersonal orientation is "the preeminent meta-orientation of Latin Americans".

How can firms balance the effort to survive and thrive financially while simultaneously providing for the needs of individuals and their families? Latin American firms are involved in people's lives as well as their work and thus must provide for both social and economic needs. Increasingly, Latin American businesses seem to have taken on responsibility for meeting expectations that were formerly placed on the community. The difficulties experienced in countries like Peru, Colombia, and Venezuela, for example, illustrate this tension and the obstacles to changing this social contract. Formerly strong paternalistic labor laws have weakened with market liberalization and no longer offer the benevolent protections of the past. The result is that employees are now less trusting of their employers. This tension presents a huge challenge for Latin American firms that were scarcely even focused on performance until recently and who now need to meet daunting business objectives.

Overview of HRM challenges in Latin America

Latin American citizens are more concerned about employment-related issues than any other social or economic issues. This concern arises out of several social and economic realities. Specifically, Latin Americans experience a constant threat of unemployment (with unemployment rates at their highest in two decades), low and unstable wages, and reduced protection of workers by union and other regulations (Inter-American Development Bank, 2004). Poverty and inequality persist, partly because wage differentials between high- and low-skilled workers have widened. Despite advances in women's workforce participation and integration, discrimination remains. Here we explore the challenges ahead for HRM in light of labor market changes, macroeconomic instability, inequality, education and training, and policies.

Changes in the employment relationship

Employment security, formerly a taken-for-granted characteristic of a paternalistic system, poses a particularly pressing challenge for HRM. The transition from paternalism to performance-driven practices such as temporary employment and outsourcing has been daunting, in part because these practices reduce employment security. Colombia's temporary workforce increased from 20 to 40 percent of the labor force between 1992 and 2001 (see Chapter 9 in this book). Some companies such as Bimbo and Telmex continue to resist this approach and have been successful with their policies. Although these firms' salaries are not very high, they guarantee employees' livelihoods until the end of their lives (Lorena Perez, cited in *Expansión*, 2003).

Another challenge created by the use of temporary employees and outsourcing is motivating and retaining crucial trained talent within both core and temporary workforces. Moving away from traditional employment practices constitutes a violation of a worker's psychological contract, resulting in diminished motivation and commitment. Building a skilled outsourced team aligned with corporate strategy is a major challenge everywhere and an especially difficult one in Latin America where it contradicts the social contract. This is a pressing issue for private domestic companies that traditionally rely on relationships of trust and commitment, which are hard to obtain from outsourced personnel. Colombians have developed an interesting solution to cope with outsourcing: OTAs, cooperative groups organized by laid-off employees with the support of their previous employers (see Chapter 9 in this book). The latter subcontract downsized workers' services, effectively transferring and transforming the employment relationship into a commercial relationship with former employees.

Another challenge related to employment security is working with unions that are currently in a transitional role, as detailed in this book's chapters on Chile, Uruguay, and Brazil (Chapters 8, 12, and 6 in this book). Latin American unions' traditional focus has been preserving employment for their members and they have built a stronghold in government-run companies. Because private companies have been more open in labor relations, unions have been prompted to reconsider their role. The union's role has also been threatened by alternative movements. A particularly interesting case is Central America's *solidarismo* movement, which emerged to defend workers' interests at a time when more traditional unions were losing leverage against large multinationals (see Chapter 7 in this book).

Changes to employment practices also impact HRM through the spreading of the informal economy. Contrary to what is typically assumed, the informal sector is not the last resort for Latin American workers without better opportunities, but is actually a preferred opportunity. In some countries, the minimum wage is more often paid to informal labor than to workers in the regular labor market. Recent studies for Brazil and Mexico document that a large majority of self-employed workers prefer this status to a formal sector job because they earn higher wages and enjoy more independence (Inter-American Development Bank, 2004). For HRM this creates a dual challenge: finding ways to attract, motivate, and retain their own workers, and protecting workers in the informal sector. Meeting these challenges will require the integration and understanding of the place of the sector within the overall economy.

Inequality, education, and demographic challenges

Inequality is a persistent challenge for Latin America. Substantial gains in profitability and service quality have accrued to firms from privatization, but the distributional gains expected from it have not reached the poorest sectors of society. The salary gap between more- and less-skilled workers in Latin America has even widened in recent years. This persistent earnings gap reflects inequality in education, which is a serious challenge for HR professionals.

Economic liberalization has not benefited less skilled workers as expected and has resulted in much reallocation of work to more skilled workers, reinforcing inequities. Leveling the playing field requires improvements in the education system, such as giving incentives for children to stay in school longer and for adult workers to go back to school (Inter-American Development Bank, 2004). The educational system is oriented toward conceptualization, not toward skill building, as is the case in most developed countries. Thus, education alone will not suffice to increase low wages.

Lack of training also contributes to inequality in salary distributions by allocating individuals to lower-paying jobs with little promotion opportunities. Training is critical for the future of Latin America's labor force, yet few countries do it well. Firms are often able to deduct training expenses (see, for example, Chapter 8 on Chile in this book) but low-skilled workers benefit little from this. Managers do receive training, which creates an interesting paradox: managers with more training and education have modernizing influences on HR, yet effective implementation of the practices that they wish to initiate requires a workforce with much more advanced skills and training. In fact, there are notable differences between what firms do in practice and what managers say they are doing, partly due to the sophisticated ways well-educated managers in firms have of presenting their HR work (Lacombe and Tonelli, 2004).

One aspect of the talent shortage is of particular concern: retention and succession management. To compete internationally, Latin American companies need to build a pool of competent managers who possess strong language command and cultural competence in both the companies' home countries and abroad. Cemex's strategy to educate globally competent executives offers an illustration of one way a company has met this challenge. This Mexican firm (the third-largest cement company in the world) bought the largest cement firm in Asia and immediately brought executives from Indonesia, Singapore, and Malaysia to spend six weeks in Mexico in order to study the culture, language, and, above all, the business style of Cemex (Furlong, cited in Castilleja, 2000). Hence, developing global leadership capability is an opportunity for HR to broaden its strategic role in firms.

Another inequality issue is the challenge of integrating women in the workplace. Surveys indicate that Latin Americans would prefer greater gender equality (Ogliastri *et al.*, 1999). Generally speaking, employment opportunities for women and their labor force participation have improved, but discrimination still exists in salaries and career opportunities. While more men hold higher positions in organizations, women tend to concentrate in support roles. Legislation is favorable to women's integration in the labor force, yet managerial actions are inconsistent with legal requirements, illustrating again the tension of functioning in a hybrid context.

On the one hand, we find that the increase in Latin American women's labor force participation during 1990–2001 was the highest among the world continents (73 percent average for all Latin American countries) according to the Economic and Social Progress Report of the Inter-American Development Bank (2004), though percentages vary widely between countries from a 90 percent increase in Chile to 32 percent in Bolivia. On the other hand, we find women segregated into areas such as politics, public administration, education, medicine, art, and ONGs/services, and absent from managerial positions in business organizations. Women's persistent absence from managerial positions is not easily explained. It cannot be accounted for by either the historically late incorporation of females into the educational system in the late nineteenth century or by the many educated professional women who voluntarily exit the workforce to be stay-at-home mothers. Thus, a challenge for HRM is to find ways to reduce organizational barriers to women's advancement.

There are many other macroeconomic challenges over which HRM has little control. Macroeconomic crises and political instability deeply affect the employment relationship as part of the social contract, and create difficulties for HR management in a culture with a preference for uncertainty avoidance. Whereas certain HR strategies and policies might make good sense in good economic times, frequent environmental shocks and the resulting pressures lead to some of those strategies being ignored. HR takes a back seat during downturns, becoming one of the functions with the greatest instability within firms.

Remaining questions for research

Important questions remain unanswered by research, adding to the challenges discussed above. One such question concerns the role of technology, which to date has played a limited role for HR in Latin America. Since a larger role for technology might reduce personal relationships, its use will need to be carefully managed by HR.

The role of time as a cultural dimension that affects work is also an important research arena. Perceptions of time differ greatly among cultures (Hall, 1960; Hofstede, 1993) and influence the relative importance accorded to people *versus* systems. This impacts technical approaches to HR. For example, schedules are important in the United States but not as important in Mexico (Graham, 2001). Latin American societies are present-oriented, making it difficult for people to consider the future. According to Zea (1992 [1952]) Latin Americans are present-oriented, partly to shut out the past, which was not within their control, and the future, which is unclear: the present exists and is within one's control.

To address these multiple challenges and research questions, recommendations by this book's authors seem to converge on increasing the strategic role of HRM. To date, Latin American HRM has experienced a steady process of professionalization, incorporating modern management principles and techniques, while at the same time keeping historical practices alive. Modern Latin American firms (particularly large and medium-sized firms) use HRM instruments, tools, and practices that are similar to those observed in more developed countries, but HRM rarely occupies a strategic position within these larger firms. There is even more room for the continued professionalization of HRM in the majority of small firms.

The call for Latin American HR professionals to become more involved in strategy is becoming increasingly legitimized through "professional" consultants using global methodologies. For example, reporting research from Mercer's survey in Latin America, Diez *et al.* (2003) recently published a *Harvard Business Review: America Latina* article entitled "Cambio de Papeles" (Change of Roles) that detailed the ways in which HR had been and should be moving into more strategic roles in Latin American companies. Not surprisingly, the authors recommend changing the image (and reality) of HR directors in Latin America from that of one who performs basic administrative tasks to one who emphasizes strategic HR management. An obstacle to this transition is the inability of firm leaders to envision HR as a contributor to firms' development and performance or to determine what they expect of HR. Nor do Latin American HR managers appear able to determine their role. This identity confusion might spring from the tensions of making decisions in a hybrid system, which by nature is mired with ambiguity. Finding a strategic fit between HR practices and the complex cultural and economic environment is challenging. Guidelines or best practices relating to HR strategy do not apply universally, nor do they necessarily follow rational discourse. Latin American firms do have expectations for human resource management but they are founded in the social contract embedded in the work culture. Understanding the importance of this context helps explain the concerns of strategic HRM, and we address this issue next.

Strategic HRM models for research in Latin America

What do we mean by strategic HRM (SHRM)? From our perspective, centered on managing people in Latin America, a relevant definition of SHRM is that of Snell *et al.* (1996: 62): "organizational systems designed to achieve sustainable competitive advantage through people." This definition is especially appropriate because it links people to the firm and we have seen in this book's chapters that HR in Latin America is person-centered.

SHRM research aims to demonstrate that HR can contribute to the profitability of firms, especially given increasing global competition. SHRM theories have been classified into universalistic, contingency, and configurational approaches

(Delery and Doty, 1996; Wright and McMahan, 1992).[1] However, the theories that fit into this classification system appear to apply mostly to the United States and cannot fully account for our observations of HR in Latin America. Below we briefly review the three approaches and discuss their shortcomings in the Latin American context. We then present two alternative approaches: contextual (Brewster, 1999) and social contract (Kochan, 1999), and discuss how they can guide emergent research in Latin American HRM.

The *universalistic* perspective maintains that using "best HR practices" will result in good firm performance regardless of the firm's strategy and the match with other HR practices (Huselid, 1995; Kochan and Osterman, 1994; Pfeffer, 1994). For example, Delery and Doty (1996) find that results-oriented appraisals, employment security, and profit-sharing have universally positive effects on organizational performance in US companies. The universalistic approach typically focuses on so-called high-performance work systems, defined by the US Department of Labor (1993) as having the following characteristics: well-developed recruitment systems, selection and training; formal systems for sharing information with workers; clear job design; local-level participation procedures; and promotion and compensation systems that reward high-performing members of the workforce. A universalistic approach assumes that these practices would still be "best" for firm performance regardless of the cultural context of the firm but there is little evidence that these are in fact the "best" practices in a non-US context. The little existing non-US evidence seems contradictory. For instance, there is inconsistency in how widely best practices are adopted by multinationals. A side effect of globalization is that the known, positive consequences of "best HRM practices" across the board have led many multinational organizations to implement such best practices (Huselid *et al.*, 1997), and thus some degree of convergence in HR practices is occurring across MNCs (Sparrow *et al.*, 1994). But we also observe cases where practices are adapted locally rather than adopted globally such as that of Intel in Central America (Chapter 7 in this book).

The issue of fit has been central to the study of HRM practices in the next two classifications, whether external fit (between HR practices and competitive strategy) or internal fit (among HR practices). The *contingency* view of SHRM suggests that the effective use of different HR practices depends on firm strategy (Jackson and Schuler, 1995; Wright and Snell, 1992). In other words, what is best is different for firms with different strategies. Yet it is not clear how this vision would transfer across national cultures. Culture alters the effectiveness of HR practices (Chapter 1 in this book). A critical contingency factor beyond firms' strategy is how historical evolution and values shape HR practices: not only does what is best vary with strategy, it also varies with national culture.

Finally, *configurational* theories propose that it is the matching of a *set* of HR practices to particular firm strategies that leads to greater effectiveness. It is the fit of the HR practices with each other and with the firm's strategy that determines effectiveness. Evidence suggests that commitment HR systems reinforce psychological links, identification between employee and organization, resulting in better performance and lower turnover (Arthur, 1994; Huselid, 1995; Ichniowski *et al.*, 1997; MacDuffie, 1995). Based on synergistic effects among HR practices, "bundles" of HR practices form employment systems that are more effective in attaining performance than such practices alone or any such practices arranged in inconsistent employment systems. Furthermore, superior performance is obtained with employment systems that agree with firm strategy. Configurational approaches are theoretically appealing but fail to address the question of whether the bundles of HR practices are equally effective in different contexts (Schuler & Jackson, 2005). If indeed the best bundle of practices varies with context, diversified firms are unlikely to be able to align all their practices in a strictly configurational way.

A serious limitation shared by these three types of SHRM theories from our viewpoint is that all of them rest on the assumption that firms act as economically rational actors, with profit maximization as their main objective. This assumption is questionable in general, but especially so in the Latin American cultural context. In Latin American firms the main goals are arguably social, with financial goals being secondary. Similarly, measures of performance are assumed to be universally applicable regardless of ownership structures, accounting systems, and technology. Yet performance is understood differently in different contexts. For example, financial success in the economic uncertainty of Latin America is often measured by survival, not profit maximization.

Evidence suggests that in Latin America there is a desire for such universalistic practices as improved training, yet the reality of competitive pressures means that such practices are not adopted. Instead, there are trends contradictory to universalistic practices: for example, increased deregulation of the labor market, increased outsourcing, reduced union membership, and an increased informal sector. Further, universalistic, contingency, and configurational SHRM theories rarely consider the larger context of government and macroeconomic reality, factors that emerge in this book's research as critical to the functioning of HR in the Latin American context. The institutional, historical, and economic frameworks are indispensable to understanding the development of business life in Latin America. Hence, we propose looking to Brewster's (1999) contextual approach and Kochan's (1999) social-contract centered approach to guide future SHRM research in Latin America. These approaches suggest that future SHRM research might look to be influential beyond the organization.

Contextual and social contract SHRM views

Brewster's (1999: 215) contextual paradigm "is ideographic, searching for an overall understanding of what is contextually unique and why". This paradigm accepts that societies, governments, or regions can affect SHRM practices, not just firms. Indeed, two important assumptions in this paradigm are that an organization's objectives are not necessarily optimal for either the organization or the society, and that the interests of all stakeholders in an organization are not necessarily the same. This seems to fit the reality of Latin American HR described in this book, where employees, organized labor, managers, and stakeholders often have differing interests. For example, the Mexican senate has recently approved a law that reduces the privileges of social security administration employees in terms of employment benefits. Previously, these government employees had demanded and received substantially more generous retirement benefits than workers in the private sector. The new law guarantees equal social security benefits for all Mexican workers. Management associations, Congress, and citizens in general have accepted the new law, but social security administration employees protested loudly. Despite their protests, the new law has taken effect (Sarmiento, 2004).

While the contextual SHRM framework has guided research in Europe, Australia, and New Zealand, it has not yet been applied to Latin America. It seems that by using a contextual lens we may better understand apparent contradictions in Latin America's HRM implementation. For instance, we saw numerous instances where acknowledged and accepted HR practices were applied differently depending on the people and their circumstances. Though this application might appear inconsistent and thus irrational, it makes sense when considered in the context of the cultural antecedents of HRM in Latin America, antecedents that give precedence to people's needs over system consistency. Similarly, labor laws can be bent to suit a firm's survival needs and therefore protect workers from unemployment, despite seeming violations of laws meant to protect them. And HR policies that may not appear economically rational (e.g., keeping employees and giving holiday bonuses during downturns) make cultural sense and can lead to increased worker loyalty and productivity. Thus, tightening the link between HR practices and performance may appear to take a secondary place. This produces yet another paradox: by attending to the cultural context in implementing HR practices, performance may ultimately be enhanced.

In sum, the contextual SHRM view emphasizes not only management actions but also external factors, including culture, ownership structures, labor markets, the role of the state, and worker unions, as integral to HRM rather than external to it. Kochan (1999) adds to this contextual theory by specifically focusing on the institutions that underlie the social contract as contextually critical for HRM. In doing so, he shifts the analysis from one of the organization to one of the employment relationship and shifts the role of the HR professional from one of creating and implementing organizational HR policy to one of contributing to societal employment policy. Thus HR research and practice have implications at the societal and policy level, not just at an organizational level. Kochan (1999: 199) suggests that to gain professional and research relevance, HR researchers should:

(1) take better account of external variables affecting employment relationships; (2) examine the effects of HRM practices and policies on the full range of stakeholders present in employment relationships; and (3) adopt the employment relationship rather than the firm as the key unit of analysis.

Kochan's suggestions bring HRM to the center of solving such societal problems as those described in this chapter, including inequality, insufficient training, increasing workforce diversity, decreased foreign investment, and recurrent political crises. By contributing to solve these societal problems, HR would also be solving many of the problems it faces more directly in organizations. In his view, HR's current emphasis on performance, understood as shareholder value, has turned HR professionals into agents of management at the expense of other traditional stakeholders in the employment relationship such as unions and workers. This narrow focus prevents HR from taking a truly strategic role in solving broader employment problems and from measuring its success in performance terms that make the most sense in the Latin American context. Focusing on the social contract can alleviate this myopia.

Social contracts can be defined as the "mutual expectations and obligations that employees, employers, and members of society in general hold for work and employment relationships" (Kochan, 1999: 201). Research stresses the importance of job security for psychological contracts and commitment (e.g. Rousseau and Schalk, 2000). As discussed in this chapter, social contracts shape HR practices throughout Latin America. The psychological contracts that accompany these social contracts may be even more important in Latin America. As shown in this book, shared beliefs regarding duties and obligations abound in Latin America. Diaz-Saenz and Witherspoon (2000), for example, explain that Mexican workers expect bonuses at holidays such as Christmas, seniority and longevity funds in their severance packages, and time off for religious holidays. Yet increasingly these expectations are not being met. Changes in the social contract include decreased security in employment, increased inequality, and reduced trust of employers. These changes imply other changes in the psychological contract.

More broadly, understanding the importance of social contracts to Latin America's society helps explain why "rational", formalized HRM systems do not adequately translate into success for Latin America's management. Formal, bureaucratic HR systems leave unmet many needs of citizens, who in turn have developed intricate and implicit informal mechanisms to provide for such needs. Anthropological studies of networks suggest that since neither firms nor governments in Latin America can satisfy the needs of the citizens, the latter have alternative methods to satisfy their needs. Specifically, social networks exist within and outside business organizations that lubricate the functioning of formal bureaucracies (Lomnitz, C., 1999; Lomnitz, L.A., 1994). Although all social classes in Latin America rely on social networks, the complexity of their implicit social contracts varies by the level of needs required. Their implicit agreements are regulated by tacit rules, sanctions, and goals. These tacit regulatory mechanisms are part of the socialization in one's culture via the family (for social networks that imply family and friends) as well as for vertical networks that exist within organizational hierarchies. Within firms these vertical networks (e.g. between managers and subordinates) balance the impersonality of bureaucratic mechanisms and lubricate business relationships. These implicit contracts are essential to understanding management in Latin America because the sanctions that accompany breaking implicit contracts are socially enforced to a greater extent than legal sanctions applicable to formal contracts. Analyzing these social networks and their effects on the employment relationship will help enrich current HRM research and address questions such as the importance of family and personal relationships for business, and more globally the intersection between social relationships and the formal economy.

Evans (1993) has suggested that HR is the "glue" that holds organizational elements together. In the context of Latin America, these elements might very well be expanded to include the environmental and contextual elements surrounding an organization. This would enhance the role of the HR professional to being a proactive liaison among various local, state, and national agents including national and multinational firms.

Applying the social contract lens to HRM challenges in Latin America

We suggest some potential research paths based on Kochan's SHRM approach that would begin to address the challenges described earlier in this chapter. There are many ways that government policies could vastly improve the employment contracts for workers across Latin America. To move forward, HR research should look at ways in which these policies could be changed and in which HR could be involved. First, focusing on the employment relationship as the unit of analysis can help find broader solutions to underemployment. For example, finding ways to more effectively place workers in the right jobs can reduce unemployment and increase the quality and productivity of workers (Inter-American Development Bank, 2004). To increase the efficiency of the job–worker matching process, private-sector HR can cooperate with policy makers in creating vacancy registries and providing job search assistance. HR research should examine ways to enhance job matching through firm and societal efforts.

Similarly, the increasing skill gap is unlikely to be closed by simply focusing on within-firm training: a more coordinated effort among employers, educational and training institutions, unions, and government will be needed. First, social institutions and firms need to develop a new system to ensure a universal basic education and to ease the transition between school and labor markets, guaranteeing workers the opportunity to develop basic skills. Future research on HR in Latin America might examine the potential role of HR in such efforts.

Further, HR can enhance career opportunities for workers by devising policies that provide incentives for workers to seek and for firms to provide high-quality training. The training should be focused on increasing productivity so that firms remain competitive in the global arena. Adult education has been a low priority in most Latin American countries and increasing it would require tax incentives. Here too, HR collaboration with government agencies seems critical to improving adult productivity by encouraging workers' skill development. Creating a favorable training environment requires a twofold effort to reform public institutions and ensure that the training already provided by firms is enhanced by worker involvement and union as well as business and government support.

To address challenges such as unemployment and outsourcing, HR can analyze how to help firms and employees cope with the volatile economic environment in which they operate. HR can help by providing counseling, job search assistance, training, employee enterprise, and community-based approaches to ease the adjustments. Along these lines, an important issue for HR will be studying how to provide more universal employment benefits, such as retirement and health insurance, which are often absent from contracts yet are highly desired by workers, especially given the economic instability and uncertainly about long-term employment (Inter-American Development Bank, 2004).

Once new policies and systems are in place, HR can continue to contribute by monitoring labor policies, enforcing regulations, and promoting harmonious employee relations. This will be key to the successful implementation of HRM practices.

Similarly, issues related to diversity such as women's inclusion in the workforce, considerations for Latin American institutions such as the family, and their consequences for hours worked, wage distribution, family-related benefits, all will affect work environments beyond any single firm. The challenges involve legal frames of reference and thinking broadly with the multiple stakeholders in the employment relationship.

In various ways, the collaboration among social institutions related to social contracts deals with ethics and its meaning at work for Latin Americans. As Latin America's companies become increasingly publicly owned and global, corporate governance will also be under scrutiny. Ethical standards set by supra-national institutions, such as the OECD or the World Bank, will impose greater transparency into interest groups in favor of shareholders. In addition, when dealing with social ethics at work, firms will need to consider the special social contract approach typical of this region. D'Iribarne (2002) describes the turnaround in Dannon's Mexican subsidiary that helped the firm improve its performance only after it had decided to take the "high-moral ground". The company understood that its low performance in Mexico derived from lack of attention to personal relationships. Hence they determined to provide their social ethics approach in a twofold way: first, by increasing employee's empowerment and their involvement in collective decision making; and second, by investing in the community and helping children in need. These changes fitted well in the context of Mexico's cultural collectivism. Social relationships improved among workers and between workers and management leading to much improved performance.

Is this Dannon case representative? To answer this question we need more in-depth case studies of local firms, focusing on best practices with an eye to meeting the social contract, to assess whether the theory presented here holds water. In general, studies should evaluate whether SHRM makes a difference in Latin America, where practices more aligned with people improve the outcomes for both employees and firms.

Perhaps there is after all a "best" approach to human resource management that is universally applicable in Latin America. That "best" way would be one inclusive of workers, society (family group in particular), and government in a *humanistic*, person-centered approach, where work is understood not only in its objective dimension (the task performed) but also in its subjective dimension (the person who performs). This guiding principle can help establish HRM practices that respect the preeminent interpersonal orientation of Latin Americans. This effort requires widespread institutional involvement.

HR research and the HR field can embrace a more encompassing perspective working with all the parties involved in the employment relationship and the institutions that govern it. HR would then become a central strategic player not just at the firm level but also at the political and social level. This constructive approach can guide HRM to solve the threats posed by global competition to employment relations in Latin America. We have presented only a few suggestions and leave this as the beginning of a conversation that should be continued by researchers interested in the SHRM area. Kochan's (1999: 211) thoughtful words apply globally: "The question is how future historians will judge our generation's success in coping with the most critical employment problems of our time." In the context of Latin America, it seems that HR cannot succeed in coping with those employment problems by universally applying HR practices within firms; it must work to apply culturally appropriate practices and to reduce the societal challenges faced by organizations.

Notes

1. We bypass the debate concerning some assumptions or postulates of the theories such as the relationship between fit and performance and mediating relationships. Our focus is on the relevant aspects of SHRM to conduct contextually relevant HRM research in Latin America.

References

Albert, R.D. (1996) "A framework and model for understanding Latin American and Latin/ Hispanic cultural patterns," in D. Landis and R. Bhagat (eds) *Handbook of intercultural training*, 2nd edn, Thousand Oaks, CA: Sage, pp. 327–348.

Arthur, J.F. (1994) "Effects of human resource systems on manufacturing performance and turnover," *Academy of Management Journal* 37 (3): 670–687.

Brewster, C. (1999) "Different paradigms in strategic HRM: Questions raised by comparative research," in P.M. Wright, L.D. Dyer, J.W. Boudreau, and G.T. Milkovich (eds) *Strategic human resource management in the twenty-first century. Research in personnel and human resource management*, Supplement 4, Stamford, CT: JAI Press, pp. 213–238.

Budhwar, P.S. (ed.) (2004) *Managing human resources in Asia-Pacific*, London: Routledge.

Castilleja, J. (2000) "Desde Asia, aprenden cómo negocia Cemex" [From Asia, they learn how Cemex negotiates] (3 May), retrieved 15 September 2004 through Elnorte.com from: http://busquedas.grupoanreforma.com/00027316

D'Iribarne, P. (2002) "Motivating workers in emerging countries: Universal tools and local adaptations," *Journal of Organizational Behavior* 23: 1–14.

Delery, J.E. and Doty, H.D. (1996) "Modes of theorizing in strategic human resource management: Tests of universalistic, contingency, and configurational performance," *Academy of Management Journal* 39 (4): 802–835.

Diaz-Saenz, H.R. and Witherspoon, P.D. (2000) "Psychological contracts in Mexico," in D.M. Rousseau and R. Schalk (eds) *Psychological contracts in employment: Cross-national perspectives*, Thousand Oaks, CA: Sage, pp. 158–175.

Diez, F., Heslop, B., and Ambrosio, L. (2003) "Cambio de papeles" [Role changes], *Harvard Business Review: America Latina* 81 (10): 26–28.

Evans, P. (1993) "Dosing the glue: Applying human resource technology to build the global organization," in B. Shaw and P. Kirkbride (eds) *Research in personnel and human resource management*, Vol. 3, Greenwich, CT: JAI Press.

Expansión (2003) "Un capital hecho de gente" [A capital made of people], Seccion: Ideas y soluciones, Ed. No. 862, retrieved 15 September 2004 through Expansion.com from: http://www.expansion.com.mx/nivel2.asp?cve = 862_27&pge = 0

Flores-Vega, E. (1995) "Bimbo la multiplicación de los panes" [Bimbo the multiplication of bread], *Expansión*, Seccion Principal, Ed. No. 677, retrieved 15 September 2004 through Expansion.com from: http://www.expansion.com.mx/nivel2.asp?cve = 677_17

Gaugler, E. (1988) "HR management: An international comparison," *Personnel* (August): 24–30.

Graham, J.L. (2001) "Culture and human resources management," in A.M. Rugman and T.L. Brewer (eds) *The Oxford handbook of international business*, Oxford: Oxford University Press, pp. 503–536.

Hall, E.T. (1960) "The silent language in overseas business," *Harvard Business Review* (May–June): 87–96.

Hofstede, G.H. (1993) "Cultural constraints in management theories," *Academy of Management Executive* 7 (1): 81–94.

Huselid, M.A. (1995) "The impact of human resource management practices on turnover, productivity, and corporate financial performance," *Academy of Management Journal* 38 (3): 635–672.

Huselid, M.A., Jackson, S.E., and Schuler, R.S. (1997) "Technical and strategic human resource management effectiveness as determinants of firm performance," *Academy of Management Journal* 40 (1): 171–188.

Ichniowski, C., Shaw, K., and Prennushi, G. (1997) "The effects of human resource management practices on productivity: A study of steel finishing lines," *American Economic Review* 87: 291–313.

Inter-American Development Bank (2004) *Good Jobs Wanted: Labor Markets in Latin America. Economic and Social Progress Report*, Washington, DC.

Jackson, S.E. and Schuler, R. (1995) "Understanding human resource management in the context of organizations and their environments," *Annual Review in Psychology* 46: 237–264.

Kochan, T.A. (1999) "Beyond myopia: Human resources and the changing social contract," in P.M. Wright, L.D. Dyer, J.W. Boudreau, and G.T. Milkovich (eds) *Strategic human resource management in the twenty-first century. Research in personnel and human resource management*, Supplement 4, Stamford, CT: JAI Press.

Kochan, T.A. and Osterman, P. (1994) *The mutual gains enterprise: Forging a winning partnership among labor, management, and government*, Boston: Harvard Business School Press.

Lacombe, B.M.B. and Tonelli, M.J. (2004) "HR managers' concerns and the experts' views: What do they say about trends in human resource management?" Working Paper, School of Business Administration of São Paulo, Fundação Getulio Vargas, Brazil.

Lomnitz, C. (1999) "Modes of citizenship in Mexico," *Public Culture* 11 (1): 269–293.

Lomnitz, L.A. (1994) *Redes sociales, cultura y poder: Ensayos de antropología Latinoamericana* [Social networks, culture and power: Essays on Latin American anthropology], Mexico: Miguel Angel Porrua, FLACSO.

MacDuffie, J.P. (1995) "Human resource bundles and manufacturing performance: Organizational logic and flexible production systems in the world auto industry," *Industrial and Labor Relations Review* 48: 197–221.

Ogliastri, E., McMillen, C., Altschul, C., Arias, M.E., Bustamante, C., Davila, C., Dorfman, P., Coletta, M.F., Fimmen, C., Ickis, J., and Martinez, S. (1999) "Cultura y liderazgo organizacional en 10 paises de America Latina. El estudio Globe" [Culture and organizational leadership in 10 Latin American countries: The Globe study], *Academia, Revista Latinoamericana de Administración* 22: 29–57.

Pfeffer, J. (1994) *Competitive advantage through people: Unleashing the power of the workforce*, Boston: Harvard Business School Press.

Rousseau, D.M. and Schalk, R. (eds) (2000) *Psychological contracts in employment: Cross-national perspectives*, Newbury Park, CA: Sage.

Sarmiento, S. (2004) "Solidaridad" [Solidarity], *El Norte* (9 August). ELNORTE, Sección Editoriales. Retreived October 3, 2004 through Elnorte.com from http://busquedas.grupareforma.com/00374634

Schuler, R.S., Budhwar, P., and Florkowski, G.W. (2002) "International human resource management: Review and critique," *International Journal of Management Reviews* 4 (1): 41–70.

Schler, R.S. and Jackson, S.E. (2205). "A Quarter Century Review of Human Resource Management in the U.S." *Management Review*, winter.

Snell, S.A., Youndt, M.A., and Wright, P.M. (1996) "Establishing a framework for research in strategic human resource management: Merging resource theory and organizational learning," *Research in Personnel and Human Resources Management* 14: 61–90.

Sparrow, P., Schuler, R.S., and Jackson, S.E. (1994) "Convergence or divergence: Human resource practices and policies for competitive advantage worldwide," *International Journal of Human Resource Management* 5 (2): 267–299.

US Department of Labor (1993) *High performance work practices and firm performance*, Washington, DC: US Government Printing Office.

Von Glinow, M.A., Drost, E.A., and Teagarden, M.B. (2002) "Converging on IHRM best practices: Lessons learned from a globally distributed consortium on theory and practice," *Human Resource Management* 41 (1): 123–140.

Wright, P.M. and McMahan, G.C. (1992) "Theoretical perspectives for strategic human resource management," *Journal of Management* 18 (2): 295–320.

Wright, P.M. and Snell, S.A. (1992) "Toward a unifying framework for exploring fit and flexibility in strategic human resource management," *Academy of Management Review* 23 (4): 756–772.

Zea, L. (1992 [1952]) "El sentido de responsabilidad en el mexicano" [The Mexican's sense of responsibility], in *Dos Ensayos sobre México y lo Mexicano* [Two Essays: Mexico and the Mexican], Mexico: Editorial Porrua, Coleccion "Sepan Cuantos ..." No. 269, pp. 105–114.

Index